Pacific Estrangement

Harvard Studies in American–East Asian Relations   2

The Harvard Studies in American–East Asian Relation
are sponsored and edited by the Committee on
American–Far Eastern Policy Studies of the
Department of History at Harvard University.

Pacific Estrangement   Akira Iriye

Japanese and American Expansion, 1897-1911

Harvard University Press, Cambridge, Massachusetts, 1972

É

183.8

J3

T74

To Mitsuko

Preface

In this book I have sought to make a modest contribution to the study of American history, Japanese history, and United States–East Asian relations by tracing the way in which the sense of estrangement across the Pacific at the turn of the twentieth century was related to the parallel development of the two countries as expansionists. Expansion is by no means the only thematic framework in which one can trace the history of United States–East Asian relations. These relations have been studied in terms of formal diplomacy, power politics, public opinion, and mutual images.* I have tried to look at United States history and Japanese history in comparative perspective by examining their interaction. Insofar as international relations by definition deal with more than one government and one people, it is necessary to transcend a narrowly uni-national, uni-archival approach, which unfortunately still characterizes the bulk of writings in diplomatic history.

The emergence of the United States as a world power and as an imperialist nation has been the subject of intensive study in the last few years, and historians have come to recognize the importance of examining the phenomenon in terms not only of domestic factors but also of currents of thought and policy in Europe. I have tried to delineate an Asian and especially Japanese ingredient in the picture. An analysis of Japanese expansionist thought provides ample examples of parallel

* The historiography of United States-East Asian relations is thoroughly explored in Ernest R. May and James C. Thomson, eds., *American-East Asian Relations: A Survey* (Cambridge, Mass., 1972). Among the most recent attempts at synthesis are Warren I. Cohen, *America's Response to China* (New York, 1971), and *Nihon to Amerika* (Japan and America), ed. Asahi shinbun (Tokyo, 1971).

thinking across the Pacific, awareness of which may enable us to transcend the parochialism that has sometimes characterized writings on American imperialism. It was not simply that the United States and other Western countries pursued imperialist policies; some of their actions were responses to Japanese imperialism. Also there were different types, informal and formal aspects, of Japanese expansionism as of American expansionism.

This leads to the book's second emphasis: the American factor in the evolution of Japanese imperialism. By emphasizing the peaceful as well as more frankly aggressive aspect of Japanese expansionism, I have sought to reinterpret the course of Meiji diplomacy. Beneath the surface of such commonly held themes as treaty revision, control over Korea, and national security lie undercurrents and subthemes approximating various shades of imperialist thought and action in the West. It is surprising how often the Japanese turned to the United States, physically and imaginatively, as a model and object of their expansion as well as a point of reference as they tried to comprehend what their country was doing in the years following the Sino-Japanese War.

These years have been given excellent scholarly treatment by specialists in United States–East Asian relations. Yet most of them have focused on China and studied America's Pacific and Asian empire primarily in terms of its interests and policies on the mainland. A plausible case can be made, however, for the view that the simultaneous development of Japan and the United States as empires was far more crucial in determining their subsequent destinies, and that American-Asian relations can be understood only when Japan as well as China is seen playing a major role as an object of American concern. The history of American involvement in East Asia indicates that the interaction between the United States and Japan has contributed to the dynamics of international relations in that part of the world. This interaction, cultural and psychological as well as political and economic, has reflected the expanding contact between the peoples.

Since the book is concerned with illustrating this phenomenon and raising some fresh questions about the nature of American-Asian historical contact, I have felt justified in not repeating in detail such landmarks as the Sino-Japanese War, the Spanish-American War, the open door policy, the Anglo-Japanese alliance, and the Russo-Japanese War, all of which have been competently examined already. Rather, my main objective has been to tell the story of Japanese and

American expansion by focusing on the problems that arose as a result of their physical and mental encounter. It is a story not so much of wars and policies as of individual endeavors, expectations, and fears. In the long run the last-named are the hardest to change, and it may be that, even in the 1970's, the language of estrangement, going back to the turn of the century, will continue to be spoken as Japanese and Americans grope anew to define their current and future relations.

Research for this study was begun ten years ago at Harvard University. Since then my research notes and my family have traveled with me to Tokyo, Taipei, London, Santa Cruz (California), Rochester (New York), and, since 1969, Chicago, where we have found a hospitable and stimulating environment to complete the writing of this book. As always I am indebted to my friends, colleagues, and former teachers for unfailing encouragement and support. Above all I should record my sense of obligation, intellectual and otherwise, to co-workers in the field of United States–East Asian relations: John K. Fairbank, Ernest R. May, Dorothy Borg, James W. Morley, and others too numerous to name. In these days of instant expertise and instantaneous revisionism, they have maintained a tradition of rigorous and honest scholarship based on multiarchival research. In the final stages of preparation for this book, I have been particularly helped by three friends: Waldo H. Heinrichs of the University of Illinois, Charles E. Neu of Brown University, and Satō Seizaburō of Tokyo University. They gave their time most generously, going over every manuscript page and giving me the benefit of their knowledge and criticism. Finally, the completion of the manuscript has been made a pleasant task by the loyal cooperation of Mrs. Helen Little who did the typing, and of the editorial staff of the Harvard University Press.

A. I.

February 1972
Chicago, Illinois

Contents

I   Introduction 1

II   The Emergence of Imperialism 26

III   Beyond Imperialism 63

IV   Japanese Continentalism and Chinese Nationalism 91

V   Confrontation: The Japanese View 126

VI   Confrontation: The American View 151

VII The Role of China 169

VIII The United States and Japan in the World Arena 202

IX   Epilogue 228

      Notes 241

      Bibliography 267

      Index 283

Pacific Estrangement

I

Introduction

"The simple truth is," Theodore Roosevelt wrote in 1900, "that there is nothing even remotely resembling 'imperialism' or 'militarism' involved in the present development of that policy of expansion which has been part of the history of America from the day when she became a nation." [1] He was wrong. The Spanish-American War had made the United States an imperialist nation, controlling overseas territories through military means. Roosevelt was wrong to imply that the new turn of events was not causing profound changes in the orientation of American expansionism. He was, however, right to assert, in this and other instances, that expansion had always characterized the nation's history. What he failed to appreciate, a failure which has not been uncommon among later writers, was that expansion could take many different forms, one of which would be imperialism, but that imperialistic expansion must not be confused with nonimperialistic types of expansion.

Historians of expansionism, American or otherwise, have been busily engaged in proposing alternative interpretations and refuting each other's theories.[2] But they have not always accepted what logic and common sense indicate: that expansion is a pervasive and basic phenomenon of man's history, but that not all expansion is imperialistic. It is hardly enlightening to assert, with a sense of fresh discovery, that the United States has always expanded, and no more enlightening to label every act of expansion "imperialism." Obviously there can be no expansion without expansionists, but the agents of expansion can be private individuals as well as armies and governments. Ideas can expand, as can goods and capital. There can be just as many motives and aspirations behind these various agents of expansion. Expansion may be undertaken peacefully, or it may be supported by force — individual, group, or national. Those at the receiving end of expansion will interact with the expansionists in a number of ways, abetting or limiting further expansion.

Put this way, there is nothing extraordinary about expansion; all peoples undertake it, and "American expansionism" has no more meaning than "American experience" or "American history." What needs investigation is not so much the existence of expansionism as its specific characteristics, its varying expressions, and its interaction with distant lands and societies. Was there a predominant type of expansion — for instance, a more or less peaceful search for markets — at a particular point in history in a certain region of the world? Was American expansion more imperialistic — that is, sustained by force and involving territorial control — in other parts of the globe? How did the various types of expansion react to one another and to different conditions overseas? In what ways did the agents of expansion define its limits, if any? What distinguished America's approaches to Asia and the Pacific from those to Europe, Latin America, and the Middle East? Exactly the same questions must be raised regarding many other countries and their interaction with the United States. Since expansion by definition covers more than one people, the study of American expansion and imperialism would not be complete without analysis of such questions.

The interaction between American and Japanese expansion in the wider Pacific region, including East Asia and the Pacific coast of the American continent, is the main concern of this book. The story, of course, cannot be traced in a vacuum, as other countries undertook their own varieties of expansion. But Japanese-American estrangement was one of the outstanding developments of the turn of the century, and it can only be understood in the context of the confrontation between the two expanding peoples. It was not that conflict between them became inevitable when they simultaneously expanded into the Pacific and East Asia. Much more important was the psychological and intellectual, as well as the political and military, impact this phenomenon had on the two peoples.

By the 1890's the United States had had an extensive and varied history of expansion, experienced in every different way. Before the Civil War, as Norman A. Graebner, Frederick Merk, and others have shown, Americans were moved by different inspirations and interests as they undertook expansion. On the one hand, they were exponents of idealistic, peaceful expansionism. They had immense confidence in the purity and wisdom of American democratic institutions and foretold their spread throughout the world, as other countries and other peoples gravitated to America, spiritually if not physically. The peaceful expansionists were opposed to the military conquest of unwilling peoples, as this ran counter to the basic credo of democracy. Men like William Ellery Channing, denouncing the annexation of Texas as contrary to the founding principles of the Republic, were not antiexpansionist. They did not say that the addition of further territory would be injurious to the United States; what they objected to was the method employed. A people should not be forced to join the Union until its general will to do so could be ascertained. The United States was essentially a republic made up of free, democratic states. One could envisage an endless expansion of the republic as the area of freedom extended, but a forceful incorporation of additional territory would subvert the basis of the American "empire" — a term often used interchangeably with "republic." According to this type of thinking, American expansion was to have its source in the mission of the United States to stand as the land of the free.[3]

On the other hand, Albert K. Weinberg's pioneering study and more recently William H. Goetzmann's comprehensive account have suggested that the early American expansionists were usually at once explorers and soldiers; they combined "the arts of civil life and the force to defend them," according to an account of an 1819 expedition up the Missouri River.[4] They were as much private profiteers as agents of the federal government, convinced alike of the civilizing value of commerce and of the country's right to territorial dominion over the West. In the 1840's proponents of territorial acquisition sought to justify their moves by resorting to the rhetoric of freedom, natural law, and manifest destiny. But these were not so much motives as justifications for action, and the basic drive was for territorial aggrandizement even at the expense of war. The reasons for this drive varied from group to group, and from time to time. The slave states of the South were eager to expand their "areas of freedom" and tended to visualize the American nation as a federally constructed entity in which states enjoyed semiautonomy. Mercantile interests in the Northeast were desirous of obtaining ports on the West coast and envisioned eventual

4

Pacific Estrangement

acquisition of the area from Mexico. The manifest-destiny expansionists were prepared to use force to capture territory even at the expense of subverting the freedom of the peoples in those territories.

Territorial acquisition was only one type of expansion in America. The decades preceding the Civil War saw the beginning of the "treaty system" in Asia in which the United States participated. The system, defining the way Asian and Western countries should conduct trade, had first been established in China with a minimum use of force by the British navy, and it was maintained without necessitating larger military involvement by Western powers. In inspiration it had been aimed at the extension of trade, not the subjugation of the Chinese, at the protection of foreign merchants, not the control of Chinese internal affairs. Still, military force had been employed, and Britain had seized Hong Kong as a colony and base of operation. This was not exactly an imperialism of free trade, an empire of influence; but neither was it a dominion sustained by power for political objectives. China was not another India. The British government sought the least possible intervention in Chinese domestic affairs, and it was not interested in reforming Chinese ways other than maintaining a stable political framework for conducting foreign trade. Most British activities in China were left in private hands. British power was represented by consuls, not by viceroys and admirals.[5]

American power was also represented by consuls, but their number was insignificant in comparison with private individuals, mostly merchants and missionaries. It is a moot question whether these latter represented anything more than their particularistic interests and private consciences. Certainly fewer of them would have gone to East Asia without the protection of the treaty system. In case of trouble they could always invoke special privileges of consular jurisdiction, and they could count on the shield, however ephemeral, of Western naval might. They were conscious of their identity as Americans, although to what extent their nationality affected their conduct is debatable. Some of them doubled as officials, as, for example, did Peter Parker, the missionary who spent considerable time as commissioner and concerned himself as much with extending American influence and obtaining overseas territories as with saving Chinese souls.

For a majority of Americans in China, however, activities in the East were acts of personal fulfillment, whether the motive be profit or mission. They were in China not to entrench American power and influence but to carry out what individually appealed to them. They were there for virtually the same reasons that their compatriots were in Hawaii, Latin America, the Near East, and Europe. Because, unlike the British, Americans were not encumbered by the burden of an existing empire, they were able to pursue their calling relatively free of imperial and national considerations. And yet as expansionists they played just as crucial a role as the manifest-destiny expansionists at home. They introduced American goods and ideas abroad and contributed immensely to relating the United States to the rest of the world.[6]

Ideas and goods, too, were agents of American expansion. Their unidirectional character should not be exaggerated. As Robert Kelley has shown, there was a trans-Atlantic community of sentiment producing what he calls "liberal-democratic" thinking.[7] Developments in England and the United States reinforced one another, and the ideas of freedom, equality, justice, and fair play were being identified with these countries. The image of America as the land of promise and of opportunity was well established and attracted not only European immigrants and savants but also Chinese laborers.

Here one comes back to the idea of mission. Americans, whether promoting or opposed to territorial expansion, believed in an image of their country, embodying what has been termed "liberal exceptionalism." Nationalism and universalism subtly merged, as Americans developed the view of themselves as the most progressive people in the world. They were the embodiment of those qualities of life that characterized progress and civilization. Civilization, according to an author for the *American Whig Review* in 1846, could be defined as "the complete and harmonious development of man in all his appropriate relations to this world — or, more fully expressed, the expanding and cultivating of all the powers and capacities of man considered as a social being; especially of those higher faculties which characterize man's proper nature; and including the refinement of the manners, tastes, and feelings." The mission of civilization was "to bring into one, the past, the present and the future — all nations and all generations." In modern Europe, "civilization has assumed a more perfect form than it had ever before attained." But American civilization was even more magnificent than European; "it is the hope of the world." In this way, the writer concluded, "we not only have duties to ourselves and our posterity to discharge, but we are entrusted with a mission for the whole race; its destinies, to a fearful extent, are placed in our hands." [8]

In speaking of America's duty, not only to its narrow national concerns but also to mankind and to civilization, those imbued with such a sense of mission were demonstrating that liberal rhetoric could exist side by side with more dynamic expansionism. Liberalism and nationalism coexisted in such a conception of American foreign relations. The two, of course, were never identical, and the idea of mission as often justified nationalistic expansion as reaffirmed the rejection of forceful aggrandizement. But the point is that these various themes and attitudes were found simultaneously in the United States in the middle nineteenth century. Expansion had many different aspects; if, in the American imagination, no limits were set to the expansion of ideas and commodities, the extension of formal American control was something else, as practical considerations intervened and prevented the outright annexation of territories. Americans, in other words, were part imperialistic and part anti-imperialistic, part nationalistic and part universalistic expansionists. As they reached the Pacific coast and extended their activities to East Asia, they were developing a wide range of ideas to conceptualize expansion and preparing themselves for deepening involvement in other parts of the world.

Territorial expansion came to a halt after the Mexican War, but other types of expansion continued unabated. The United States, declared William H. Seward in 1854, "expand, not by force of arms, but by attraction." As examples he pointed to various parts of the world which had felt America's influence and thus invited its expansion:

The influences of the United States on the American continent have resulted already in the establishment of the representative system everywhere, except in Brazil. . . . In Europe they have awakened a war of opinion, that, after spreading desolation into the steppes of Russia, and to the base of the Carpathian mountains, has only been suppressed for a time by combination of the capital and of the political forces of that continent. In Africa, those influences, aided by the benevolent efforts of our citizens, have produced the establishment of a republic, which, beginning with the abolition of the traffic in slaves, is going steadily on toward the moral regeneration of its savage races. In the Sandwich Islands, those influences have already effected, not only such a regeneration of the natives, but also a political organization, which is bringing that important commercial station directly under our protection. Those influences have opened the ports of Japan, and secured an intercourse of commerce and friendship with its extraordinary people. . . . The same influences have not only produced for us access to the five ports of China, but also have generated a revolution there [the Taiping uprising], which promises to bring the three hundred millions living within that vast empire into the society of the Western nations.[9]

He could also have pointed to such illustrations of peaceful expansionism of the 1850's as the Clayton-Bulwer treaty, which gave no exclusive rights to the United States over the prospective canal route in Central America, and the Canadian reciprocity treaty of 1854, which specified free trade between the two countries in certain commodities.

Not all American expansion was nonimperialistic. A prototype of formal imperialism was James Buchanan's effort as secretary of state and president to offer military protection to American merchants in Central America. The abortive McLane-Ocampo treaty foreshadowed the later Roosevelt corollary entrenching American power and authority in political and economic affairs of that region.[10] In Asia and the Pacific the fine line between informal and formal empire became even thinner as the United States sought to maintain a paramount position in Hawaii, opposing any other nation's control over the islands. President Franklin Pierce and Secretary of State William L. Marcy desired eventual annexation of Hawaii. Missionaries who had earlier gone there under the universalistic inspiration of evangelism now settled down to a life of political and economic influence, and they began considering themselves less agents of the Holy Spirit than of the American nation.[11] Similarly, while Commodore Matthew C. Perry's "four black ships" did not quite amount to a massive imperialistic onslaught, neither was he attempting peaceful persuasion, which the Dutch had tried without success. Perry advocated the seizure of Okinawa as a move to demonstrate American interest and power in the western Pacific. Considerations of American prestige and strategy, not simply or even primarily commercial interests, dictated his approach to Japan.

Yet the predominant strain in American foreign relations at this time was peaceful expansion, in particular, the expansion of trade and shipping. Two-thirds of American trade, amounting to 687 million dollars in 1860, was with Europe. Imports almost always exceeded exports, but there was considerable pressure for further lowering tariffs to obtain raw materials for industrialization. Trade deficits were offset by the expanding merchant marine. In 1856 United States merchant marine tonnage reached 4,871,652, of which 700,000 tons consisted of steamers. The British tonnage for that year was 4,841,000.[12] This achievement was buttressed by the growth of American exports to Britain, consisting chiefly of raw cotton and wheat. Britain paid for these imports to a large extent by investments in the United States, which almost doubled between 1840 and 1860. While capital movements were overwhelmingly toward the United States, American technology was making its impact upon other countries. The 1850's saw the arrival of European industrial commissions to study the American system of manufacturing and personnel relations.

While trade with Europe grew steadily, the universalism underlying economic expansion dictated development of a strong effort to achieve similar successes in other parts of the world. "I know," Seward remarked in an address in 1860, "that when you consider what a magnificent destiny you have before you, to lay your hand on the Atlantic coast, and to extend your power to the Pacific ocean and grasp the great commerce of the east, you will fully appreciate the responsibility." He talked of an empire of free trade, linking all parts of the world commercially. Since most Western countries had already been thus interconnected, it was natural that such a rhetoric should include a sweeping vision of their expansion to the non-West, especially Asia. In language that would be echoed time and again by Japanese expansionists several decades later, Seward asserted that "empire has, for the last three thousand years . . . made its way constantly westward . . . and it must continue to move on westward until the tides of the renewed and of the decaying civilizations of the world meet on the shores of the Pacific ocean." [13]

Such expressions reveal the enrichment of the vocabulary of American expansion in the East by the events of the 1850's such as the opening of Japan and the second Anglo-Chinese War (1856–1860). The use of force in both instances was considered insignificant in view of the great opportunities it brought about in Japan and China. American expansion in Japan was couched in the language of liberal expansionism that could be reconciled with the use of force because of the image of Japan before the Perry expedition. Here was a country, said the *American Whig Review,* so backward that the people "hardly go forward a year during a century." [14] And yet there seemed nothing inherently preordained about such backwardness. As the *Democratic Review* put it on the eve of the expedition, "naturally a trading nation, [the Japanese] are debarred from external trade; an inquiring nation, they are denied the means of research; a progressive nation, they are forced to be stationary; an ingenious nation, they are deprived of the benefits of ingenuity; an ambitious nation, they are reduced to arbitrary distinctions which paralyze all individual enterprise." [15] The Japanese caused Americans little philosophical difficulty as the Shogunate grudgingly but without risking war yielded to Perry's pressure. Here was a case of bringing backward peoples to higher reaches of civilization and of bringing Americans to vast opportunities for commercial and other kinds of contact with those peoples. "Under the auspices of an expedition," the *North American Review* averred, "the world's knowledge of Japan has just now been doubled, and the world's respect for Japan will increase in proportion." [16] This respect usually derived from the discovery, *Harper's Monthly* said, that the Japanese seemed to have "an aptitude for acquiring the civilization of the West to which no other Oriental race can lay claim." [17] Because such was the case, the implications of the use of force could be ignored without disturbing the consciences of American liberal expansionists.

The case with regard to China was somewhat different. One of the themes common in the 1850's was the alleged difference between Chinese and Japanese. According to the *Atlantic Monthly,* China was "so palsied, so corrupt, so wretchedly degraded, and so enfeebled by misgovernment, as to be already more than half sunk in decay," while Japan showed "real vigor, thrift, and intelligence." [18] If the Japanese, who hitherto had seemed no better than the Chinese, could be viewed as stirring themselves to change under the pressure of American initiative, could the Chinese be expected to respond likewise? The decade of the 1850's saw the colossal turmoil of the Taiping uprising as well as the tribulations of another war with Europe. Stuart Creighton Miller has shown that there was much less criticism of British policy toward China in the United States now than during the Opium War. As the *New York Times* said, "by force, and force alone, can the Chinese government and people be compelled or persuaded to accept and recognize the principle of International Law." [19] Probably as a result of the successful "opening" of Japan, there was greater receptiveness to the employment of military force to change China.

In a sense the period between the end of the Civil War and the 1890's was a golden age of America's peaceful expansionism. It saw no foreign wars, no territorial aggrandizement through force, no direct intervention or establishment of a protectorate abroad, and no increase in armament. Rather, the period was characterized by a tremendous growth of foreign trade, an influx of immigrants as well as an outpouring of Americans as travelers, missionaries, and advisers, and the founding of a number of educational institutions by Americans overseas.[20] Seward's earlier dream for an empire of influence was coming true. Men who inherited his leadership of American diplomacy, such as Hamilton Fish, James G. Blaine, and Grover Cleveland, while less ambitious and less given to sweeping rhetoric than Seward, shared the same vision of America's nonimperialistic expansion. They shunned military adventurism and territorial aggrandizement and concentrated on protecting Americans' right to trade, fish, and engage in business abroad.

Although the economic expansion of these postwar years cannot be related entirely to foreign policy, in a negative sense the latter promoted the former. By avoiding costly adventures and territorial annexations, the United States government left the field open to private exertions. Private expansionism reached new heights in the 1870's and 1880's as Americans interested themselves in cultivating new opportunities for profit. After 1874 imports rarely exceeded exports in dollar values, a condition reflecting not only the high Republican tariffs but also the quantitative expansion of export trade. There was a general decline in prices after 1873; even so, the dollar value of exports increased from 569 million dollars in 1874 to 845 million dollars in 1890. It is interesting to note, however, that manufactured items still claimed less than 20 percent of total United States exports during this period, the bulk of exported items being agricultural products. At least 80 percent of exports went to Europe, and another 10 percent to Canada and Mexico. South America and Asia still accounted for a small portion of the overall export trade of the United States. This partly explains why American expansion was overwhelmingly informal and peaceful. American goods tended to concentrate in areas where they could be marketed without the protection and enforcement of American power.

Yet even at this period of comparatively peaceful orientation of American expansion, the Pacific Ocean represented something of an exception. In Pearl Harbor and Pago Pago the United States obtained exclusive control over potential naval bases, and the whole of Hawaii and part of Samoa fell into its sphere of influence. In 1875 a reciprocity treaty with Hawaii forbade that government to grant most-favored-nation treatment to other countries, in direct contradiction to the principle of equal opportunity the United States was stressing in East Asia. The determination to preserve the American orientation of Hawaii, not only economically but ethnically and politically as well, was expressed by Secretary Blaine, who asserted in 1881, "The United States regards the Hawaiian group as essentially a part of the American system of states. . . . [While] favorably inclined toward the continuance of native rule on a basis of political independence and commercial assimilation with the United States, we could not regard the intrusion of any non-American interest in Hawaii as consistent with our relations thereto." [21] He was opposed to the importation of coolie laborers from British colonies as they would subvert the character of the islands. Whatever the rationalization, the crucial fact remains that in Hawaii, American behavior was never totally peaceful but displayed characteristics of imperialistic expansion. The same was true of the advance into the Samoan Islands, where, with economic interests far less significant than in Hawaii, the United States nevertheless obtained exclusive use of the harbor of Pago Pago. Some, like Minister John A. Kasson in Berlin, advocated the establishment of an American protectorate which "would give to us the control of their foreign relations." His government was not willing to go that far, but neither was it averse to competing for influence in that distant region against the formidable imperialistic policies of Britain and Germany. Kasson was wide of the mark when he lamented, in 1885, what he took to be America's inaction in the Pacific: "The Pacific Ocean should have been an American sea . . . touching at numerous islands having American plantations, and covered by the American flag." [22] Although the ocean was not quite an American sea, United States action there was far more assertive than elsewhere — a fact destined to have profound consequences for its relations with Japan.

In East Asia proper American expansion was generally private and peaceful. Trade with China suffered a decline after the Civil War, amounting at most to only 2 percent of the total American exports. More impressive were the activities of missionaries and educators, who began to make their presence conspicuous. Whereas there were only two hundred American missionaries in China in 1870, by 1900 the number had grown to a thousand. As the Ch'ing Dynasty went through periods of restoration, reaction, and reform, some were employed in positions of influence in government and education. Among them was W. A. P. Martin, who was to spend sixty years in China. He was comparable to the Englishman, Robert Hart, in that both became officials employed by the Chinese government and contributed immensely to the country's reforms. But, whereas the British navy stood behind Hart's work as inspector general of the Maritime Customs Administration, Martin's influence was almost entirely his own. As he worked as president of the T'ung-wen kuan, a school founded in 1861 to train translators, his sole aim was to educate Chinese officials in the arts and technology of the West so that they could deal with Westerners in diplomatic relations.[23] Martin even severed ties with the Presbyterian board in New York to devote his energy full-time to secular education in China. He was instrumental in introducing Western subjects to the traditional Chinese examination system, and the sciences began to gain wider acceptance as a respectable field of study. Basic to his work was the conviction that knowledge — in his case scientific knowledge in particular — was universally valid and that he should be an instrument of disseminating it in a society hitherto little touched by it. It is hard to find a more representative figure of nineteenth-century universalistic expansionism.

It was in Japan that America's liberal expansionists were able to witness the immediate fruits of their labor. David Murray was employed by the new Meiji government to organize a modern educational system, and American missionaries founded more girls' schools at this time than were created by the Japanese government. Young Japanese of the 1870's and the 1880's, fresh out of the tumult of the 1860's, flocked to American missionaries and teachers to absorb the ideas and techniques of the West. Pragmatic considerations alone did not lead them to Western teachers. The latter offered refreshing insights and novel opportunities for inquiry and philosophy to young Japanese, most of samurai origin, who had failed to find in traditional studies appealing challenges to their existence. Americans who imparted a zeal for learning and for good living, like William Clark who taught at the Sapporo Agricultural School, were immensely popular and influential. It was not so much practical knowledge as a brush with infinite knowledge and spiritual depth that excited the Japanese. In this sense American educators were conveyors of universalism.

American merchants in the treaty ports of Asia represented a different type of expansion. They, along with other Western merchants, controlled the host countries' foreign trade in more than one way. Not only did the treaty tariff system, making for low import duties over foreign goods, exist, but Western merchants controlled exchange transactions, selection of native commodities for export, setting of prices, and their marketing overseas. There were few Chinese and Japanese merchants in the West before 1890, and the marketing of Chinese and Japanese silks, teas, and other items was entirely in the hands of foreigners. For instance, in 1884, when Japanese trade amounted to about 63 million yen, it was reported that 86 percent of the exports and 95 percent of the imports were handled by foreign merchants.[24] Teas and silks were Japan's major items of export, but their selection, shipment, and sale abroad were controlled by foreigners. With little knowledge of market conditions overseas, the Japanese operated at the mercy of price fluctuations and whimsical tastes of foreign consumers.[25] Some were interested in posting trade agents in New York and other cities to exert some control over Japanese trade, but, because of a lack of experience, expertise, and capital, their efforts did not immediately bear fruit.

As earlier, there was much interest in the United States in developments in East Asia. A familiar theme in American writing in the 1870's and 1880's was the "awakening" of Japan. After the Meiji Restoration of 1868 the Japanese began behaving as though directed by American notions and expectations of how they should conduct themselves. As a whole the American liberal mind embraced these developments with enthusiasm. It reached out to Japan to entertain an image of the progress of civilization. Henry M. Field's *From Egypt to Japan,* first published in 1877 and going through thirteen editions within nine years, provides a good example. The travelogue was written, according to its author, "to bring them [other peoples] nearer, and to bind them to us by closer bonds of sympathy. If these pictures of Asia make it a little more real, and inspire the feeling of a common nature with the dusky races that live on the other side of the globe, and so infuse a larger knowledge and a gentler charity then a traveller's tale may serve as a kind of lay sermon, teaching peace and good will to men." This was not only his message to his American readers; it was also the framework through which he viewed non-Westerners. Thus, he said of the Islamic religion: "at its heart the system is cold, and hard, and cruel; it does not acknowledge the brotherhood of man." Field dichotomized the world between East and West, and his visits were to the Eastern half. Cairo had "all the peculiar features of the East." When the hold of Islam was broken, "the Eastern world may be moulded into new forms. Then will the Oriental mind be brought into an impossible state . . . and it may yield to the combined influence of civilization and Christianity." English laws, as administered by British colonial governors, "will educate the Hindoos to the idea of justice, which, outside of English colonies, can hardly be said to exist in Asia." As the people of India proved, "The Asiatic nature is torpid and slow to move, and cannot rouse itself to great exertion."

"The question of English rule in India," the author continued, "is a question of civilization against barbarism. These are the two forces now in conflict for the mastery of Asia." But the former was bound to "conquer" the world. Field was fully prepared to match words to what he thought he found in Japan. The "sudden revolution" taking place there was "one of the most remarkable things in history, which, in a few years, has changed a whole nation, so that from being the most isolated, the most exclusive, and the most rigidly conservative, even in Asia, it has become the most active and enterprising." The change "has taken [Japan] out of the stagnant life of Asia, to infuse into its vein the life of Europe and America. In a word, it has, as it were, unmoored Japan from the coast of Asia, and towed it across the Pacific, to place it alongside of the New World, to have the same course of life and progress." [26]

These expressions reveal that America's liberal expansionists, who delighted in Japan's "awakening" and "progress," were not averse to seeing backward areas of the world come under the control and influence of civilized powers. This may explain their surprisingly muted response to European imperialism, which was just then entering a new era. No detailed study of American opinion exists regarding such instances of the new imperialsim as the British occupation of Egypt and the establishment of French protectorate over Annam. On the whole it would seem that in the United States there was no intense and widespread condemnation of European imperialism. America's liberal expansionists could tolerate Europe's political and military control over Africa, the Middle East, and Asia because it was couched in the rhetoric of civilization. As a New York paper noted, "civilization gains whenever any misgoverned country passes under the control of a European race." [27] Although few yet advocated that the United States

should take part in this civilizing mission, there was intellectual recep-
tivity to the idea of Western expansion, forceful as well as peaceful,
into the non-West. To be sure some remained skeptics. Writing for
the *Andover Review* in 1885, W. Barrows, a theologian, argued that
the use of force could not be justified even for the sake of the spread
of civilization. "Does civilization allow violence," he asked, "and may
an inferior people be forced by a superior into a higher grade?" Even
if all the barbarous and semi-civilized peoples were to be moved up-
ward in the scale of progress, he was not sure that "the common processes of force and manoeuvre and seizure" could be defended.[28] Another Christian writer, Josiah Strong, was more representative of
American thinking. In *Our Country,* published in 1885, he confidently
foretold the coming of the age of Anglo-Saxon supremacy in the
world. "Is there reasonable doubt," he asked, "that this race, unless
devitalized by alcohol and tobacco, is destined to dispossess many
weaker races, assimilate others, and mold the remainder, until, in a
very true and important sense, it has Anglo-Saxonized mankind?" Distinguished from other races by Protestant Christianity and civil liberty, the Anglo-Saxons, according to Strong, were destined to overwhelm others both in quantity and quality. The result would be the
triumph of liberty, Christianity, and civilization on earth.[29] Such an argument could as easily rationalize imperialism as echo the more traditional liberal expansionism.

Regardless of the methods visualized and the rhetoric employed, expansion was almost without exception conceived of as a unidirectional
phenomenon. To quote Josiah Strong again, the time was coming
when "this race of unequaled energy, with all the majesty of numbers
and the might of wealth behind it — the representative, let us hope,
of the largest liberty, the purest Christianity, the highest civilization
— having developed peculiarly aggressive traits calculated to impress
its institutions upon mankind, will spread itself over the earth." [30]
Others talked of the dissemination of American ideas and goods
abroad, or the spread of Western civilization to non-Western lands.
Expansion was unidirectional because Western superiority and American supremacy were taken for granted. Primitive, semi-civilized, and
dormant societies of Asia and Africa were to partake of the benefits of
Western civilization through the coming of energetic Westerners to
these lands. Whether they used force or not, they were agents of history which, according to E. A. Allen's four-volume *History of Civiliza-*

tion (1888), revealed "the various steps by which man passed from the lower stages of enlightenment to that advanced stage that we call civilization." [31]

This cultural monism underlying American expansion of all varieties ill prepared the nation for coping with a totally different phenomenon: expansion undertaken by non-Western peoples. Historians of Western imperialism usually forget that Asians were also expanding. In purely economic terms, Asian goods were expanding to the American market much more rapidly than were American exports to the East. Moreover, there was a great deal of intra-Asian movement of men, as Chinese, Japanese, and others became more and more mobile. The Chinese, in particular, had had a long record of migration overseas, and by the end of the nineteenth century their small communities were thriving in Southeast Asia, Hawaii, and the West coast of the United States. To be sure there was no ideological underpinning comparable to the rhetoric of American expansionism. Chinese universalism was more self-sufficient than American, and there was little necessity to argue for the universal applicability of Confucian institutions, since Confucianism was a symbol of status which one gained with effort, not something to be imposed upon unknowing and unwilling peoples. Also the bulk of Chinese emigrants to Hawaii and America were contract laborers, bound to their creditors for a term of years, whose primary goal abroad was to pay off their debts and return home. The fact remains that the Chinese, even at this time, were just as mobile as Westerners, and their presence in distant lands was as conspicuous as the enclaves of Westerners in Asia. If the latter phenomenon is called expansionism, then the former suggests Chinese expansion. Wherever they went, Chinese abroad met strenuous and often impossible working conditions with patience, hard work, and kinship ties which provided a means for mutual association and help. Pockets of small communities dotting the surface of the earth were an index of the Chinese people's remarkable capacity for cultural transplantation and peaceful expansion. When one speaks of the "decline" of China in the nineteenth century, one's view should be balanced by the "rise" of these overseas Chinese communities.[32]

It is little to be wondered at that, in the vocabulary of American expansionism, whether liberal or imperialistic, there was no room for Chinese expansion to the United States, of all places. Theoretically, if America's liberal expansionists had been truly universalistic, they should have recognized the logic of welcoming Asians to the United States to partake of its allegedly superior civilization. In 1849, for instance, a Protestant publicist had written in glowing terms of the spread of Anglo-Saxon civilization in the Pacific created by the coming together of Westerners and Asians on the West coast of the United States. "May it not be," he asked, "that the causes which have thronged the Atlantic states with European immigrants, will crowd the Pacific states with the teeming population of the Asiatic nations? And as Germany, France, and Ireland have been leavened, in a measure, with republican and evangelical principles, and will be in a greater degree by the reflex influence of their emigration; so, may it not be that China, India, and even Japan, shall receive missionaries, in due time, from the converts among their native emigrants to the American coast?" [33] Few shared such a vision after the Civil War. While a small number of Japanese and Chinese officials and students were received with enthusiasm, there was no thought that America would be an object of Asian expansion. This explains the feeble resistance in the United States to the anti-Chinese agitation on the West coast. As Stuart Miller has shown, anti-Chinese prejudice was not confined to California, whose exclusionist legislation went scarcely checked by the rest of the country.[34] Fundamentally this was because the Chinese were regarded as a stagnant, stationary people, the exact opposite of the energetic, expanding Americans. "The China of today is far behind the China of Marco Polo," a writer noted in Harper's.[35] Americans, regarding themselves as expansionists, were unable to envision the possibility of the expansion of Asians toward the United States. Although there were far more Chinese in the United States than Americans in China, expansion was to be unidirectional, from higher to lower civilization, from America to China.

As yet there was no comparable Japanese expansion, but forces were already stirring in Japan that were destined to affect the shape American expansion would take. Interpretations of early Meiji Japan usually stress the new leaders' pragmatic concern with immediate national issues, as well as their overriding commitment to "enrich the nation and strengthen the army." In foreign affairs, historians point virtually unanimously to two basic problems: Korea and treaty revision. The Japanese government is generally pictured as having sought the revision of the existing unequal treaties and military security vis-à-vis the Korean peninsula as the fundamental national goals. Such a view ignores the far more significant undercurrent in Japanese thought, concern with expansionism, that paralleled the growth of expansionism in other parts of the world. The speed with which the Japanese absorbed Western concepts and methods of overseas expansion was the key to their successful self-transformation.

It is true that there had been an indigenous tradition of expansionism in Japan. When, in the 1870's, Japanese publicists began calling for expansion overseas, they could and did point to the record of the sixteenth and seventeenth centuries, when Japanese merchants, warriors, and adventurers ventured out to Southeast Asia and even beyond. After the "closing of the country," there had been no physical reaching out to foreign lands, but the idea of overseas settlement and colonization never died. As the long period of internal peace and economic development caused an increase in population, interest in finding vacant spaces for resettlement increased. Ezo — or Hokkaido, as it came to be known — loomed as just such a territory. From the end of the eighteenth century on, treatises on the subject of "colonization" referred to the desirability and feasibility of settling the northern island with a surplus population. Kuroda Ken'ichi, whose 1942 monograph remains the standard work on the subject, asserts that this interest in colonization was quite independent of Western colonialist literature.[36]

After the Meiji Restoration, two new developments added to the growing concern with the subject of expansion. One was the introduction of the Malthusian theory of population, which began to be discussed in Japanese newspapers and journals around 1877.[37] Taguchi Ukichi, one of the most influential economists of the day, addressed his journal, *Tokyo keizai zasshi* (Tokyo economic magazine), established in 1879, to the population question. Statistics were scanty and unreliable, and at first there was only superficial acquaintance with the Malthusian theory, but the image of an overcrowded Japan created a receptive audience for Malthus' ideas. By the 1880's practically all authors on the question of Japanese economic and political development at least paid lip service to the famous formula of the population's geometrical increase in contrast to the arithmetical expansion of food productivity. The perception of Japan as a country with too many people and too little food, if not at the moment then at least in the near future, was already widespread.

Another development was the more general admiration of the

West and search for the sources of its wealth and power. Of all aspects of Western life and institutions, ranging from modern armament, constitutionalism, and factories to schools and churches, none impressed the Japanese more than the phenomenon of expansion. It was not simply and even primarily the military might of the Western nations that excited them. Military superiority, after all, was easy to understand. In their eagerness to equal the West, the Japanese were curious to know what lay beneath its power. Their conclusions, arrived at after several years of direct and indirect observations of Western countries, all pointed to the phenomenon of expansion: the West's ability to let its resources and energies overflow national boundaries and reach far corners of the earth. Expansion frequently took the form of colonialism, but to early Meiji Japanese other activities such as foreign trade and emigration also seemed a vital part of the expansion of the West. The terms "expansion," "colonization," and "emigration" were often used interchangeably, indicating that in the Japanese view these were all aspects of Western power and influence in the world.

These two threads of thought combined with specific diplomatic issues in China and Korea and brought about the beginning of Japanese continental activities. The Tokyo government sought to establish a position of influence in Korea that was at least comparable to that exercised by China, while Japanese merchants and adventurers (shishi) entered these countries to do what Westerners were doing. Their exploits have been extensively chronicled and given excellent scholarly treatment by Marius Jansen, Motoyama Yukihiko, and others. They have noted the early Meiji and even late Tokugawa origins of Japanese continentalism and pan-Asianism. Yet it would be misleading to focus on these phenomena to the exclusion of other kinds of expansionist ideas and activities. Historians usually cite men like Satō Nobuhiro, Ōi Kentarō, and Tarui Tōkichi to illustrate nineteenth-century Japanese expansionism, but there were many others, now almost forgotten, who contributed to the literature of Japanese expansionism and whose arguments do not fit the picture generally presented.[38]

That Japanese expansionism was not confined to Asia can be seen in the number of Japanese overseas. It is recorded, for instance, that in 1880 there were 86 Japanese in Hong Kong, and that nine years later the number was 243.[39] While there were nearly 5,000 Japanese in Korea and several hundred in Shanghai in the late 1880's, in 1885 only

6 Japanese residents were counted in the important port city of Hankow.⁴⁰ In January of the same year 850 men, women, and children left Yokohama for Honolulu, to be followed by another thousand in June.⁴¹ Certainly these were all cases of Japanese expansion as the term was understood by the Japanese at that time, and the statistics indicated that the incipient Japanese expansion overseas was global, not merely continental. They also revealed that territorial imperialism was not what was usually meant when the Japanese talked about expansion; they were far more interested in the overall economic expansion of the country after the pattern of the West.

The theme of economic strengthening through trade and emigration came to be stressed more and more strongly in Japan in the 1880's, just at a time when Americans were beginning to take some positive measures in the Pacific to consolidate their interests. One of the earliest extant expressions of Japan's peaceful expansionism was a pamphlet printed in 1883 by Hashimoto Jūbei, a licensed examiner of silks. Having toured Europe from 1880 to 1882, he returned home convinced of the need for massive national effort to extend Japan's silk industry and trade. He warned his countrymen against assuming that domestic political movements would contribute to the nation's strengthening and enrichment. Only by building a solid material foundation for national power, he argued, could people talk of carrying out political reforms at home and extending diplomatic prestige abroad. By material foundations of the state he meant "the encouragement of industry and development of commercial organizations." The situation was such, however, that "today our commercial world is chaotic and filled with vicious merchants. . . . The real power in commerce is in the hands of a few European and American merchants in Japan, and it seems extremely difficult to regain power from them." Even with respect to Japan's main item of export, silk, it was the foreign merchants who set prices, while Japanese producers and merchants were totally ignorant and helpless. As a way to change the situation, Hashimoto urged the establishment of a public market in Yokohama dealing in silks and an inspection station to determine their grades. Only through such efforts could the Japanese find ways to export their commodities directly, without going through the hands of foreign merchants. Only then would it be possible for Japan to engage in the "economic warfare" which was raging all over the world.⁴²

The expression "economic warfare" was one of the most commonly used in Japanese writings at the time. Hashimoto described it as "a war without warfare." The great powers seemed to be waging invisible, peaceful wars without resorting to armed clashes. Victory in such warfare depended on economic rather than primarily military factors. It was of little consequence that certain nations had more soldiers or ships. Of much more fundamental importance was what Hashimoto called "skill or lack of skill in economic management." From his point of view, the effort to regain control over the export of silk was far more important than building ships.

Similarly, another author, Ōgoshi Seitoku, who had also spent several years in England and France, wrote in 1889 that "the way to enrich the nation is to develop industry at home and extend transportation and trade abroad." He was particularly interested in the import trade, as it was in Japan's interest to obtain raw materials and other goods cheaply. He, too, noted that the bulk of imports to Japan was handled by foreigners, so that Japanese consumers had no idea of the adequacy of the quality and prices of foreign goods. Western merchants in Japan were very "arrogant"; they treated the Japanese as though they belonged to an inferior breed of men. Thus, in general commercial transactions as well as in casual relationships, Western merchants were developing a peculiar style of human relations. This, Ōgoshi reasoned, must be because foreign merchants who came to Japan had first done business in India, China, and other parts of Asia and were accustomed to despising Asians. At the same time, Japanese merchants as a whole were no better than Westerners; both were avaricious, cunning, and untrustworthy. The only way to gain the respect of the West in commercial dealings was to improve the quality of individual Japanese merchants. In an important passage, the author asserted that military strengthening was no solution to the problem. "The strengthening of army and navy," he wrote, "is for the defense of the country, not for challenging foreign merchants or extending commercial rights. I have never heard of any country expanding its armament without regard to its position and economic conditions merely to extend commercial rights." Because foreign trade markets were like battlefields, Japanese must find out what weapons and what means "the enemy" — foreign merchants — employed in the battle. The only way to do so was for Japanese resolutely to enter the battlefield, in other words, to go abroad in search of markets, prepared to wage peaceful but serious warfare with foreign merchants.[43]

Such reasoning led logically to the conclusion that Japan's salvation lay in expansion, broadly defined. From the foregoing quotations, it is easy to see that Meiji Japanese viewed even commercial work abroad as something requiring soldierly determination. One was about to enter the world arena and exert every effort to expand economic opportunities; one was going to share in the national task of expansion. Thus, the "opening of the country" meant not only the coming of foreigners but also the going out of Japanese, and this expanding of the Japanese overseas was undertaken with self-conscious determination. Compared with this task, the build-up of armament or revision of treaties, themes usually stressed by historians, were far easier tasks. We miss the essential meaning of early Meiji history unless we take note of the fact that this was the period in which forces converged to make Japan push outward, not primarily in search of territory to conquer, but as part of the necessary expansion of the country.

While they pondered the need to expand activities abroad, many Japanese were impressed with the fact that Chinese were already active in many parts of the world. As Ōgoshi remarked, the people "most to be feared" as potential competitors in Japan's quest for overseas activities were the Chinese. In such places as India, Siam, Singapore, Hawaii, Australia, and the Philippines — areas of the greatest potential for Japanese trade — Chinese were already active. They lived on meager wages and dealt not only in Chinese but also in foreign goods. They had a strong sense of community and cooperated closely with one another. They, rather than Westerners, could develop as the strongest rivals of Japanese abroad. Similarly, in 1887 Mutō Sanji pointed out in his influential tract, *Beikoku ijūron* (On emigration to the United States), that the Chinese had contributed much to the development of California. They had migrated to a land about which they had had little previous knowledge and were now competing with the whites in the enjoyment of natural resources. Mutō had visited Hawaii and the West coast in 1885 and was very impressed with the prevalence and spread of the Chinese everywhere: "Wherever there were white people, there were also Chinese." There was no reason why the Japanese could not do likewise, especially now that agitation against Chinese laborers in the United States was widespread.[44]

Considering the success of Chinese overseas and the spread of anti-Chinese movements abroad, Mutō felt that the time was opportune to undertake massive emigration and resettlement of Japanese. He was confident that the superiority of Japanese to Chinese was already well recognized by Westerners, and that, unlike Chinese laborers who had been excluded from the United States, Japanese were well liked by whites. Mutō was particularly convinced that Japan's lower, laboring classes made fit candidates for migration to California and other Western states of the United States. They were impoverished in Japan, and their future was uncertain. It was in their interest as well as in the interest of the capitalists to resettle large numbers in the rich land of California. The capitalists should establish emigration companies and actively sponsor a program of resettlement. "It will be enormously profitable to export our cheap labor to the United States where labor is expensive," he asserted. He warned, however, that those going to America must be prepared to stay permanently. It was in part because the Chinese were sojourners, interested only in making money, that they were being mistreated. Japanese must resolve to settle and contribute to the making of riches in a new country.[45]

Expressions such as these reveal that even before the 1890's the Japanese were concerned with much more than the immediate questions of treaty revision and Korea. Actually, these were part of the growing interest in expansion, and when they talked and thought about it, the Japanese were as likely to have peaceful expansion in mind as more militant varieties. Nakae Chōmin's celebrated booklet, *San suijin keirin mondō* (Argument among three drunkards), published in 1887, reveals that, in spite of the lack of consensus about the kinds of expansion to be undertaken, agreement regarding the need to relate Japan to the rest of the world in a positive manner did exist.

In this tract the author presents three discussants, representing three divergent views on the course Japan should follow in external affairs. The first speaker represents the view that the whole wide world is a gemeinschaft: "I happen to be in Country A and so am a citizen of that country. If I move to Country B, I will become a citizen of that country. . . . Since I live on the globe which is the native land of mankind, everywhere in the world is my living place." The basic principles of association with other people are liberty and friendship, and only these principles should dictate how Japan as a country should relate to others. Since various peoples of the world, at least of the democratic countries, are inspired by these principles, there can be no war or conflict among them. At least this will be the general situation if all countries follow these ideals. Japan, in particular, has no reason not to follow them, being a small country with limited resources, and given the fact that no spot on the globe is available for Japanese expansion even if the Japanese should want to undertake forceful expansionism. On the contrary, they should dedicate themselves to the goal of making Japan a peace-loving country where morality and civilization flourish. There should be complete free trade with all nations. Then Japan may very well prove to be the first country taking decisive steps toward making the world one family. "In the nineteenth century, it is madness to try to build up national prestige through armament, make aggression the national policy, and become the owner of the whole earth by plundering other peoples' lands and massacring them." As an example of a country that does not engage in such madness, Nakae points to the United States where the people laugh at other countries' territorial ambitions and mutual jealousies and instead "concentrate on developing industry and accumulating riches."

The second speaker takes a diametrically opposed view. He notes that the civilized nations are those strongest in arms and most aggressive in overseas expansionism. At a time when their troops and ships are rampant in European fields and Asian waters, it is idleness to talk of liberty, freedom, and universal brotherhood. Fortunately, Japan already is on its way toward economic enrichment and military strength. It should now take the next step and seize overseas territory, in particular, parts of China. If Japan acquires one-third to one-half of China and settles Japanese farmers, artisans, merchants, and teachers there, Japan will become a great power comparable to England and Russia. Japan can then be a continental empire, and the capital may be moved to some point on the Asian continent. As for the islands of Japan proper, they may as well be given to the idealists to experiment with their freedom and democracy! Unless part of China is taken, Japan will have no resources with which to pay for advanced technology of the West, a necessary condition for the country's civilization and strengthening.

The third speaker, presumably representing the author, criticizes the other two for their extreme and exaggerated views, insisting that world conditions are neither as alarming as the second says nor as conducive to optimism as the first implies. Rather, Japan's wise course lies in maintaining a defensive armament against attack but otherwise cultivating its economic resources in order to enrich the country in conditions of peace. "The best strategy for our diplomacy is to maintain friendly relations with any and all countries, persist in defensive military planning unless an emergency situation necessitates otherwise, avoid costly overseas expeditions, and increase the welfare of the people." One should never think of attacking China but instead consider it a great potential market. If Japan does not boast of its prowess or demonstrate national egoism, it will not be feared by China, which will make unlimited resources available.[46]

These three views, the first representing non-nationalistic universalism, the second nationalistic particularism, and the third non-aggressive nationalism, represented the alternatives open in the 1880's. They all envisaged some sort of expansion as a necessary condition for Japanese existence. One was frankly imperialistic, and the other two advocated economic expansionism, one being more willing than the other to give up the national framework in the process of expansion and consider international relations like those among individuals. Small wonder that their discussion produced no agreement on how Japan should relate itself to the rest of the world. In a cryptic postscript, the author casually mentioned that the three discussants never had another opportunity for discourse. "People say," he wrote, "that the Westernized gentleman [the first speaker] has gone to America, and the brave hero [the second] has left for Shanghai. Mr. Nankai alone remained, unmoved, and sipping his wine." Only the future would tell in what way the ideas of these three gentlemen would be implemented by the people and the government to define the nature of Japanese expansion in the world.

II

The Emergence of Imperialism

In 1887 Nakae Chōmin expressed a generally held view in Japan when he excepted the United States from the imperialistic powers and referred to its policy as peacefully and economically oriented. Eleven years later, in 1898, another Japanese liberal, Kōtoku Shūsui, was denouncing the United States as no different from others, saying there was no nation in the world that was not selfish and aggressive.[1]

Such contrasting opinions characterize the changes that were taking place in Japanese-American relations. The simultaneous emergence of the two countries as imperialists seriously affected their respective courses of expansion. In searching for clues to explain the origins of the territorial empires of the United States and Japan, historians have almost totally neglected the interaction between the countries. This interaction was not simply military and economic; it was also ideological and psychological. Above all it was racial and cultural, and it determined the way in which the two peoples would expand in the Pacific and East Asia. To ignore these factors is to treat the emergence of Japanese and American imperialism in a vacuum.

For instance, historians have noted the convergence of American and European thinking toward the end of the nineteenth century, as Americans and Europeans employed similar words and concepts to justify their imperialism. Julius W. Pratt and Richard Hofstadter have commented on the transmission of Social Darwinist thought across the Atlantic, providing American imperialists with theoretical rationalizations.[2] More recently, Ernest R. May has convincingly demonstrated that the leading exponents of imperialism in the United States had close social and intellectual ties to British imperialists, and that such writers as Charles Dilke, James Anthony Froude, and John Robert Seeley were immensely popular in America.[3] There existed, in other words, an intellectual baggage from which Americans could draw bits of ideas to explain and promote overseas expansion. But why should this have been the case? Why should they have justified their interest in imperialism by referring to European currents of thought and events? Earlier, Americans might have adopted a more unique rationale, such as manifest destiny, and stressed differences between greedy European imperialism and their own expansionism. Toward the end of the century, however, they were more willing to use the same arguments as Europeans, and considered it less strange that they should be thinking in the European framework of thought and vocabulary. There was an implicit assumption that both belonged to the same perceived world.

Nowhere was the convergence of European and American thinking more clearly demonstrated than in the outpouring of writings on civilization in the last years of the century, and in the defense of imperialism in the name of civilization. Theodore Roosevelt, for instance, wrote to Henry White during the Boer War, "I feel it is to the interest of civilization that the English-speaking race should be dominant in South Africa, exactly as it is for the interest of civilization that the United States themselves, the greatest branch of the English-speaking race, should be dominant in the Western Hemisphere." White himself wrote that "it is in the interest of both branches of the Anglo-Saxon race that we should be supreme on both American conti-nents." [4] As the racial connotations in these remarks indicate, civilization was becoming a parochial notion, representing the interests of Americans for some writers, Anglo-Saxons for others, and the white race for still others. This was symptomatic of the growing concern with the future of Western supremacy in a rapidly changing world. Herein lie the clues to American imperialism and to Japanese-American estrangement.

"The world is getting so small," a writer for *Science* magazine wrote in 1892, "that the thought and life of one portion of it can no longer be a matter of indifference to another, even the most remote." [5] Practically every writer, in Europe as well as in the United States, agreed that the steamship and electricity, items most commonly cited as symbols of modern technology, had changed the physical appearance of the earth. These inventions had revolutionized human communica-

tion and brought into closer contact distant regions of the world. As
Josiah Strong wrote, "steam and electricity have had so profound an
influence on modern civilization. . . . [Men] have been brought into
much closer relations and the world's rate of progress has been won-
derfully quickened." [6] One could, of course, respond to the situation
in a traditional way. Charles Morris wrote in his *Civilization: An Historical Review of Its Elements* that "underlying . . . civilization are
found traces of progress from the state of the primitive savage to that
of cultured man." He reviewed the rise and fall of individual civilizations and, as had so many earlier writers, described the "steady decadence" and "stagnation" of Asia. Nevertheless, while individual civilizations decayed, human civilization seemed to have steadily
progressed. There had "never been any actual ebb in the tide of
human development," Morris wrote, but "every step has been a step
forward, even though made by the foot of barbarism on the neck of
prostrate civilization, which it seemed to crush into the earth." Thus,
he concluded, "Mankind is . . . tending to become one great being,
made up of discrete parts, yet linked together as intimately by bonds
of sympathy as the human organs are by bonds of sensory nerves." [7]
Similarly, in his *History of Civilization,* E. A. Allen asserted that "man
has lived on the earth for a very long time, while . . . his starting point
was very low in the scale . . . he has lived a life of progress. . . . A true
idea of the dignity and worth of man is gained only when we take
these broad general views of his antiquity and his growth in culture
. . . [We] have faith that in the future, as in the past, man will live a
life of progress." [8]

Others were far less certain of progress and the unity of human experience. More and more writers were stressing conflict rather than
harmony among different peoples, and the threat posed to Western
civilization by new forces within and without. The history of the
world appeared to them to be more ominous and less stable than pictured by innocent Americans.[9] The world, again according to Josiah
Strong, was likely soon to "enter upon a new stage of its history — *the
final competition of races, for which the Anglo-Saxon is being
schooled.*" [10] Charles Eliot Norton wrote, "we are brought face to
face with the grave problem which the next century is to solve, —
whether our civilization can maintain itself, and make advance,
against the pressure of ignorant and barbaric multitudes." [11] Hiram
M. Stanley asserted, in the magazine *Arena,* "It is a truth which it is

perfect folly for us to ignore, that our civilization is in the most vital part of its decadence," and in the same issue another author declared, "What is history but a record of wrecks, sometimes swift, sometimes slow, and of drifting, water-logged empires, which survive because the storms have not yet been fierce enough to sink them." [12]

Such pessimism and the stress on conflict often affected thinking about America's future in Asia and the Pacific. American-Asian relations could be viewed within the framework of Western-Eastern relations at a time when Western technology was rapidly transforming life in the East. Perhaps the best exposition of this problem came from the pen of Charles H. Pearson, an Englishman of long residence in Australia. His *National Life and Character*, published in 1893, provided the point of departure for many writers, European and American. In it Pearson asserted that the white race, by spreading all over the world, was imparting scientific knowledge and organizational skills to the yellow and black races, and that in time the latter would emerge as no longer docile objects of exploitation but as serious competitors to the former. "The day will come," he wrote, "and perhaps is not far distant, when the European observer will look round to see the globe girdled with a continuous zone of the black and yellow races, no longer too weak for aggression or under tutelage, but independent, or practically so, in government, monopolising the trade of their own regions, and circumscribing the industry of the European." Such a day would mark the end of Western expansion, and the white race would be confined to its original home. Worse, it might find its seas visited by the fleets of non-Western countries, its conferences attended by their representatives, its turf and salons crowded by darker citizens, and its social fabric torn by intermarriages with other races. When Western expansion was arrested, Pearson thought, and non-Western counterexpansion began, the character of mankind would be profoundly altered. Westerners would be forced to "a stationary condition of society" and might see their societies become garrison states. "It is now more than probable," he concluded, "that our science, our civilisation, our great and real advance in the practice of government are only bringing us nearer to the day when . . . we shall ask nothing from the day but to live, nor from the future but that we may not deteriorate." Deprived of its vigor and strength, the West would cease to be Western.

There was a streak of fatalism in Pearson, as he saw Western expansion and non-Western counterexpansion as inevitable developments. He did, however, believe that "if we cannot change manifest destiny, we may at least adapt ourselves to it, and make it endurable." Expansion was not to cease, for that would be against the natural disposition of Westerners. The solution, however temporary and illusory, lay in spreading Western ideas as well as technology. If the non-Western world should appropriate the nobler concepts of Western civilization while absorbing its materialistic aspects, then the non-white races might prove to be less incompatible with the white. Even so, it would mean that the West no longer was the sole center of civilization, but that it was diffused over vast areas of the globe. "With civilisation equally diffused, the most populous country must ultimately be the most powerful; and the preponderance of China over any rival — even over the United States of America — is likely to be overwhelming."

For Pearson, as for other writers on the subject, diversity within the West was much less important than its overall unity. "For civilized men there can be only one fatherland," he wrote, and they had taken "their faith from Palestine, their laws of beauty from Greece, and their civil law from Rome." Russians, Germans, Anglo-Saxons, and Frenchmen were all heirs to the tradition. The central paradox of his thesis is obvious. Modern civilization, originating in the West, the only home of civilization, became, when diffused over wide areas, a menace to the West and therefore to civilization itself. But the extension of civilization was a vital part of Western history and could not be arrested. Western civilization was destined to atrophy because of its own vitality.[13]

Not everyone agreed with Pearson's diagnosis of the future of Western civilization. His book typified a negative awareness of Western unity, one derived from the perceived menace of the non-West. Few were willing to accept his conclusions. But the problems he dealt with, those relating to contact between West and non-West, were drawing increasing attention and creating a climate of opinion favorable to the development of common assumptions and outlooks on both sides of the Atlantic. The number of books and articles published in these years on civilization in general and on East and West in particular revealed that Americans, no less than Europeans, were becoming interested in the question of the future of Western civilization. American expansionists undoubtedly benefited from the fact that more and more Americans were coming to look at the world as

Europeans were viewing it. One of the themes of Josiah Strong's *The New Era* was the contrast between East and West, and he pictured American expansion as part of the expansion of Western civilization. Andrew Raymond, president of Union College, echoed Pearson when he wrote in 1899, "the century just closing, by reason of its discoveries and inventions, multiplying facilities for intercourse, has brought face to face as never before, and in mutual antagonism, the two great types of civilization described in general terms as the Eastern and Western world." The latter needed "all the intelligence and strength and high purpose" it could muster to survive the conflict.[14]

By far the best American essay on the subject was a long article Alfred Thayer Mahan wrote for *Harper's* in 1897. East and West, he said, had existed apart as they had sprung "from conceptions radically different." Evidence was everywhere, however, that "the Eastern world . . . is rapidly appreciating the material advantages and the political traditions which have united to confer power upon the West." The result would be that instead of torpor and death the East would be characterized by vigor and life. Therefore, "we stand at the opening of a period when the question is to be settled decisively, though the issue may be long delayed, whether Eastern or Western civilization is to dominate throughout the earth and to control its future." When the non-Western regions of the world bestirred themselves, their numerical superiority to and religious difference from the West would become crucial factors. If the West was not to perish, efforts must be made to "receive into its own bosom and raise to its own ideals those ancient and different civilizations by which it is surrounded and out-numbered." It was most crucial for Westerners to understand that "Our own civilization less its spiritual element is barbarism; and barbarism will be the civilization of those who assimilate its material progress without imbibing the indwelling spirit." Mahan's sense of desperation was revealed when, totally disregarding the tenet of his thesis, he asserted that the "great armies and the blind outward impulses of the European peoples are the assurance that generations must elapse ere the barriers can be overcome behind which rests the citadel of Christian civilization." It was as if he had lost confidence in the efficacy of Christian civilization to survive and had fallen back upon brute force to defend "the commonwealth of peoples to which we racially belong." [15]

The theme of conflict between East and West was also developed

by Benjamin Ide Wheeler in "Greece and the Eastern Question."
The Eastern question, he wrote, was not merely a problem of the disposition of the crumbling structure of the Ottoman empire. "It is a
question which in its reality concerns the perennial antithesis between
Occidentalism and Orientalism, and which in its practical statement
for us and ours means this: Who is to lead, who is to champion, who is
to represent Occident in its inevitable conflict with the Orient?" He
elaborated on the differences — the immutable distinction — between the two civilizations:

The Occidental conception of life as active and creative, inhering in active
and self-moving autonomous personalities, begets the political idea of what
we call self-government. The idea which represents personality as self-directed
in the fulfillment of its own purposes becomes, when applied to politics, the
idea that communities shall be self-governed in things belonging to themselves. . . . The opposite thereto is the upshot of Orient. A potentate seated
on a very high throne under a very broad canopy, and loaded with very costly
jewels, with prostrate subjects bowing in obeisance before him, — that is the
tableau of Oriental government.

Wheeler was not certain that the Occident was inherently superior to
the Orient, but he reiterated a universalistic faith in the value of the
Anglo-Saxon political concepts. "Government shall find its sanctions
in expressing the purposes and interests of the community governed.
Equal justice, personal rights, distributed government, immanency of
law, — this is the Occidental idea which the Anglo-Saxon spirit offers
to champion before the world." [16]

These writings reveal that in addition to the old notion of peaceful,
universalistic expansionism, cultural particularism in the service of nationalistic expansion was developing. It is not that one first became
convinced of the stakes of Western civilization and then called for
American assertiveness. Such a sequence would be hard to prove.
What seems to have happened is that imperialism came to be justified
in the framework of an emerging perception of the West's struggle to
maintain its strength and superiority. America's expansion could be
seen as a necessary chapter in the West's effort to preserve its civilization. Imperialism became more comprehensible and defensible than
before as the rhetoric to justify it was more readily acceptable.

Indirect evidence, at least, for this can be provided by the fact that
imperialistic sentiment grew strong enough to affect official policy

only toward the end of the 1890's, a period which coincided with the accelerating tempo of Asian politics and the emergence of Japan as an imperialist nation. Until the middle of the decade American policy and opinion were still largely influenced by the tradition of liberal, economic expansionism. As Thomas McCormick has argued, Grover Cleveland typified this tradition and fought a heroic battle to preserve it.[17] He rarely talked about civilization and Western supremacy. Rather, he defined policy in terms of specific national interests and broad universalistic rules. When trouble arose regarding the rights of American fishermen in Canadian waters, Cleveland asserted, "the violation of American fishery rights and unjust or unfriendly acts towards a portion of our citizens engaged in the business is but the occasion for action, and constitutes a national affront which gives birth to or may justify retaliation." This was essentially an old idea, and it did not involve any change in attitude toward expansion. Cleveland saw no need or justification for military and territorial expansionism. His concern was with the traditional one of promoting the welfare of the country through commercial expansion. He was an ardent supporter of tariff reduction and of financial conservatism. Through such means he hoped that the American economy would expand and benefit all segments of the population. He was opposed to high protective tariffs as they would raise consumer prices at home and deprive industry of much needed foreign raw materials. "When we give to our manufacturers free raw materials we unshackle American enterprise and ingenuity, and these will open the doors of foreign markets to the reception of our wares and give opportunity for the continuous and remunerative employment of American labor." Likewise, a sound financial system would help establish a stable basis for American economic relations with the rest of the world. "I not only want our currency to be of such a character that all kinds of dollars will be of equal purchasing power at home, but I want it to be of such a character as will demonstrate our wisdom and good faith, thus placing upon a firm foundation our credit among the nations of the earth." [18]

The second Cleveland administration (1893–1897) was beset by domestic economic problems and foreign crises. The latter were epitomized by the two major episodes of the time: the abortive Hawaiian annexation and the Venezuelan dispute. Historians have been struck by the contrast between Cleveland's responses to these events. Toward the Hawaiian question he consistently maintained an anti-annexationist stand, viewing the annexationist movement as morally wrong and unrelated to American interests. During the Venezuelan dispute with Britain, on the other hand, he startled the world by a forceful enunciation of America's stand and an adamant demand that Britain arbitrate its boundary dispute with Venezuela. It was as if the peaceful, quietist president became all of a sudden a champion of aggressive nationalism. In fact, however, these two responses were not contradictory. Both represented the same concern for protecting American rights and interests in the framework of economic expansionism. Cleveland saw no reason why Hawaii ought to be annexed to the United States; America's basic interests seemed contradicted by a hasty annexation without ascertaining the justice of the situation and weighing the cost of such expansion. Similarly, he regarded Britain's stubborn stand, what he considered its territorial expansion in Venezuela, a violation of the basic principles of peaceful expansionism. Just as the United States would abjure taking the Hawaiian Islands, so Great Britain should refrain from making unjust claims. Arbitration, on which he insisted even by threatening retaliation in case of British refusal, seemed the only way to settle the boundary dispute. There was no assertion that the United States intended to use force to impose a particular boundary definition on Latin America, or that it would act as the arbiter of all American questions. The only assertion was that the United States expected other nations to be bound by the same principles to which it adhered. As he wrote to Minister Thomas F. Bayard in London, "instead of threatening war for not arbitrating, we simply say, inasmuch as Great Britain will not aid us in fixing the facts, we will not go to war, but do the best we can to discover the true state of facts for ourselves, with all the facilities at our command." [19]

Ernest May has suggested that Cleveland could not have acted the way he did had he felt the "foreign policy public" opposed his type of nonimperialistic expansionism.[20] There continued to exist a core of nonimperialistic consensus which, while expansionistic in the traditional, economic manner, was opposed to territorial aggrandizement and costly overseas adventures. Because of this consensus the Cleveland administration was able to stifle attempts by advocates of imperialism to annex the Hawaiian Islands and obtain overseas bases and coaling stations. In 1898, however, these influenced policy and launched the United States on a career as an imperialist power. Reasons for the shift have been endlessly debated among historians, and it would serve no useful purpose to reiterate them here. One factor which has not been sufficiently explored is the interaction between American policy and opinion on one hand and the course of Japanese expansion on the other. In the United States resistance to imperialism temporarily weakened, at least in part, because of the aroused public interest in Asian and Pacific affairs that seemed to dictate a greater American role than before. A rhetoric of civilization was readily available to legitimize new action in the East.

There was a striking parallel between American expansionist thinking on the eve of the Spanish-American War and Japanese opinion prior to the Sino-Japanese War. Both exhibited concern with the need to extend national interests commercially and peacefully, and both showed awareness of racial and cultural diversity. Imperialistic sentiment was growing in the two countries, and calling for force to expand territorially, but this was never the major strain in either Japan or the United States. No matter what the means employed, Americans and Japanese were visualizing expansion into the same areas of the world.

Inagaki Manjirō, who studied under John Robert Seeley at Cambridge and published his *Japan and the Pacific* in English in 1890, joined a growing number of foreign-affairs experts in Japan by writing the influential book *Tōhōsaku* (Eastern policy) upon his return. Based on his earlier work, it reiterated the familiar arguments for peaceful expansion. "The powers compete for wealth in peacetime and in arms during war," he wrote. Although these types of struggle differed in external manifestations, at bottom both revealed the essential fact of modern times: competition among nations. Peacetime competition was the law of international life. "If a nation wants to establish long-range plans and aim at achieving strength and prosperity, it must try to become the center of world commerce and industry, by implication becoming the focus of world politics." Japan was uniquely fitted to emerge as such a center, situated as it was at the crossroads of world commerce where goods from the East met those from the West. The Pacific Ocean "is bound to emerge in the coming century as a great theater of world politics and trade." Japan was destined to play a key role in the drama. With the United States in the east, China in the west, Russia in the north, and Australia in the south, the nation could not help prospering if only it set its mind to taking advantage of such a favorable situation. All that was needed, Inagaki pleaded with his countrymen, was to establish "a fundamental principle of diplomacy" and work together to implement it. More specifically, Japan should import raw materials from Australia, the Asian countries, and the United States and industrialize itself, in order thereby to augment the nation's economic potential.[21] Here was unqualified peaceful expansionism.

Ōishi Masami, a prominent politician, was also moved to write after a trip to Europe. In substance he agreed with Inagaki that Japan's geographical location was extremely favorable to its economic growth, and that material wealth was the basic determinant of national power. But he felt the nation was still far behind Western countries in that respect. There was no industry to speak of, the home islands were filled with unemployed people, and capital accumulation was infinitesimally small. The only way to change the situation was to undertake massive programs of peaceful expansion. One was to develop shipping. Japanese ships ought to dominate trade routes in Asia and the Pacific, so that the nation would emerge as the Great Britain of the East. Students should be sent abroad to acquire necessary skills for industrialization, and foreign capital should be imported for the same end. Overseas emigration, in particular, should be encouraged by the government. Reduction in the size of the population was an absolute necessity for raising the standard of living of people at home and for creating overseas markets for Japanese goods. Ōishi was not calling for forceful territorial aggrandizement, although he did not rule out territorial acquisition through purchase. Essentially he was advocating peaceful migration of Japanese overseas, especially to South America and to the South Sea Islands. Overseas Japanese settlements would help reduce the population in Japan proper and contribute to the extension of trade by creating markets for Japanese goods. Such expansion must not be left to the haphazard efforts of a few individuals but should be carried out under close governmental supervision. The protection of overseas Japanese was essential; for this purpose as well as to gain the respect of other nations, the navy should be augmented. The merchant marine must also be expanded; in 1889 only 1,030,000 out of 12,268,100 yen worth of freight charges incurred in Japanese trade accrued to Japanese shipping. Above all, the people must arouse themselves from inertia and resolve to brave the seas to transplant themselves across the ocean.[22]

Overseas expansionism became a cardinal theme of Japanese

writing in the years immediately preceding the Sino-Japanese War of 1894. Basic arguments for expansion had already become familiar, but their authors were quite aware of the complexity of the problem. It cannot be sufficiently stressed that expansion and not military conquest or colonization was what was generally spoken about. These latter were never completely excluded as possibilities, but they were considered a minor part of the far more fundamental goal of national expansion. In a book entitled *Kaigai shokuminron* (On overseas colonization), published in 1891, a respected economist, Tsuneya Seifuku, asserted that what the title implied was not so much territorial annexation or colonization but such things as "working abroad, settling overseas, foreign trade, fishing, and all such activities as the Japanese will be engaged in abroad, depending on overseas living for their food." Expansion in this broader sense, he pointed out, was Japan's absolute necessity because this was what the Western nations were doing and would continue to do unless checked by Japanese expansion. Moreover, Japan had a tradition of overseas expansion — a theme more and more writers would stress. According to this view, the Japanese had been an expanding, adventurous people, spreading out in the whole world until their activities were stifled by the negative policy of the Tokugawa regime. The time had come for them once again to go abroad and combine their labor with land and capital overseas so as to create markets for Japanese goods and send back their earnings to enrich the home country. "Overseas emigration is the foundation of a rich state and strong army." Massive national efforts were needed to compete with the expanding Western peoples. "In war our army could take on Russia's expeditionary force. But in the peacetime struggle for survival we must take on the whole of the white race. In war our navy could take on the combined fleets of Britain and France. But in the struggle for survival the whole nation must compete with the fleets of the entire world." Tsuneya concluded that for all practical purposes the areas suited to Japanese emigration and settlement would be South America and the south Pacific. In these areas climatic and soil conditions would suit Japanese habits, native populations would accept Japanese without taking advantage of them, indigenous governmental control would not be too severe, and emigrants would be within reach of the home country's navy.[23]

The stress in Ōishi's and Tsuneya's books on South America and the South Seas merits attention. It has been customary to consider

Japanese expansionism as directed primarily toward the Asian continent, in particular Korea and China. Whatever the concern with these
areas in connection with Japan's military security problems, the thrust
of expansionism, as revealed in the writings of the period, lay elsewhere. The Asian continent was generally viewed as much less attractive climatically and socially. There were already too many people
in China and Korea, and the Japanese there would have to compete
with hard-working, low-paid Chinese and Koreans. The Chinese were
pictured as admirable settlers overseas, and the presence of their communities throughout the world indicated that the yellow race could
expand and successfully wage a struggle against other races.[24] But by
the same token the Chinese were formidable competitors, and few
Japanese could support the idea of massive emigration to China.

The case for southern expansion was eloquently presented by a
book entitled *Nanyō saku* (Policy toward the south) written by Hattori Tōru. He had visited the Marshall Islands in 1877 and made several voyages in the South Seas afterward. These trips convinced him
that what Japanese expansion required was a southern policy: "policy
for commerce, trade, settlement, and colonization of the southern
islands." China, North America, and South America were naturally
good markets for Japanese goods, but it was the countries and territories of the south Pacific that promised the most to Japanese adventure
and ingenuity. These areas were rich in natural resources and enjoyed
open spaces. Japanese did not have to struggle to find a niche in civilized society, as in San Francisco or Vancouver. Rather, they would
find native populations awaiting Japanese goods and investments and
eager to dispose of their riches to Japanese visitors and settlers. From
small commercial beginnings, Japanese would be able to develop extensive trade, establish close connections with the natives, and spread
Japan's civilization and influence. The Marianas, Carolines, Mar-
shalls, and Philippines were among the most promising in this regard.
Japanese should do in these islands what Germans were doing in
Samoa. This was the so-called "peaceful policy." Military aggression
and outright territorial conquest were out of the question; great powers were trying to effect colonization and expansion through peaceful,
commercial methods. There were still South Sea islands which were
like empty houses, to which Japanese would be most welcome. Westerners were fast spreading their influence and control over this region,
and the Japanese should not be left behind. Hattori was particularly

concerned with the future of the Philippines. Should Germans predominate, as appeared likely, the islands would forever be closed to Japanese expansion. Japan should send agricultural settlers and gradually seek to tie the Philippines closely, economically and politically. "It would be to our great advantage if our countrymen moved outside the limits of the nation, scattering themselves in overseas settlements and colonies, engaged in their respective activities, provided food for themselves, but still maintained contact with the mother country so that while they were physically abroad they would internally be still part of Japan. . . . I sincerely hope that we can create a new Japan in the South Seas." [25]

Southern expansion was also stressed by Watanabe Shūjirō, whose *Sekai ni okeru Nihonjin* (Japanese in the world, 1893) was the first comprehensive account of modern Japanese expansion, comparable to Seeley's *Expansion of England.* He, too, favored expansion into the South Seas as more timely and less costly than adventures in the Korean peninsula. Watanabe, however, was frankly an imperialist, advocating territorial expansion in the Pacific. "As we incorporate lands in the South Seas," he said, "we could either occupy them or purchase them. This is how the European powers have added new territories. Why should we alone be governed by moral scruples in international affairs?" Basically he was one with other expansionists in believing that Japan could never be a great and energetic country so long as its people were confined to the home islands. They all looked to the example of Western power and influence. "It is no accident," he concluded, "that the Europeans are so powerful in the world. It is because the nations of the white race cooperate and compete with one another in carrying out their enterprises throughout the world, overcoming all difficulties and obstacles. If Asians are to equal and eventually supersede Europeans, they, too, must combine and endeavor to engage in activities in the world. Japan, situated at a strategic location in Asia, has an immense responsibility. The Japanese people must realize that they are not simply citizens of Japan; they must belong to the world." [26]

While Watanabe was willing to advocate the use of force to incorporate some islands in the Pacific, most writers at this time stressed peaceful migration and settlement, which they were convinced would obtain the same result — the expansion of Japan — at less cost and with less serious diplomatic tension. In 1892 Takeuchi Seishi, having just returned from a trip abroad, wrote a six-hundred-page treatise entitled *Shin rikkoku* (The founding of the new nation). His tour of Europe and the United States had impressed him, he wrote, with the dedication of Western countries to colonialism, and with the fact that the thrust of their expansion was toward the Pacific. Japan must follow suit; it must develop as an expansive, powerful race, scatter its people all over the earth, and concentrate on the extension of overseas settlement and trade. Only then could the Japanese be the white race of Asia, the superior race in the world. Every vacant space on the globe, however, was already under the control of the white race, and there was no hope that Japan could obtain a colony. "We cannot just plunder another country's territory by force, like the European powers are doing." The best solution was peaceful emigration without regard to the question of political sovereignty. In this regard Southeast Asia and South America were among the most suitable areas for Japanese settlement. The southern islands were closer to Japan, and those of them that were under Spanish control could be peacefully developed by Japanese in the hope that eventually they might become intimately associated with Japan. South America, although much farther away, provided a great opportunity for Japanese enterprise. If a number of Japanese with a large amount of capital were to undertake resettlement, the rich soil and resources of the region would amply reward their effort. It would not be beyond the realm of possibility, Takeuchi wrote, to create a prosperous new Japan in South America, matching in civilization, economic progress, and natural beauty the giant in the north.[27]

One result of the increasing movement for overseas emigration was the establishment, in 1893, of a Colonization Society. The inspiration came from socially and politically prominent men who had traveled abroad and recognized the urgency of their cause. The initial founders included Shiba Shirō, who had written the influential *Kajin no kigū* (Chance meetings with fair women) introducing the theme of Japanese overseas to romantic literature, and Tsuneya Seifuku, Shiga Shigetaka, and Inagaki Manjirō, authors already mentioned. Scholars such as Taguchi Ukichi, officials like Komura Jutarō, politicians such as Shimada Saburō and Kaneko Kentarō, and writers including Miyake Yūjirō were among the list of two hundred people who attended the organization meeting on March 11.[28]

In a statement setting forth reasons for founding a colonization society, they asserted that overseas emigration and settlement as well as colonization were the means through which the European powers were competing with each other in a struggle for power and wealth. Japan must follow suit. The nation already had an abundant population, and unless it sought suitable outlets, very soon all vacant spaces would be filled by other peoples. Moreover, Japan's insular location admirably fitted its aim as an emigrating country. "We cannot rule out the possibility of establishing overseas settlements by the use of force and seizing somebody else's territory. But the least objectionable way is to find an appropriate area abroad and colonize it through peaceful methods." Emigration would encourage the shipping industry, thus contributing to the growth of naval power. Japanese overseas would help expand their home country's trade not only by consuming home products but also by acquainting the native populations with Japanese goods. The money they sent home would add to the capital needed for industrialization. The statement concluded, "Overseas settlement is a vital aspect of the national policy, adopted at the Meiji Restoration, of elevating our spirit, broadening our vista, introducing new knowledge, and reforming people's minds." [29]

From such a perspective, it is easy to see that the United States, too, was viewed as an object of Japanese expansion. By this time school textbooks and general accounts had familiarized a generation of Japanese with an image of America as a land of fantastic wealth and unlimited opportunities. "In recent years this country [the United States] has grown increasingly rich and strong," said a history textbook. "Its trade flourishes, steamboats navigate the Pacific Ocean, frequenting Japan and China at regular intervals, and transcontinental railroads connect the Pacific coast with the Atlantic coast. Truly it may be said that the United States occupies a commanding position in the East Asian trade." [30] Another school reader on world history concluded, "In recent years the nation [the United States] has grown rich and powerful, and its trade has been expanding rapidly. All the world's ships visit its shores. People are well fed, and there is harmony between upper and lower classes." [31] When such an image was combined with an increasing self-consciousness of Japan as a Pacific nation as well as the growing realization of the need for overseas trade and emigration, it was natural that the United States should come to be viewed as an ideal land for potential emigration and settlement.

In 1893 Nagasawa Setsu published a book entitled *Yankii* (Yankees). It was a first of its kind, a combination of historical and geographical descriptions of the United States and detailed accounts of how Japanese had fit into American society and might do so in the future. The book opens with a portrait of the Puritans who as English migrants are contrasted to Japan's potential emigrants to the United States. "If we compare what the Japanese today are calling overseas settlement and the history of colonization in America, we become aware of tremendous differences in spirit. . . . Those who truly wish to be pioneers of overseas settlement must be prepared to overcome hardships and difficulties as America's pioneer settlers did." It is, the author asserts, "our people's most sincere wish to make our country as rich as America, and expand our country as extensively as America has expanded." To do so the Japanese must learn from the persevering spirit of the Puritans. They must also learn from the lessons of Chinese laborers, who were being discriminated against and expelled from the United States primarily because they had successfully competed with American workers. In time they would be totally removed to Mexico and South America — unless Japanese got there first!

How the Japanese could peacefully expand in America and not be frustrated like the Chinese was the book's major concern. There were more Japanese in the United States, Nagasawa noted, than in any other foreign country with the exception of Hawaii. Four thousand Japanese had gone there in search of wealth, education, and opportunities. They were engaged in agriculture, commerce, household service, or mining. Many who wanted to earn their living while going to school became "schoolboys" and worked in private residences in the early morning and then later in the day. These domestic servants were earning over one dollar a week, enough to keep them at school. But their growing number, especially on the West coast, had drawn the ire of native agitators, labor leaders, and politicians, and the Japanese immigrants might be subjected to the same kinds of discriminatory treatment as Chinese. To combat discrimination, the best strategy was to obtain the vote so as to constitute a sizable political force with which American politicians would have to reckon. Since they could not obtain the franchise without citizenship, the author suggested that Japanese go to the East coast, establish residence, acquire citizenship, and then return to the West coast to vote. This was a roundabout way of carrying out Japanese overseas settlement; but, "if it is as essential to plan massive expansion on the Pacific coast as it is in Hawaii, then we must do everything possible to realize the goal." Lacking such determination, it would be useless to think of creating a new Japan in the American West. The Japanese might as well invest their capital and manpower in Mexico or South America.

The author was convinced, at any event, that Hawaii should be a primary target of Japanese expansion. The revolution of 1893 seemed to give Japan a good opportunity to interest itself in the islands. "It should be easy to spread our influence to the Pacific," he wrote, "if the government should decide to make expansion the nation's major diplomatic goal and send an emissary to Hawaii to negotiate the granting of political rights to the Japanese, and if resolute and brave individuals should emigrate en masse to Hawaii, open stores, engage in agriculture, and invite further immigrants." Should Hawaii be annexed to the United States, the latter's prohibition of contract labor would be applied to Hawaii, and, without political rights, Japanese life would be jeopardized. Once these rights were acquired, Japanese influence would increase and Hawaii could become a key station for further expansion into Mexico, South America, and Australia. "Where else but in Hawaii can the Japanese race hope to compete truly and frontally with the white race?" Since all this would come to nothing unless Japanese were determined to remain abroad, banking, cultural, and recreational facilities should be established in Hawaii to serve the social and economic needs of the Japanese. Otherwise they might hurry home as soon as their contracts were terminated. Since, moreover, most of the Japanese already in Hawaii were unschooled and ignorant, it was imperative to found schools for their children. In this way, Hawaii would truly become a springboard of Japanese expansion abroad.[32]

On the eve of the Sino-Japanese War, therefore, there existed a growing movement and a well-developed literature for Japanese expansion. Tokutomi Sohō best summed up the sentiment in his articles written in the early summer of 1894, just before the outbreak of hostilities. Like so many others, he talked of expansion, but he was thinking of peaceful expansion in all directions, and not primarily of forceful conquest on the Asian continent. On June 3 he recalled the activities of countless Japanese overseas: "there is no corner of the earth where you do not encounter your countrymen." Within the next twenty-five years it seemed certain that "there will be established new Japans wherever the waves of the Pacific washed, the lights of the southern polestar reached, or the warm Black Currents enveloped." Unless Japanese expanded, other peoples, especially the whites and Chinese, would seize the earth's best territories and stifle Japanese energy. Then came Sohō's long remembered, ringing declaration: "Certainly our future history will be a history of the establishment by the Japanese people of new Japans everywhere in the world." [33]

The Sino-Japanese War has often been regarded as an outcome of Japan's premeditated plan to expand into the continent of Asia. Certainly the war cannot be dissociated from Meiji Japan's preoccupation with the Korean peninsula, whether with its presumed importance for Japanese security or with penetrating its political and economic life in order to entrench Japanese influence. It is wrong, however, to consider Korea in isolation. In the history of Japanese expansion, the value of Korea was never highly estimated. Even in 1894 that kingdom was considered vital to the national interest primarily in noneconomic terms. As Foreign Minister Mutsu Munemitsu wrote, when Japan dispatched 8,000 troops to Korea in June, it was preferable if some tangible material benefits could be reaped as a result of such action. Otherwise public opinion might not condone the hasty sending of soldiers that was bound to provoke Chinese retaliation. For this reason, Mutsu thought, it was necessary to press the Korean government for railway, telegraph, mining, and other concessions.[34] Such candid remarks attest to the uncertainty felt by Japanese leaders that military action in the peninsula would help what had by now become a national consensus: economic expansion.

For those like Taguchi Ukichi, Shiga Shigetaka, and Tokutomi Sohō, who had consistently advocated Japanese expansion overseas, war with China probably had as much symbolic as practical meaning, which the nation must utilize to achieve specific economic objectives as well as security goals. War and, if possible, victory would help coalesce national resources and exhibit the people's energy and channel these to further acts of expansion after the war. As Tokutomi wrote on July 23, two days before the beginning of hostilities, "I do not advocate war just for the sake of it. I am not advocating plundering of other lands. But I insist on war with China in order to transform Japan, hitherto a contracting nation, into an expansive nation." The war, he went on, would help establish a beachhead for Japanese expansion in Asia, and the world would come to recognize the nation as one of the expanding countries. Then and only then would his people be able to hold their own in the world arena of peaceful competition. In mid-September, as the battle of the Yellow Sea approached, Tokutomi hoped that by defeating the Chinese the Japanese would gain self-confidence in order to create an expansive nation.[35] Kayahara Kazan, who was soon to emerge as Tokutomi's rival in Japanese journalism, was also writing at this time of the war's long-range implications. Small and new Japan, he said, was about to conquer large but ancient China. The result would make Japan a world power, enabling it to expand into and dominate the Pacific while at the same time carrying out the mission of transmitting modern civilization to the Asian continent. In the minds of these writers victory over China was not viewed narrowly in the context of the Korean question or broadly in terms of continental expansion. There were far greater implications; as Kayahara wrote, the experience was bound to teach the Japanese people to wipe out their provincialism and develop a global outlook, starting a new career of expansion in commerce, industry, and education. "The door has been opened," he declared, "for our ambitious people to go and work in all areas of the world. . . . We cannot let the whites and Chinese dominate the global battlefield in the war of intelligence and commerce." [36]

By the end of November, Japanese victory was in sight, and there was much talk of the fruits of war. As the Japanese people drank the sweet cup of military victory, they began entertaining dreams of empire. They talked of taking Manchuria, Taiwan, and Korea. They felt that the nation was embarking upon empire-building just like the other great empires of the world. There is no question that the war made Japan imperialist, controlling overseas territories by force and seeking even greater influence in the affairs of Korea and China.[37] In the context of the expansion of Japan, however, it is necessary to recall that the war and the subsequent territorial acquisitions never completely replaced the earlier emphasis on peaceful, economic expansion. If anything, there was renewed determination to carry through the latter objective now that Japan was being recognized as a power.

Again, Tokutomi Sohō provides the best example. He advocated the taking of Liaotung peninsula primarily for security reasons. His lamentation over the retrocession of the area to China under the pressure of the Dreibund has forcefully impressed subsequent writers, but he was actually much more interested in Taiwan. He regarded the island as essential for Japan's expansion, whereas Manchuria was important as a shield against Russia: "it is the fundamental principle of Japanese expansionism to defend the north and develop in the south." If Japan had Taiwan, he said, the nation would be provided with a base from which to penetrate the South Seas: the Philippines and the Dutch East Indies. Japan would then be in a position to compete with Britain in the region. Tokutomi was quite certain that Japan could expand through emigration and trade now that it had attained world recognition as an energetic country and it was no longer necessary for Japanese to feel inferior. World markets and living space would be open to them. They must at any rate realize that the war with China was but a prelude to "a far more complicated and difficult war in peacetime." Having fought the Chinese army, the Japanese must be prepared to wage peaceful competition with the entire world. They must be spiritually renovated and determined that the nation, after thirty years of domestic reconstruction, was now ushering in a new age of global action, of worldwide enterprise. Not only should Japan strengthen its armed forces after the war to guard its newly acquired possessions, it must also develop industrial capacities, and its government must do its utmost to cope with the new problems of expanding navigation, trade, colonization, and overseas settlement.[38]

Tokutomi's publishing firm, Minyūsha, served for a time after the war as one of the most effective popularizers of the notion of expansion in mid-Meiji Japan. Now that the nation had proved its vigor and ambition, it did not seem excessive to indulge in the hope that the Japanese empire might come to approximate the British. In a pamphlet entitled *Ensei* (Expeditions to distant lands), Minyūsha editors asserted that Japan was at a threshold of empire-building, just like Britain after the Armada. As Britain's greatness was derived from its overseas activities and trade, so the new Japan must spread outward and develop new markets in distant lands. The Japanese must become "manufacturers, traders, and emigrants." "Our new territories, new voyages, and new markets require new people. It should not be difficult to create new Japans by settling our abundant people. Is it not the mission of our expeditionary people to open a new epoch in Japan's trade and colonization?" [39]

As such expressions revealed, the Sino-Japanese War gave the Japanese what they most needed: self-confidence as a first-class power. They would henceforth cease to view themselves and be viewed by

Westerners as a small Asian country, an object of foreign exploitation. The war, wrote Matsumoto Kunpei, an economist trained in the United States, had exhibited to the world that Japan was a civilized and progressive country, with a people endowed with intelligence and knowledge. Europeans and Americans had looked down upon them as a little, contemptible people, but now they knew they had been wrong. The whites would surely come to regard Japan as a great power. This reputation, he said, was the most important capital with which the Japanese should plan their postwar development.[40] This could take many forms. According to Matsumoto, the principal goal ought to be commercial expansion. The only way to preserve the reputation won by war was through the economic strengthening of the nation. More specifically, Japan should try to wrest control over its trade from the hands of foreign merchants, systematize the processes of production, selection, and testing of goods for export, and establish retail stores abroad specializing in Japanese commodities.[41] Similarly, Ōkuma Shigenobu, always sensitive to changing currents of opinion, urged his countrymen to realize in actuality what the Treaty of Shimonoseki gave them on paper — mainly the economic penetration of China. Now that Japan had joined the ranks of the treaty powers, with concessions, settlements, and rights similar to those enjoyed by the Western powers, what was needed was an indomitable will to compete with the latter in China.[42] It was with the same sense of timing, self-confidence, and determination that the Japanese after 1895 sought to govern the newly acquired colonies of Taiwan and the Pescadores, entrench its power and influence in the Korean peninsula, obtain spheres of influence in China, and enter into exclusive arrangements with other imperialist powers to safeguard their respective interests in Asia. Great-power status also dictated that Japan possess a first-class army and navy; accordingly, postwar armament expenditures were phenomenally increased, from the average of 21 million yen before the war to 73 million yen in 1896 and 110 million yen in 1897.

Implications of such developments for Japan's foreign relations were obvious, and historians have minutely traced the course of Japanese diplomacy from the Sino-Japanese War to the Russo-Japanese War ten years later, through such landmarks as the Boxer incident and the Anglo-Japanese alliance.[43] There are also abundant studies of the impact of Japanese colonialism and imperialism upon domestic politics, industrialization, and intellectual life.[44] What has not been sufficiently recognized is the relation between Japanese expansionism and American expansionism. To some contemporary observers, however, this was one of the most obvious results of the war. When the Japanese, sharing the expansionist thinking of Tokutomi, Kayahara, and others, visualized postwar expansion, they set their eyes as much on the islands and territories of the Pacific as on the Asian continent. Hawaii and the Philippines, North and South America, Australia and the South Sea islands were frequently mentioned as good targets for extending Japanese trade and emigration.

Press coverage on developments in Hawaii continued to be extensive. Japanese newspapers were aware that the 20,000 Japanese already in the islands easily overwhelmed the white settlers in number, and that behind them stood an expanding navy, as symbolized by occasional visits to Honolulu of the cruiser *Naniwa* to look after their interests.[45] Shortly before the Sino-Japanese War, the *Tokyo Nichinichi* reported that the provisional government of Hawaii would likely soon give Japanese residents the right to vote.[46] Though nothing came of such rumors, newspapers continued to print articles throughout the war tracing internal developments in Hawaii.[47] In July 1895 *Nichinichi* referred to the growing political and economic influence of the Japanese, challenging the supreme position enjoyed by the whites in the islands. The war seemed to have made the former confident and even arrogant, the paper said, and there was notable white reaction against them.[48] In the pamphlet *Ensei*, cited earlier, it was noted that the United States was seeking to annex Hawaii for naval and commercial reasons. But the editors hoped that the islands would remain an independent republic. Obviously such a condition was better from the point of view of Japanese commerce. "No matter what relations or special circumstances exist between Hawaii on one hand and the United States and England on the other . . . we must try to coordinate Japanese and Hawaiian interests and turn Hawaii into a well-developed, commercial area." Because of Japanese immigration, the islands had become "our branch house." The Japanese, therefore, should consider them among the most suitable for postwar expansion.[49]

The importance of the Philippines likewise increased, now that they became next door to Japan in newly acquired Taiwan. In a pamphlet entitled *Firipin guntō* (The Philippine Islands), the Minyūsha sought to arouse public interest in territorial expansion in that direction. Writing a preface to the booklet, Tokutomi Sohō insisted that three hundred years earlier some brave Japanese had already visited and settled in the Philippines. Now that Japan had acquired Taiwan and Spanish rule was weakening, the Japanese should not shrink from the manifest opportunity and prod their government to take vigorous action. In the book itself, the editors noted that with the opening of a Nicaraguan canal impending, the commerce of the world was bound to shift from the Atlantic to the Pacific; as a consequence, the Philippine Islands would occupy a strategic position commercially. Since neither Britain nor Germany appeared likely to want them (no mention was made of the United States), the Japanese should develop a colonization plan, send as many merchants as practicable to the Philippines, open up trade routes for Japanese goods, establish a close relationship with the natives, and prepare for an opportunity to assert Japanese influence. The most influential foreign element was Chinese, as Chinese immigrants controlled the economic life of the islands, although they were persecuted by the Spaniards. The Japanese should step into their position, not necessarily with a view to immediate territorial seizure but in order to effect Japanese economic penetration.[50]

Strikingly similar ideas were thus developing in Japan and the United States. Each country's expansionism manifested self-consciousness about civilization and race. There was a premonition of a coming struggle for power in Asia and the Pacific, areas visualized in the two countries as primary targets for expansion.

The rapid turn of events in the East served to keep Americans interested in world affairs, just as they began to clamor more and more loudly for intervention in Cuba. The foreign policy public was enlarging and stayed large for several years as a result of the conjunction of these developments. Those who demanded that the government do something for the Cubans were likely also to be interested in the Sino-Japanese War and its outcome. Few of them were imperialists before 1898 in the sense of advocating forceful acquisition of territories, but their concern with foreign affairs was such that they could support an aggressive policy once it was launched.

Among the events that held the interest of the American public and predisposed it in favor of expansionism, the rise of Japan as a power was one of the most significant. It was no accident that Hawaii provided the first serious crisis between the two countries. It had all the factors — racial antagonism, jingoism, struggle for influence and power away from the home-base — that were to characterize the subsequent decades of Japanese-American antagonism. The whites in Hawaii, controlling the government after the coup of 1893, were alive to the danger from the islands' Japanese population whose mother country had won an impressive victory over China. They had taken steps to preserve their rights by restricting the vote to the native Hawaiians and the propertied classes, and there was no wavering from the determination to keep Hawaii racially mixed but economically and politically dominated by whites.[51] The best way to do so was to seek annexation to the United States or, if this was impossible in the immediate future, to obtain its military protection. Confident of such support, the Hawaiian government began taking steps to discourage and reduce Japanese interests, the most spectacular of which was the *Shinshū Maru* incident of early 1897. This involved the refusal to permit the landing of Japanese laborers who had come on that ship. They were subjected to investigation and more than two-thirds of them, numbering 463, were ordered returned to Japan. Two more incoming ships were treated similarly, and altogether 1,199 Japanese prospective immigrants returned home, humiliated and angry.[52]

There was no Japanese plan to "take over" the Hawaiian islands, as alleged by some then and since.[53] But the *Pacific Commercial Advertiser* of Honolulu was not very mistaken when it expressed the fear of Japan's swallowing up Hawaii.[54] From the point of view of the Japanese, both at home and in Hawaii, the islands belonged as much to them as to any others willing to come and work. Peaceful emigration to and gradual enhancement of economic and political influence in Hawaii had become a test case of postwar Japanese expansionism. No wonder, then, that Japan took strong exception to the treatment accorded to *Shinshū Maru* passengers. Shimamura Hisashi, the senior diplomat representing his country in Hawaii, believed that repetition of similar incidents would result in total exclusion of Japanese from the islands, and that Honolulu authorities were acting as they were in the belief that the United States would support them and sooner or later agree to annexation. The matter was so grave for the future of Japanese expansion in the Pacific that Shimamura urged the dispatching of a warship from Japan in order "to exhibit our power and protect 26,000 Japanese, almost one-fourth of the total population of Hawaii." [55] Foreign Minister Ōkuma Shigenobu fully shared such views. A strong exponent of energetic overseas expansion, he needed little

prodding to lodge a strongly worded protest with the Hawaiian government, and to ask the navy to send a warship to Honolulu. Accordingly, the *Naniwa* was dispatched, with a representative of the Foreign
Ministry on board to observe Hawaiian-American relations.[56] As
Ōkuma wrote to Shimamura, the expedition was a demonstration of
force to the Hawaiian government, warning it to settle the dispute
speedily instead of prevaricating in the hope of eventual annexation
by the United States.[57]

Ironically, the strong stand taken by Japan gave the final impetus to
the American annexation of Hawaii. Pro-annexationist newspapers,
which had not been successful in swinging public opinion before 1897,
could now phrase the issue in terms of Japanese hegemony over the
islands. Anticipating the popular argument ten years later, San Francisco's *Chronicle* and *Examiner* began talking of Japan's design to
take over Hawaii by sending soldiers disguised as laborers.[58] The
McKinley administration, coming to power just as the *Shinshū Maru*
incident occurred, was much more receptive to expansionist thinking
than its predecessor, and the Republican Party had made a partisan
issue of the Hawaiian question. The sending of the *Naniwa* gave im-
perialist-minded Republicans an opportunity to reopen the annexation issue and push for speedy action. Theodore Roosevelt, Assistant
Secretary of the Navy, wrote to Mahan saying, "If I had my way we
would annex those islands tomorrow." He was becoming aware of the
rise of Japan as a Pacific power and convinced that annexation offered
an expeditious way of avoiding war between Japan and Hawaii, which
could drag the United States in before the latter was ready.[59] Secretary of the Navy John D. Long went farther: he gave instructions to
the naval force at Honolulu to proclaim a provisional protectorate if
Japan showed signs of resorting to force.[60] Even so strong an anti-
imperialist as Senator George Hoar supported Hawaiian annexation
in order to forestall Japanese action.[61] According to his autobiography, he was converted to this view following talks with President
McKinley, who stressed the Japanese question as the key to the Hawaiian issue.[62] As early as May 6, 1897, Representative William H.
King of Utah introduced a joint resolution for annexation of Hawaii,
saying, "the ascendancy of European or Asiatic influences and forces
[in Hawaii] would work its destruction and prove perilous to the liber-
ties of its people, especially the Americans and native Hawaiians." A
month later the administration took the matter in its own hands and

signed a treaty of annexation with Hawaii. As Julius W. Pratt has shown, the Senate Foreign Relations Committee and the House Foreign Affairs Committee endorsed the treaty as a preventive measure, to forestall the islands' falling into Japanese hands.[63] The rhetoric of race and civilization provided a perfect vocabulary to rationalize such action. According to the Foreign Relations Committee's report, "the present Hawaiian-Japanese controversy is the preliminary skirmish in the great coming struggle between the civilization and the awakening forces of the East and the civilization of the West. The issue is whether, in that inevitable struggle, Asia or America shall have the vantage ground of the control of the naval 'Key of the Pacific,' the commercial 'Crossroads of the Pacific.' " [64] No statement could have better expressed the expansionism not only of the United States but of Japan.

The Japanese would have used almost identical language to justify their interest in Hawaii, although they would have viewed themselves not as the champion of the East but of the Westernizing forces of the world. Minister Hoshi Tōru in Washington wrote in February 1897 that in terms of national security the Hawaiian Islands could not be equated in importance with Korea and Taiwan. Security, he said, would not be a good reason for protesting against American annexation. What was at stake was the future of the Japanese already in Hawaii and those who would follow. Their rights would be jeopardized if America's immigration and naturalization laws were applied to the islands as a result of annexation. Contract laborers would no longer be allowed entry, and those already there would suffer perpetual subordination to the whites. Japan would have to do its utmost to prevent or at least to delay the union of the islands and the continental United States.[65] Foreign Minister Ōkuma fully agreed. He was, he said, "opposed to [the] annexation under any circumstances," and hoped the European powers, especially Britain, would act together with Japan to put pressure upon the United States against incorporating the islands.[66] The Foreign Office in London was sympathetic, Under Secretary T. H. Sanderson saying, "it would be contrary to our interests that Hawaii should be annexed to the United States." But Britain would not move for fear that any such action would arouse hostile sentiment in America and accomplish no useful purposes.[67] Japan was left to protest alone to the American government, as soon as the treaty with Hawaii was signed, on the ground that the maintenance of the status quo in the Pacific was essential for the preservation of Japanese-American friendship.[68] Protests alone seeming ineffectual, Minister Hoshi suggested that Japan might immediately occupy the Hawaiian Islands, "by dispatching without any delay some powerful ships under the name of reprisal," in other words, on the pretext of retaliation against the Hawaiian government's treatment of Japanese.[69] Even Ōkuma was not willing to go that far. What he desired was preservation of the status quo. If force were the only effective method, now that the United States had signed an annexation treaty with Hawaii, Japan faced the risk of war. He had to admit that Japanese interests in Hawaii were not worth war. As he telegraphed Hoshi, "Continuation without interruption or disturbance of our intercourse with United States is of vastly more importance to Japan than interests that will be menaced by annexation. Consequently good policy dictates that our opposition to annexation should be within limits of diplomacy." [70]

This was tantamount to admitting defeat and impotence in the face of vigorous American expansionism. Hawaii was the first instance where Japanese expansion was frustrated, and its implications were not lost on some observers. Akiyama Masanosuke, the diplomat who had been sent to Hawaii on the *Naniwa* during the Honolulu crisis, was so disgusted by the government's helplessness regarding the annexation issue that he attempted suicide on his return. To him the whole episode was a signal defeat of Japanese expansionism.[71] Another diplomat, writing from Mexico, was distressed for the opposite reason. He felt the use of force, actual and threatened, by Japan in Hawaii gave the impression that its expansion overseas was not entirely peaceful. Such an impression would do untold damage to the cause of Japan's commercial expansion and settlement in Latin America.[72] The Japanese press generally expressed displeasure with the turn of events. According to the nationalistic *Kokumin shinbun,* there were four views on the matter. The first advocated strong action against the American annexation of Hawaii, even at the risk of war. The second suggested that Hawaii be made a neutral country under the joint protection of the powers, an opinion which was gaining support. The third view would concede Hawaii's political destiny to the United States on condition that a new treaty be signed between Japan and America, defining Japanese rights broadly. This, said the *Kokumin,* was the most pervasive opinion, reflecting official policy. The fourth view was even more pessimistic. Recognizing the Japanese government's powerlessness in the situation, it would suggest that the nation do nothing beyond seeking assurances that the existing rights and interests by Japanese in Hawaii would be honored by the United States.[73]

What in fact happened was something even less than this fourth alternative. After a debate lasting nearly a year, the American Congress finally approved annexation, not through treaty but through a joint resolution requiring a simple majority. Japan withdrew its protest in December 1897, and Hawaii paid $75,000 to indemnify the *Shinshū Maru* passengers and others who had been expelled. But nothing was done to codify the rights of Japanese immigrants. Quite ironically, the annexation of Hawaii brought about a second wave of Japanese immigration, so that the Japanese population in the Islands more than doubled between 1896 and 1900, reaching 61,000 that year.[74] Their migration thence to the West coast of the United States was to pose the most serious question between the two powers of the Pacific.

The Hawaiian episode was a chastening experience for the self-consciously expanding people of Japan, and they became aware of the obstacles and dangers, as well as opportunities, in the path of expansion. It was in part for this reason that officially at least Japan took a more moderate attitude toward the Philippine question in 1898, as the battle of Manila Bay signaled the extension of American power in the southwestern Pacific. Nevertheless, now more than ever before, the fate of the two empires became intertwined. In East Asia and the Pacific, their interaction would be more direct than in the past, and each expansive move by one would be closely watched by the other. Hitherto almost exclusively concerned with such matters as tariff revision and extraterritoriality, Japanese-American relations would now be those between rival empires.

Historians of American imperialism have tended to overlook the Japanese variable in the intricate equation making up the story of expansion into the Pacific. Recent works by Walter LaFeber, Thomas McCormick, William A. Williams, and others have served to map out the general social, economic, and intellectual picture of the 1890's that prepared the nation for expansion after 1898.[75] Marilyn B. Young and David Healy, echoing the earlier study by Julius W. Pratt, have shown how an image of China as a potential market was linked to acquisition of the Philippines.[76] Ernest R. May has suggested that insular imperialism was undertaken by the McKinley administration to preserve the Republican Party, as the President perceived the public clamoring for expansion and the responsible opinion leaders becoming unwilling to criticize it.[77] One factor which has not been sufficiently stressed is the possibility that, because of the Japanese crisis in Hawaii in 1897, the United States in 1898 was becoming much more assertive in Pacific affairs. To be sure, as John A. S. Grenville and George B. Young have shown, in 1896 there was already a naval war plan that visualized attack on Manila in case of hostilities with Spain.[78] What stands out is the conjunction of all these developments; an identical war plan would produce different results if carried out under different circumstances. While the United States navy contemplated war with Spain in the Philippines, it was also becoming concerned with events in other parts of the Pacific and East Asia. In December 1897, Admiral Frederick V. McNair, commander of the Asiatic squadron, wrote to Admiral George Dewey, soon to replace him: "Since the Hawaiian question has arisen, the attitude of the Japanese toward Americans has not been friendly. The Department [of the Navy] desires to be forewarned by telegraph of any prospective increase of Japanese fleet in the Hawaiian Islands, or other significant movement of Japanese forces. . . . Japan is extensively increasing her naval force, mostly from acquisitions abroad." Having decided upon Hawaiian annexation, the United States was fully prepared to make good its position as a Pacific power. Reflecting the assertive, expansive mood of the period, Navy Secretary John D. Long instructed Commodore Dewey in February 1898 "to make inquiries . . . what he regards as the best attainable port in China, in case negotiations should be entered into for obtaining the same concessions in some Chinese port, for the benefit of our ships, and the extension of our commerce, as are enjoyed by some of the other nations." [79]

Given these developments, it was not at all surprising that the conflict with Spain over Cuba should come to have immediate implications for America's position in the Pacific. Dewey was under constant instruction to fit out his squadron for attack on the Philippines once hostilities with Spain commenced. He reported on March 31, "the vessels have been kept full of the best coal obtainable, provisioned and ready to move at twenty-four hours notice. . . . I believe I am not over-confident in stating that with the squadron now under my command the [Spanish] vessels could be taken and the defenses of Manila reduced in one day." [80] Because of the anarchic situation in the islands, it was a foregone conclusion that once Dewey's fleet defeated the Spanish, American forces would have to occupy part of the territory in order to maintain order and prepare for counterattack. When in May, Rear Admiral Montgomery Sicard, president of the Naval War Board, suggested construction of batteries and taking other measures "looking to a permanent defence" of Manila, President McKinley gave his unqualified approval.[81] He authorized military occupation and directed the secretary of war on May 19 to take effective steps to preserve law and order in the Philippines.[82] The army of occupation, en route from California to Manila, stopped over in Honolulu in June and was given a rousing reception. It was as if Hawaii and the Philippines were emerging as two outposts of American empire in the Pacific.[83] To defend the Philippines against foreign interference, the strategic importance of Hawaii was looming large. As Admiral Sicard said in a memorandum written in August, "if, not only battleships, but a large body of troops were assembled at Hawaii . . . and the whole armada, naval and military, [were] in a state of readiness for landing promptly against any enemy about the Philippines, the intention and power of the United States to repress internal or external disorders in that region would be apparent, both to the insurgents and to foreign Powers." [84]

The United States was emerging as an imperialist power, incorporating Hawaii and, it appeared likely, the Philippines, and even contemplating the seizure of a base in China. "Are we," the *Cleveland Leader* asked, "become a different people from our ancestors, or are we yet the same race of Anglo-Saxons whose restless energy in colonization, in conquest, in trade, in 'the spread of civilization,' has carried their speech into every part of the world and planted their inhabitants everywhere?" In a striking parallel to Japanese attitude right after the Sino-Japanese War, Americans at the end of the Spanish war affirmed their devotion to peaceful expansion even while rejoicing in victory brought about by force. "The spirit of the people once having looked outward, American enterprise will seek new fields of conquest, — not by arms, but by trade and legitimate adventure. Our navy has revealed to ourselves not less than to the rest of the world our rightful place among the nations." [85] The juxtaposition of forceful and peaceful expansionism presented a fresh challenge not only to Americans as they tried to adapt themselves to the new situation in the Pacific, but also to Japanese, who were watching the fateful turn of events in the Philippines with the utmost concern.

Official Japanese policy was quite clear. Foreign Minister Ōkuma instructed the legations abroad on September 8, 1898: "While we would prefer, in terms of selfish interests, to see the Philippine Islands maintain their old status quo and thus belong to Spain . . . if they are to pass into the hands of a power other than Spain, and if Japan is not to take them, then we think American possession of the islands would be most convenient from the point of view of maintaining the peace in East Asia." [86] *Jiji shinpō*, probably Japan's most respectable and influential daily, which under the editorship of Fukuzawa Yukichi reflected the views of the urban, educated, business-oriented, politically alert sectors, endorsed the general policy. In an editorial of May 7 it was asserted that, since the Philippines were close to Taiwan and a key to Japan's southern expansion, it was desirable to send Japanese settlers to the islands. While Mexico and Brazil might also be suitable for colonization, the Philippines would be best on account of their vastness and small population. "If we continue to send emigrants and create Japanese villages and towns, the result would be almost like extending the limits of our empire." Japan must first send out a survey mission to investigate geographical conditions to select areas convenient for Japanese settlement. To protect Japanese pioneers, the editorial concluded, it was essential to dispatch some warships. In another editorial, however, it was recognized that the Japanese navy was still small, and that the nation had to turn to Western countries, especially Britain and the United States, for ships, cannons, and machinery. It was therefore imperative to remain on good relations with them, particularly since mutual economic relations seemed compatible. Thus *Jiji shinpō* wholeheartedly expressed support for the United States in its war against Spain. The war, it said, should be made an occasion to strengthen ties between Japan, Britain, and the United States and also to augment the Japanese naval force.[87]

Quite in contrast to such affirmative views was the tone of the antigovernment *Yorozu chōhō*. This paper, influential among radicals and those liberals who did not share Fukuzawa's business orientation and general complacency, was at one with the rest in stressing the need for peaceful expansion and in particular overseas migration. Instead of spending their time in boarding rooms of Tokyo, *Yorozu chōhō* once asserted, Japanese should consider venturing out to Singapore or San Francisco.[88] From such a premise, the paper consistently spoke out against the American annexation of the Philippines. On May 19 it editorialized that the Japanese people should make their concern regarding the disposition of the islands heard. The Philippines, it said, had for three hundred years been closely tied to Japan, and they were much closer to Taiwan than to Cuba. If the United States asserted the doctrine of two spheres, then it had no business meddling in Asian affairs. Japan should try either to put pressure upon Spain to effect administrative reforms of the islands or assist their independence even through the use of force. Kōtoku Shūsui, who made his debut in Japanese journalism at this time, wrote on the editorial pages of *Yorozu chōhō* in the same vein. He was unalterably opposed to excepting the United States from the general considerations governing conduct of nations in the world. In a notable essay entitled "The diplomacy of sentimentalism," he sought squarely to challenge writers such as Fukuzawa who were arguing that the American incorporation of the Philippines might be a good thing as the United States was not the avaricious imperialist that other powers were. Such an attitude, according to Kōtoku, was basing vital considerations of national interest on sentimentalism and emotionalism, not on rational calculations and cold facts. He repeatedly insisted that while Anglo-Saxons as individuals were praiseworthy in their dedication to liberty, peace, and morality, as nations they were no different from others. Their governments were no less selfish. "Unfortunately I see no nation in the world today that is morally oriented." [89] Consequently, it was nonsense to yield the Philippines to the United States under the illusion that that country was more ethically disposed than Russia, Germany, or France. Before the Japanese agreed to a scheme, advocated by *Jiji shinpō*, for an alliance with Britain and the United States, they must think carefully about the implications of such a course of action for Japanese interests.[90] These interests, as Kōtoku saw them, dictated southern expansion. American possession of the Philippines might endanger Japan's "avenue southward" and stifle the latter's commercial rights in the South Seas. In an editorial written for *Yorozu chōhō* he insisted that Japan should aim for, first, "the extension of Japanese interests at present and in the future," second, maintenance of the balance of power in Asia, and, third, the welfare and happiness of the Filipinos. The ideal way to realize these goals would be to seek an independent Philippine republic, but if this was difficult, Japan could promote an autonomous regime in the Philippines under Spanish rule. Either way Japan would be assured of an influential position in the islands and further south, instead of seeking its access to the South Seas blocked by the United States or another power.

Such ideas were not limited to alienated radicals, as can be seen in an article Ariga Nagao wrote for the prestigious *Gaikō jihō* (*Revue diplomatique*) in August 1898. The author, a respected scholar of international law, had founded the journal six months earlier. In this article he argued that, apart from the question of justice and injustice, the premeditated incorporation of the Philippines, "Japan's southern neighbor," into the United States had serious practical implications. Most fundamentally the question of the future of Japanese expansion was involved: "If the United States should take the islands, Japan will forever have to renounce its desire to expand in the south." Japanese leaders and officials, the writer said, had looked on lands to the southward as the most promising area for expansion, and even if Japanese acquiescence in the American annexation of the Philippines might purchase American and British friendship, this was not worth the cost of foreclosing Japan's future expansion in that direction. The best solution, according to Ariga, was somehow to persuade Spain to retain the islands so that when an opportune moment arose Japan could incorporate part or all of them.[91]

Kōtoku's and Ariga's dream was frustrated, as the United States proceeded not only to annex the Philippines but to apply to them a tariff and immigration policy, restricting foreign trade and immigration. But ironically the decision for annexation was made by default, in the absence of viable alternatives. Having driven the Spaniards from their colonial position in the Philippines, the McKinley administration felt there was no choice but to exercise American power in order to maintain law and order and to avoid foreign intervention. There was no solid imperialist consensus among officials and opinion leaders in 1898–99, committed to overseas territorial acquisitions, as evidenced by the unwillingness to turn Cuba into an outright American colony. Unlike Cuba, the Philippines were far away, among the Asian colonies of the great powers, and for that very reason formal colonial control by the United States seemed required to protect the interests of Americans and Filipinos alike. The constant reiteration of idealistic themes, that Americans were there for "liberty and law, peace and progress," as McKinley declared, revealed that they had constantly to convince themselves that they were doing the right thing.[92]

No matter what the rhetoric, the net effect of America's Pacific imperialism was to forestall Japanese expansion in the same regions. But the Japanese government, remembering the Hawaiian imbroglio, was determined to accept the inevitable gracefully. "Southern expansion is our ideal, but it is not to be carried out right now," said an army spokesman, reflecting the official policy.[93] Openly to oppose the American annexation of the Philippines or to aid Emilio Aguinaldo's rebel troops, it was felt, would bring about a serious crisis in Japanese relations with the United States. This was a risk that could not be taken in view of the developing tension in China. Between November 1897 and April 1898, Germany, Russia, France, and Britain had one by one obtained leases and concessions from China, producing fear of a pending break-up of the Ch'ing empire. Under the circumstances, Japan could not jeopardize its friendly relations with the United States. Timing was the crucial factor that explained Japan's feeble response to American expansion in 1898, compared with that in 1897.[94]

Nevertheless, the Japanese were fascinated by the situation in the Philippines where Americans, hitherto considered the symbol of man's struggle for freedom, were using force to suppress Filipino rebels. The United States, long viewed as a peaceful expansionist par excellence, was now developing as a colonial power. Only if one subscribed to the belief that there could be no trouble between the two countries, or accepted the American rhetoric of civilization and mission, could one accommodate oneself to the new fact. Such was the opinion of *Jiji shinpō*, generally behind the Ōkuma policy. It had initially believed that the United States would grant independence to the Filipinos after the war, but was ready to accept the new situation when American intentions became known. It admitted in an editorial that there seemed to exist no inherent necessity for America to annex the islands, now that the United States had successfully revealed its moral influence to the world, while recovering its economic strength internally. However, "there seem to be no limits to man's desires," and the American people were no exception. Moreover, "the noblest desire of man is to use his excess energy for the happiness of others," and this was what they were trying to do in the Philippines. Since the United States stood for peace, it was to be expected that its incorporation of the Pacific islands would add to the number of peacefully oriented powers in the East and contribute to the lessening of international tension.

The theme of continued friendship between the United States and Japan, reiterated time and again by the government, did not find a strong echo in Japanese public opinion. There was general recognition that America had become a major power in the Pacific and East Asia. With this happening just at a time when the Japanese were witnessing the European powers' scramble for bases and concessions in China, they pictured America's emergence as an imperialist as part of the same phenomenon. Japan was itself acting as a full-fledged imperialist, but this did not diminish the potential antagonism between the two countries. "Imperialism has conquered America which has defeated Spain," Takayama Rinjirō wrote. He had thought that the United States was a commercial and peaceful country, but it seemed to be disregarding economic considerations in joining the worldwide push for colonies. Earlier, the government in Washington had decided, despite the national profession of the principles of liberty and justice, not to oppose Germany's seizure of Kiaochow Bay. Was not the United States, too, driven by self-interest? International affairs were never determined by moral or humanistic considerations, but solely by selfishness. Japan must resolve to maintain its independence and extend its power abroad, in order to remain an expansive nation.[95]

The year 1898, Takayama wrote, had been one of crimes. It opened with the powers' encroachment on China and was closing with the emergence of American imperialism. Both were instances of Western penetration of Asia. History was at last becoming global, the Eastern and Western hemispheres were joined together, and mankind was being molded into one unit. The United States was a symbol of the new age. Having departed from its Monroe Doctrine, it had expanded into the Eastern hemisphere under the name of Anglo-Saxonism. The taking of the Philippines just because a ship was sunk in Cuba was essentially no different, no less criminal, than Germany's plundering of Kiaochow, or Russia's and Britain's taking of Port Arthur and Weihaiwei. All these seizures indicated the coming conflict of races. The last years of the nineteenth century had witnessed the unprecedented ascendancy of the power of the white race. The Aryans were everywhere in Asia, subjugating alien races. In their search for opportunities for aggrandizement they were totally ignoring moral considerations. The last battle for the survival of the Turanians was fast approaching. Japan was the only remaining bastion of that race. The twentieth century was certain to witness as great a racial conflict as had taken place in the fifteenth.[96] The first stage of Pacific confrontation between Japan and the United States was already bringing forth a language of estrangement and conflict that was to define their relations for decades to come.

III

Beyond Imperialism

American presence in Hawaii and the Philippines brought with it a greater willingness to assert and use national power in Asia. This was part of the imperialistic expansion of the United States in the period after the Spanish-American War. Nowhere was the new assertiveness more dramatically expressed than in China, where combined pressure from imperialism and domestic turmoil was producing the last great upheaval of the nineteenth century. Having extended military control over the Pacific Ocean, it was not surprising that the United States should decide to exercise its power on the Asian continent.

Already in February 1898 the Navy Department had considered the establishment of a naval base on the China coast. In November of that year Minister Edwin Conger in Peking recommended that the United States take possession of a good port in China, "from which we can potently assert our rights and effectively wield our influence." The following March he suggested the taking of a port in Chihli province with a view to establishing an American sphere of influence there. The American Asiatic squadron, which had depended on British ships and bases for coal supplies during the war with Spain, now insisted that the creation of a coaling station in north China was necessary, and in January 1899 the Navy Department's bureau of equipment recommended the acquisition of Chusan island, off Shanghai. The suggestion was warmly seconded by Secretary of the Navy Long in July 1900.[1]

By this time the Boxers had arisen in Shantung province and were spreading and attacking foreign lives and property throughout north China. America's response to the Boxer uprising was the same as that of the other imperialists in one basic respect: the use of force to suppress the rebels and protect their own and other foreign nationals in China. Logistically the task was easier now that the newly acquired islands in the Pacific could be utilized as stepping-stones for dispatching troops and ships. Politically and intellectually there was little hesitation in joining the allied expedition as the United States government and foreign policy public had grown accustomed to viewing their country as a world power. What Marilyn Young has aptly called a "rhetoric of empire" was very evident in the years immediately after the Spanish-American War. As Frank Hackett, Acting Secretary of the Navy, telegraphed Rear Admiral Louis Kempf, the senior American officer in China, in June 1900, the Department "directs the protection of American National interests as well as that of the interests of individual Americans. Whatever you do let the Department know the plan of the concerting powers in regard to punitive or other expeditions or other measures, and keep it informed of the force that you will require in order that this Government may properly discharge the obligations which its large interests put upon it." [2] On July 13 the American Association of China, with headquarters in Shanghai, resolved to request the home government "to use all the forces available . . . in immediate service in China for the restoration of order, the protection of its citizens and the securing of guarantees . . . against a recurrence of such grievous outrages as they are now experiencing." The resolution was forwarded to President McKinley with a message, expressing confidence that, "if the horrors which have confronted those in Peking and elsewhere, and the grave peril which faces all our race in China were but comprehended by our countrymen, our Government would receive most generous support in dealing with the situation on the large scale which it demands." [3]

The American contingent participating in the international relief expedition to Peking, undertaken in July and August, numbered only 2,500 soldiers, in a multinational force of 14,000. America's use of force was not "on a large scale," certainly not as extensive as desired by American missionaries and merchants in China. This resulted in part from the overriding concern with pacifying the Philippine Islands. [4] But one basic fact remained: the United States acted as one of the powers engaged in penalizing the Boxers. Nor was this an end in itself. Much thought was given to augmenting American power in China by obtaining a territorial base. On the modest side, Major General Adna R. Chaffee, commanding the American land forces, suggested in December that the United States seek the concession of the Temple of Heaven grounds in Peking. As he cabled the War Department's adjutant general's office, this was a good place to station the legation guard. "In time of threatened trouble, five thousand troops could be camped inside wall temporarily." But then he went on to say, "If influence United States is to be pushed along any particular line, Chili [sic] Province and westward seem to me offer fairest field remaining uninfluenced by other powers." [5] A different locale was suggested by A. W. Bash, representing the American China Development Company of New York, which held a concession to build a railway between Hankow and Canton. Writing to Assistant Secretary of State Alvee A. Adee in August, he stressed "the importance to our company of securing a point in Amoy as the deep sea terminal of the Hankow-Canton Railway." Japan had claimed special interests in Fukien province, in which Amoy was situated, on account of its proximity to Taiwan, but Bash was confident that the company's vested rights in the area were more substantial than Japan's. "The interests of the Development Company can safely be said to be by far the greatest single American interest in China." They could best be asserted while American troops were present; once they were withdrawn, the United States government would not be "in any position to wield the great influence it can now . . . and all American interests in China [would be] absolutely made void. Therefore the present is the most opportune time to make sure of a maintenance of our rights." [6] Finally, toward the end of the year, territorial acquisition was made official policy when Secretary of State John Hay decided to see if Japan objected to an American lease of Samsah Bay in Fukien province.[7] Japan did, and nothing came of it. The episode was not an isolated instance of American assertiveness in China in this year of turmoil.

In the end, however, the United States did not develop as an imperialist power in China. It would be easy if one could reduce international relations in East Asia to a simple equation of imperialist power politics. Such was not the case. The earlier emphasis on economic expansion, carried out without the burden of territorial control and diplomatic entanglements, continued. The tradition of a more or less peaceful, economic approach to Asia did not just evaporate after the war with Spain. It became bound up with the new territorial expansionism, but in China it generally prevailed over the latter, in effect defining the United States as a nonterritorial expansionist vis-à-vis that country and placing China beyond the immediate limits of American imperialism. The open door policy of John Hay expressed this assertion of the earlier brand of commercial rather than military penetration of China.

It is not necessary to detail the never-ending debate about the making of the open door policy. The immediate circumstances have been clearly delineated by Tyler Dennett, Marilyn Young, and others, while writers such as Walter LaFeber, Thomas McCormick, William A. Williams, Jerry Israel, and L. N. Zubok have provided the broader historical context.[8] Conceptual ambiguity remains, however, as later developments have tended to becloud the relation between the open door policy and America's emergence as an Asian power. The Hay policy was undoubtedly important as an assertion of the nation's power and status in East Asia; its enunciation indicated that the United States would play a role in that part of the world. But the way this would be done, as John Hay made abundantly clear, would be not through the stationing of troops or acquisition of bases in China, but through the protection and extension of peaceful commercial activities.

The open door policy in this context can be regarded as a codification of the peaceful, liberal expansionist strain in American foreign affairs. It was an expression of what the Democratic Party platform of 1900 termed "expansion by every peaceful and legitimate means." It was at once idealistic and expansionist, unconcerned with military enforcement and directly related to economic power. The very fact that no substantial military power backed up the policy indicated that here was a continuation of the earlier tradition of expansionism. It had envisaged America's peaceful expansion through traders and missionaries; it had as a whole opposed territorial expansion and the use of military force for extending power for its own sake. What happened in 1899 and 1900 demonstrated the strength and vitality of America's peaceful expansionism that tended to limit the more narrowly power-oriented, particularistic type of expansion. To be sure this tradition had not been sufficiently influential to check the territorial expansionism of 1898–99, and even after 1900 more imperialistic modes of expansionism were undertaken in the Caribbean, as witnessed by the exercise of the right of intervention in Cuba, establishment of virtual control over Panama, and institution of customs receivership in Santo

Domingo. In this region there was much greater commitment to imperialism, buttressed as it was by the perceived need to build an isthmian canal and safeguard its route. The United States, which in China was insisting upon an open door, nonchalantly closed the door in Puerto Rico by incorporating it to the American economic system, and in Cuba through a reciprocity tariff arrangement. American control over the isthmian canal was envisaged as virtually unlimited, while at the very time the United States was insisting on equal treatment on the Russian-built Chinese Eastern Railway in Manchuria.

American imperialism in the Caribbean was no less imperialistic than the imperialism of other powers. It is all the more interesting, therefore, that American expansion in Asia retained the earlier, nonimperialistic characteristics. The Pacific Ocean, standing between the Caribbean area and the Asian continent, exhibited the traits of imperialism as well as peaceful expansionism. Trade patterns in Hawaii and the Philippines were closely integrated into the American tariff system, and the open door was out of the question. All who had been citizens of the short-lived Hawaiian Republic — mostly natives and whites — automatically attained American citizenship, whereas in the Philippines the people continued to be subjects of the American empire.

There were thus different patterns of American expansion at the beginning of the twentieth century. How far and in what ways the expansion would continue was the subject of serious debate within the United States. Woodrow Wilson wrote in the concluding pages of his five-volume *History of the American People*, that the nation's colonial empire had been acquired "without premeditation" on the part of the statesmen. But, he said, they had instinctively grasped that "they had come to a turning point in the progress of the nation. . . . It had turned from developing its own resources to make conquest of the markets of the world." Thus Wilson saw little to lament about the coming of a new era in America's external affairs. Asia "was the market all the world coveted now, the market for which statesmen as well as merchants must plan and play their game of competition, the market to which diplomacy, and if need be power, must make an open way." The possessions in the Pacific came to Americans "as if out of the very necessity of the new career set before them." This power was to be used in the achievement of the same ends for which America had been known: commercial expansion and humanitarian goals. Wilson was proud of American behavior during the Boxer crisis. "America played her new part with conspicuous success. Her voice told for peace, conciliation, justice, and yet for a firm vindication of sovereign rights, at every turn of the difficult business. . . . [The] new functions of America in the East were plain enough for all to see." [9] The "new" functions in fact were not new at all; in Wilson's view, the United States was using the recently acquired empire and power for realizing its traditional aspirations. The tension this kind of nationalistic universalism presented is obvious. It could revert to traditional universalism, emphasizing liberal ends rather than empire, or to more nationalistic imperialism, justifying power for its own sake. In Wilson's case the limits of American expansionism were set by regard for traditional liberal commitments. His subsequent championing of Philippine autonomy and Chinese modernization grew naturally out of his beliefs.

Wilson's ideas were not very far from those of Charles A. Conant, the American counterpart to England's John A. Hobson. Like Hobson, Conant believed that modern imperialism was derived from the advanced nations' accumulated domestic savings which the capitalists sought to invest in profitable fields overseas. Although Hobson was convinced that labor suffered from this type of financial imperialism, for Conant labor and capital were one in promoting and benefiting from overseas economic expansion. He came close to the moralism of Wilson in considering continued economic growth an essential condition for the survival of Western civilization. That civilization, particularly its Anglo-Saxon branch, had fostered the cause of modern social progress and freedom, ideals which were to be transmitted to the rest of the world through economic expansion. This, said Conant, "is a law of economic and race development." The United States could not shirk from its responsibilities; it must join the "struggle for the maintenance of free markets and equality of opportunity in the undeveloped countries." While it was preferable to use only peaceful means for this end, the nation must not hesitate to take up the burden of territorial empire if it were not to fall into economic stagnation and race atrophy. Thus, toward China, Conant insisted that the United States either sustain Britain's policy to stand for an open door, or, if this was difficult, "follow the narrower policy of the continental countries" in establishing a sphere of influence and seizing bases and tracts of territory.[10]

Paul S. Reinsch was also quick to contemplate the meaning of American imperialism. In *World Politics at the End of the Nineteenth Century*, published in 1900, he correctly grasped the essence of the new expansionism, characterizing it as "national imperialism." "The older ideas of the solidarity of humanity, of universal brotherhood, have largely lost their force, and have been replaced by a narrow national patriotism." Reinsch was not as convinced as Wilson of the meaning of American imperialism after 1898. The United States, he wrote, "was drawn into Oriental politics and incurred far-reaching duties, without any clear recognition among the public, or even among statesmen, of a national purpose or policy." For him the basic American principle in external affairs was still commercial, and he saw no need why this should change. He wrote: "the fundamental principles of American policy ought to be the fostering of commercial relations and the strengthening of industries at home, rather than the acquisition of vast reaches of territory. . . . [We] ought to be slow to enter upon a policy of ambitious territorial expansion, which would weigh down our industries with the cost of maintaining an extensive colonial service and naval establishment, without any proportionate gain."

Reinsch, however, was as much concerned with the future of Western expansion as of American expansion. Now that the United States had expanded territorially into the East, he pondered the question not only in narrowly national terms but also in terms of the future of civilization. It is suggestive to note that, despite his opposition to extensive colonization, he little doubted the inevitability of Western expansion. "Did it not represent the real demands of the human race [for industrial progress] imperialism could not have become the force it is in modern politics." Imperialism was part of the gradual globalization, the process of industrialization of the non-West through the expansion of Western ideas and technology. "Asia is the principal prize, because with its marvellous resources and its great laboring population it is bound to become the industrial centre of the future." From here, the question naturally followed about the future of Western civilization itself, once it was extended to the whole world: "the questions to be solved involve not merely commerce and industry, but the deeper interests of civilization as well. The whole cast of thought that characterizes the West, its ideals and principles, may be modified by the intimate contact with the Orient into which it is now being brought by imperial expansion." In a thoughtful chapter entitled

"The Meeting of Orient and Occident," Reinsch echoed the concern of Pearson, Mahan, and others who had expressed similar ideas in the 1890's. "The meeting of the Orient and the Occident, long foreshadowed, had finally taken place, and the settlement of accounts between the two civilizations cannot be longer postponed. . . . Is the Western spirit to conquer or to be conquered, or is there to be a peaceful union of the two ancient civilizations, combined into a higher harmony?" [11]

For Reinsch, Russia presented the greatest menace to the continued vigor and supremacy of Western civilization. The "semi-Asiatic" character of Russia, "is becoming still more Oriental." Russia seemed consciously opposed to Western ideals of democracy and individualism. Given Russian expansionism in Asia, this was a serious cause for concern. Should Russia expand and assimilate China, "Orientalism will be furnished with a strong political organization to aid it in impressing its character upon the world." In thus viewing Russia, especially its connection with China, as the key to international politics and the future of world civilization, Reinsch was joined by other Americans. The great question of the twentieth century, said Franklin H. Giddings, a professor at Columbia University, "is whether the Anglo-Saxon or the Slav is to impress his civilization on the world." Josiah Strong fully agreed and developed the theme in his book *Expansion.* The contest, according to him, was between Eastern and Western civilizations. The Slav represented the former. He was "an Asiatic." His mental characteristics and historical roots were the opposite of those of the Anglo-Saxon race, of which the United States was the most powerful example. It was extremely revealing, Strong wrote, that Russia and America should now face each other across the Pacific Ocean, for it was there that the drama of the new century was most likely to be played. The Anglo-Saxon was destined to win the contest and turn the ocean into "an Anglo-Saxon sea." Viewed in such a context, it was inevitable that the United States should have extended its sway over Hawaii and the Philippines at the end of the nineteenth century. To fight for the noble heritage of Western civilization, that was the historical mission of American imperialism in the Pacific. That mission would not stop with the extension of naval power throughout, and the governing of inferior races in the ocean. It would also involve the Westernization of China. "Unless prevented by Russia," Strong said, "England and America will give to China the blessings of European civilization, the triumph of which represents the liberation of the individual, not only politically, but religiously and intellectually. Bring the East thoroughly under the influence of the West, and it would be impregnated with a new life." [12]

Alfred Thayer Mahan, from whom Strong borrowed many ideas, gave his authoritative support to such views of Russia and China in *The Problem of Asia*. He argued that Russia, representing the world's land powers, was consciously opposed to sea powers, including Britain, Germany, Japan, and the United States. China was a potential land power, but its absorption into the Russian empire would be a disaster not only to the sea powers but to civilization. The concern with the future of Western civilization, which Mahan had eloquently expressed in 1897, was now even more intense in view of American expansion in the western Pacific and East Asia. China was the prize of all powers intent upon expansion, and the interaction of these powers was likely to draw the United States more and more deeply into Asian politics, at the same time bringing China into closer contact with the West. For Mahan the implications of all these developments for American policy and civilization were obvious. A process had begun,

which must end either in bringing the Eastern and Western civilizations face to face, as opponents who have nothing in common, or else in receiving the new elements, the Chinese especially, as factors which, however they may preserve their individuality . . . have been profoundly affected by long-continued intimate contact, and in such wise assimilated that the further association may proceed quietly to work out peacefully its natural results. . . . [The] incorporation of this vast mass of beings, the fringe of which alone we have as yet touched, into our civilization, to the spirit of which they have hitherto been utter strangers, is one of the greatest problems that humanity has yet had to solve.[13]

These views reveal an interest in China in terms both of its potential modernization and of America's stake in it, which would become increasingly more intense. In the period before the Russo-Japanese War, however, the growing concern with the China question did not imply a negative image of Japanese-American relations. In a sense there was a lessening of tension as the relation between the two countries was more one of compatibility than conflict in Asia. During the Boxer episode the Japanese were allies of the United States and the two countries "succeeded in controlling the international policy," according to Brooks Adams.[14] "Cannot the Japanese send us protection?" a typical American missionary asked in July 1900, just as the Tokyo government was deciding to dispatch 20,000 troops to China. The sentiment was echoed in the United States. "If the Western powers would remain in the background," said the *Springfield Republican*, "and let Japan apply whatever force is needed to relieve the present situation, there will be less danger of a general war and more chance of restoring peace and order at an early day." [15] After the suppression of the Boxers, Americans in China and at home turned their attention to Manchuria, where Russian soldiers posed a threat to the principle of the open door. In this context, too, Japan was seen more often as an ally, "a partner" as Mahan said, of the United States than as a potential rival. Even though Japan was trying to do in Korea what Russia was doing in Manchuria, the American government and public were far more concerned with what was happening in Manchuria than with the Korean situation. In the anticipated racial and economic struggle in Asia, Japan was frequently characterized as more Westernized and therefore less hostile to the Anglo-Saxon powers than the Russian empire.[16] Even a person as critical of Japanese policy in Korea as Horace Allen, American minister in Seoul, confided in 1901: "If it is true that Russia intends to quiet matters by handing over Korea to Japan I think it will be a move for general peace and not without benefit to Korea." Three years later, just before the outbreak of the Russo-Japanese War, he wrote to W. W. Rockhill, minister in Peking, that Japan had made a mistake in not absorbing Korea, whose people "cannot govern themselves." "Let Japan have Korea outright if she can get it," Allen said, "I am no pro-Japanese enthusiast as you know, neither am I opposed to any civilized race taking over the management of the kindly asiatics [sic] for the good of the people and the suppression of the oppressive officials, the establishment of order and the development of commerce." [17]

Insofar as Japan was seen as a threat to the United States, it was in connection with the latter's Pacific possessions. After the Spanish-American War the navy saw a great need to divert part of the fleet to Asia, and in 1903 an Asiatic fleet was formed, comprising one-third of the existing naval strength, including cruisers and battleships. The navy also called for the construction of a chain of bases extending from the eastern United States through the proposed canal, Hawaii, Guam, to the Philippines and preferably a port in China. But this time Japan's menace to Hawaii and the Philippines was considered much more potential than actual. Writing a report on the Japanese forces in China at the time of the international relief expedition to Peking, Major Charles H. Muir remarked that the Japanese soldier "receives almost no pay, but is actuated by a most intense patriotism and pride in his position as a soldier. . . . The compulsory service and strict physical requirements with the system of reserves, allows Japan to put a large body of trained men in the field at short notice. And if Japan can keep the armament and equipment on a par with her soldiers she is a most valuable ally and a most formidable enemy." [18] In 1901 the Navy General Board considered the possibility that Japan, despite its current troubles with Russia, might make up with that power and strike southward toward the American possessions.[19] Both army and navy continued to follow closely the buildup of Japanese armed forces, but at this time there was no fear of an immediate collision. Otherwise, the United States navy would have been alarmed by the signing in 1902 of the Anglo-Japanese alliance which at least theoretically had the effect of combining the navies of the two powers in Asia. But the United States was inclined to view the three nations as at peace.

This feeling of security reflected trends in Japanese policy and opinion which retreated from the earlier, more belligerent attitude toward the United States. This was the result in part, but only in part, of Japan's preoccupation with the Russian question. The story of Japan's road to war has been recounted colorfully and authoritatively, and there is little need to repeat it.[20] Unfortunately, historians have tended to isolate Japanese-Russian relations and treat them in terms of their clash in Korea and/or Manchuria. When arguing about the "character of Japanese imperialism," they often do so in the framework of the war with Russia. Among Japanese writers in particular, scholarly debate has on occasion taken the form of asking whether the ultimate source of the war with Russia lay in Korea or in Manchuria. Obviously it was both. There was near-unanimous consensus in Japan that national security demanded Japanese control over the Korean peninsula, and that this could never be safeguarded as long as Manchuria remained under Russian power. A memorandum written by an officer of the General Staff in February 1901 noted that Russia's occupation of Manchuria following the Boxer affair would virtually divide up China, threaten Korea's independence, damage Japanese security, and violate the peace of East Asia. To prevent these developments it was incumbent upon Japan to resist Russian hegemony over Manchuria, even at the risk of war. Specific researches for planning for war against Russia were begun later in the year. In the meantime naval strength was built up to cope with the increases in the Russian navy. Diplomacy, too, was guided by the need to guarantee that in case of hostilities with Russia other powers would remain uncommitted or maintain friendly neutrality. The conclusion of an Anglo-Japanese alliance in 1902 was a great achievement in that sense; although not a military alliance to prepare against Russia, it obtained Britain's endorsement of Japan's policy in Korea as well as British neutrality in the event of a Japanese-Russian conflict. By 1903 Japanese leaders concluded that diplomatically and militarily they could realistically press Russia to concede Japanese supremacy in the Korean peninsula. Their resolve, adopted in April, to resort to war unless Russia yielded, led inexorably to war in less than a year.[21]

Insofar as Japan was diplomatically and militarily preoccupied with the Russian question, the United States tended to be viewed from that perspective. The government in Tokyo was generally satisfied that the two nations on opposite sides of the Pacific were pursuing similar policies toward the Russian menace in Manchuria, and that the United States could be counted upon to maintain friendly neutrality in case of an armed clash between Japan and Russia. Japanese diplomats in Peking and Washington frequently saw their American colleagues and officials to solicit their opinions and coordinate action. Summaries of American press opinion were forwarded to Tokyo regularly.[22] In 1901, when a staff member of the Japanese General Staff wrote a memorandum examining possible attitudes of the powers in case of a Russian-Japanese war, he did not even find it necessary to pay attention to the United States. After analyzing in detail how France, Germany, and England would react, he casually wrote, "other European powers and the United States will of course remain neutral." This reflected the army's lack of concern with the United States.[23] Neither was the Japanese navy particularly conscious of rivalry with the American navy. The proposal for naval construction submitted for Diet consideration in 1903 talked of the need to keep up with the European powers in expanding the navy. It was observed that the United States was emerging as an important naval power, but it was not expected that much fleet strength would be put in the Pacific. Only the Russian and British navies seemed to count.[24]

Struggle with Russia over the Korean and Manchurian questions was only part of Japan's external affairs. Because diplomatic and military matters concerning Russia dominated Japan's official foreign relations, it does not follow that they overshadowed all else. Japan, like the United States, was at once an imperialist and a nonmilitary expansionist. It was engaged in preparation for control over Korea that was clearly imperialistic. The nation's army, with the support of the government, was contemplating the use of force to assert predominance over a neighboring kingdom and to eliminate foreign influence. But this was only a fraction of the expansion being undertaken and planned by the Japanese, and not all of it involved an overt use of force. The areas of more subtle expansion were pregnant with future implications and had direct relevance to Japanese-American relations.

Japanese thinking can perhaps best be seen in three books on imperialism, all published in 1901: Kōtoku Shūsui, *Nijusseiki no kaibutsu teikokushugi* (Imperialism, the monster of the twentieth century); Takimoto Seiichi, *Keizaiteki teikokushugi* (Economic imperialism); and Ukita Kazutami, *Teikokushugi to kyōiku* (Imperialism and education). Of these Kōtoku's book is best known today, but at that time its influence was no more than that of the other two. All three were timely, coming just when the Japanese people debated the course of their empire, formal and informal, and when they were viewing themselves and the Americans as two latecomers to the ranks of imperialists.

Kōtoku's book opens with the famous passage: "The fashion of imperialism is spreading like a prairie fire. . . . Even the United States seems to be copying it. As for Japan, after the great victory in the Sino-Japanese War the people, both high and low, have been fanatically turning toward it like a wild horse trying to throw off his yoke." Imperialists in Japan and elsewhere are like drunken men, intoxicated by patriotism and militarism, which are nothing but expressions of their animal instincts. They bleed people white with taxes, expand armaments, divert productive capital for unproductive ends, cause prices to rise, and invite excessive imports. These are all for the sake of the state. Government, education, commerce, and industry are sacrificed to patriotism, which is the root of militarism and imperialism.

Echoing the argument of contemporary British anti-imperialists, Kō-toku asserts that war, armament, and imperialism retard economic progress and destroy civilization. Prosperity cannot be achieved through territorial acquisitions, national greatness does not come from aggression and plundering, and civilization never progresses by means of dictatorial rule. In an important passage, the author says what he objects to is imperialism in the sense of colonialism and territorial aggrandizement, not expansion itself. The economic expansion of a people should be welcomed, but not the extension of the limits of empire which can be achieved only through the use of force and suppression of other peoples.

Like the American anti-imperialists, Kōtoku argues that imperialism does not really bring about the expansion of national life. On the contrary, it only means the expansion of the interests and self-esteem of a handful of military men, capitalists, and politicians, obtained at the expense of the well-being of the majority of the people. From such a viewpoint, the book gives a harsh indictment of the United States:

The action of the European powers in Asia and Africa, and the territorial expansion of the United States in the South Seas are all carried out through militarism and armed forces. . . . If the United States truly fought for the freedom and independence of Cuba, why does it try to violate the freedom and independence of the Philippines? To use force to suppress another people's desires and plunder their territory and wealth — does such a thing not bring shame to America's glorious history of civilization and liberty? . . . If in the future the United States should be faced with a crisis of national existence, it would result not from the narrowness of its territory but from its unlimited territorial expansion, not from the lack of power in external affairs but from corruption and social decay internally. . . . They [i.e., Americans] are competing with one another to enter the evil path simply to satisfy their ambitions, interests, and patriotic zeal. I not only fear for their future troubles but feel sorrow for liberty, justice, and humanism.

If Japan were not to fall into the same error, it must renounce imperialism through the use of force. Instead it should stress, as Britain did before the age of imperialism, the expansion of the people through trade, production, and the spread of civilization. A nation's happiness and greatness, Kōtoku concludes, do not lie in the vastness of its territory, but in the high level of its morality, not in the strength of its armament but in the nobility of its ideals, not in the number of ships and soldiers but in the abundance of products.[25]

A second edition of Kōtoku's book was issued within twenty days. By then newspapers and journals had printed their reviews, reflecting tremendous national concern with the book's subject matter. The reviews were either entirely or partially laudatory, but rarely, if at all, unfavorable. Antigovernment and radical organs such as *Yorozu chōhō* and *Rōdō sekai* (The world of labor) wholly endorsed the author's ideas and heaped high praise, and Nakae Chōmin expressed his complete agreement with Kōtoku's analysis. The so-called imperialism, Nakae wrote, "is militarism pure and simple . . . the most miserable state of affairs in all history." Influential dailies such as the *Mainichi, Yomiuri, Hōchi*, and *Jiji shinpō* praised the book as a sharp and readable account of the imperialism that was spreading all over the earth. The major point of criticism raised by other reviewers went to the heart of the question: Kōtoku's definition of imperialism. He saw it as characterized by militarism and territorial aggrandizement, pushed for their own interests by a handful of men who would resort to the rhetoric of patriotism to arouse the animal instinct inherent in all men. This was too narrow a view for some readers, who argued that not all patriotism was evil, and that not all imperialism was practiced by vicious men. Moreover, not all phenomena in the world could be described in terms of the harmful effects of imperialism; cosmopolitanism, pacifism, economic development, and utopianism were apparently growing in strength. According to such critics as Kayahara Kazan and Taoka Ryōun, all were part of the same global development. Mankind, according to Kayahara, was becoming conscious of unity through the diversity of individual cultures and nations; and imperialism should be viewed not simply as evil militarism but as an instrument through which peoples of the world could develop a cosmopolitan outlook while refining their individual characteristics. Taoka, too, though sharing Kōtoku's hatred of imperialism, asserted that this was but a stage in man's evolution toward unity and equality. While less sentimental, reviewers for *Asahi* and *Tokyo Nichinichi* criticized the book for failing to see that the imperialistic outlook was not a product of blind impulses but an expression of basic national energy, made manifest through the organization of the nation-state.[26]

These writers were grappling with a worldwide phenomenon that had become all too visible after the decade of the 1890's. They were not simply concerned with the Manchurian crisis, nor were they talking merely of Japanese interests in Korea; they were trying to gain a sense of world movements so that their country could chart a correct course. Kōtoku gave them a book that became a classic in expounding the negative features of imperialism. Takimoto Seiichi's *Keizaiteki tei-kokushugi*, by contrast, viewed the economic aspects of the phenomenon and sought to justify imperialism as a necessary policy for national expansion. Published just four days before Kōtoku's, Takimoto's book presented the other half of the picture. As he said, "armed commercialism" was the order of the day, and "any nation which intends to maintain its independence and promote its expansion must be ready to wage this [economic] struggle." Imperialism, from this point of view, was not a machination of a few greedy individuals and groups, but a fundamental necessity for national sovereignty and welfare. No wonder, then, that the most imperialistic countries were also those that were internally united and practiced "industrial democracy." Kōtoku's model of imperialism was British and American; Germany provided Takimoto's best example. Here was a nation in which the government sought to harmonize the interests of various segments of the population so that they would be united behind the struggle in the world arena. It was nonsense, according to this author, to talk of economic cosmopolitanism. Rather, in the new mercantilistic age, the economy was at the service of the state, which would expand its territorial limits to create a self-sufficient, protected economic system. Now that Japan had Hokkaido and Taiwan, they should be made the bases for further imperialistic expansion in order to make the nation the great empire of the East. Unless it became one, the whole of Asia would fall into the hands of Western empires. Imperialism, in this sense, was a necessary, defensive policy, not an impulsive militaristic adventure.[27]

Kōtoku's and Takimoto's books dealt with modern imperialism from two diametrically opposed viewpoints. There is little doubt that they reflected a division in Japanese opinion concerning the future of national expansion. Most people, however, would not have sided with either of these extreme positions. What the Japanese government was doing and the people were supporting was a cross between imperialistic expansion and more peaceful, economic expansion. Ukita Kazutami's book *Teikokushugi to kyōiku* represented the middle position. By profession a philosopher, Ukita was active as one of the influential popularizers of ideas and commentators on current affairs. The book reprinted some of the articles he wrote for *Kokumin shinbun*, edited by Tokutomi Sohō, who obviously endorsed many of Ukita's views. He starts out by saying that imperialism is the only way to maintain the nation's independence and participate actively in world civilization and politics. The new modern imperialism is represented by Britain, Russia, and the United States, and differs from the old imperialism of the Spanish or Dutch type. The latter is aggressive, political, militaristic expansionism, whereas the former is fundamentally economic and propelled by the people's energy rather than by the state. Modern imperialism does often carry out territorial aggrandizement, but this is basically because of the struggle for survival among races. Certain races and countries simply do not have the will to remain independent, but their incorporation into stronger nations will advance world civilization as a whole. There are, in other words, ethical factors in imperialism, and Japan should try to be an ethical imperialist.

Most of the earth's surface, Ukita continues, has already been absorbed by the imperialist powers. If Japan is to adopt a policy of imperialism, it can do so only through lawful expansion of Japanese rights in relation to the West and assistance to Asian countries to carry out reform programs and achieve independence. The Japanese government should be prepared to promote such expansionism so that the people will migrate abroad and plant seeds of future success. He asserts that, since the Japanese variety of imperialism must take an economic and peaceful form, there will be no limits to such expansion save those conditioned by the level of education of the Japanese people.

"The areas for our expansion," according to Ukita, "obviously are confined to the Asian continent, the New World, and the South Seas." While Japan must persist in "peaceful, economic, and commercial" expansion in these parts of the world, it must be prepared to make an exception in the case of Korea, as its "independence" is a fundamental national policy. Even this is not aggressive imperialism, since Japan only desires a preponderant economic and political position in the peninsula. Interests are not comparably extensive in China, and Japan will gain most by encouraging that country's reform and modernization. On the other hand, it is desirable to settle and protect Japanese people in the Pacific and the New World. In this task Japan "is destined to compete with American imperialism." Such competition, however, is "peaceful competition." The Japanese can achieve victory only by inculcation in practical subjects such as commerce and economics. Pragmatism and efficiency ought to be the guiding principles of Japanese public education. Individual students must learn to develop their personal morality, integrity, and perseverance so as to equip themselves for the peaceful competition of imperialism. Only if they develop "internalized, spiritual, autonomous, and self-reliant" morality, will they be able to guide Asia's hundreds of millions along the path of modernization and to go out and live in the South Seas and the American continents.[28]

Records of Japanese expansion prior to the Russo-Japanese War show that Ukita correctly predicted the general outline it was going to follow. Apart from Korea, there was no premeditated design to extend the limits of Japan's formal empire to the continent of Asia or to the Pacific Ocean. Japanese imperialism did not take so aggressive a form as that urged by Takimoto. Neither did the nation completely renounce its right to assertive expansion, as Kōtoku insisted. Beyond the clear limits of imperialistic policy in Korea, the Japanese were practicing and rationalizing their expansion much as Ukita suggested.

His idea that the basic thrust of Japanese imperialism in China should be to help the latter reform was a theme stressed by many other writers. In 1902 Itakura Naka, a former member of the Diet, wrote that after Japan established its control — political, economic, and cultural — over Korea, the next step should be to expand in China by spreading civilization to the Chinese people.[29] In 1903 Satō Torajirō published two books in the same vein: *Shina keihatsu-ron* (On developing China), and *Shinseikei* (New politics and economy). The author had traveled widely in the South Seas and once tried, unsuccessfully, to establish a small Japanese settlement on the British colony of Thursday Island, off Cape York in northeastern Australia.[30] He was probably the first to use the term "heiwateki hattenshugi" (the principle of peaceful expansion) self-consciously. The second book named was an exposition of this principle. Although admitting the necessity of developing Taiwan as a formal colony and preserving Korean "independence," Satō argued that in other parts of the world "the expansion of national power and rights must be carried out through peaceful means. It must take the form of the extension of specific rights, influence, and interests." China was most likely to be the coming battleground of "peaceful warfare," to be waged by economic weapons. Japan could win the struggle because of its unique advantages: the same cultural roots as China, the short geographical distance between the two countries, and their close historical ties during the past several thousand years.[31] The pan-Asianist theme in the service of peaceful expansionism was also stressed in *Shina keihatsu-ron*. The time seemed opportune, the author argued, for Japan to undertake positive assistance for China since the Chinese were apparently welcoming reform and development. Japan could do for that country what the United States had done for itself in the middle of the nineteenth century. Japan should act as China's "teacher and father" and the two should be closely united, not in imperialistic relations but through the Japanese people's combined effort to engage in the development of China. To do so, however, they must get rid of their sense of superiority. "The first step toward developing China is for the Japanese to become like Chinese," instead of trying to remake China in the image of Japan.[32]

Such expressions have often led historians to detect pan-Asianism and continentalism as major themes of Japanese expansion even before the Russo-Japanese War. They must, however, be put in proper perspective. As Satō said, the Japanese at that time were extremely ignorant of China. So many of them were interested only in the West. Consequently, little fruit of Japanese activity could be seen in China.[33] The observation was essentially accurate. Compared with the precise military planning for confrontation with Russia in Korea, and with the accelerated flow of Japanese emigrants to regions of the Pacific, expansion in China remained largely on paper. The blueprint, reiterated by government and business spokesmen, called for "southern expansion" — penetration of southern provinces, in particular Fukien and Chekiang, which were opposite the island of Taiwan. In this area it was hoped that Japan would be able to obtain mining and railway concessions and to engage in educational and cultural activities. Little of this, however, had materialized before the outbreak of war with Russia in early 1904. Though the Tokyo government had, as early as 1898, drawn up a proposal for railway construction in south China, no serious negotiations were begun until 1903.[34] The plan was to build a line between Amoy, Foochow, and Wuchang, and another between Nanchang and Hangchow. These railways, if built by Japanese capital and technology, would have facilitated the penetration of south China. But it was impractical to carry out such costly undertakings, and Japanese policy was primarily confined to preventing other powers from building railways or engaging in mining in the area.

Neither was there much to show for Japan's cultural expansion. Actually, the flow of men was from China to Japan; an increasing number of Chinese youths went to Japan to seek education at all levels even before the termination of the Confucian examination system in 1905. In 1903 Chinese students in Japan, most of them in Tokyo, numbered a few thousand, half of whom paid their own transportation and fees. As Liang Ch'i-ch'ao, the leading reformist, noted, there was no ship coming from China which did not bring students to Japan.[35] By comparison, there were far fewer Japanese educators in China. The fate of Buddhist proselytization undertaken by Japanese priests is especially interesting. The idea had semiofficial backing, as the government in Taiwan encouraged missionary activities by Japanese Buddhists in Fukien and adjoining provinces as part of "southern expansionism." The first missionaries were sent out in 1898. But the number never grew to more than a handful, and those who went to China operated with meager financial resources. Unlike the Christian missionaries from Western countries, they were not under the supervision and support of home boards.[36]

If economic and cultural expansion into China was more ideal than reality, there was not even a conception for military control over China. Neither the Japanese army nor the navy had a clear plan to expand beyond Korea into the continent of Asia. Because of the Russian occupation of Manchuria the army expected that the Chinese government and people would support Japanese action to challenge Russian power.[37] But the aim of Japanese action was always considered to be the restoration of China's integrity. The idea was that, once Manchuria was freed from Russian control, the threat to Japan's position in Korea would be removed, and that the other powers would support Japanese action in order to secure this end. China would regain its territorial integrity and be made an open market for foreign commerce. An important memorandum written in June 1903 by Major General Iguchi Shōgo, chief of the general affairs bureau of the General Staff, is a good example of army thinking. He stated "[We would aim at] expelling Russia out of Manchuria, opening up Manchuria as an open market for the commerce of all nations so as to balance their interests against one another, neutralizing Manchuria to prevent its falling into a particular country's hands, securing our occupation of Korea in order to prevent Russia's southward thrust, and making Russia restore the lease of Port Arthur and Talien to China."

He added that, in order to block any Russian intention of expanding into the Pacific, Japan might try to occupy Vladivostok. This was the only reference to Japanese territorial control of any land outside Korea.[38]

The Japanese navy's essential goal before 1904 was the augmentation of the fleet. According to its estimates, as of 1902 battleship tonnages of the major powers were as follows:

Britain	561,900	Italy	124,153
France	246,096	U.S.	119,120
Russia	193,311	Germany	115,968
Japan	129,715		

Navy Minister Yamamoto Gonbei, in view of the possibility of war with Russia, established a ten-year naval expansion program. Approved by the Diet in 1903, the plan called for the building of three new battleships, three heavy cruisers, and two light cruisers by 1913, totaling 85,000 additional tons. As Yamamoto explained to the cabinet in October 1902, naval expansion was essential in view of the revealed weakness of China and the occupation of its coast by the powers. The size of expansion must depend on the principle of overwhelming the strongest hypothetical enemy, probably Russia. If Japan expanded its naval strength efficiently and sufficiently, Yamamoto was hopeful that not only war with Russia but also Russian control of China and Korea could be avoided. Altogether, naval strength was designed to "maintain forever the prestige of the Empire, guarantee the peace of East Asia, protect the development of our commerce, and develop needed natural resources." [39] The navy was not interested in territorial expansion at this time. The objective was relative superiority over the Russian Far Eastern fleet, and the possibility of war was always considered in connection with the need to prevent Russian naval predominance.[40] As for China, leading naval strategists and officers such as Satō Tetsutarō and Akiyama Saneyuki reflected their reading of Mahan in viewing the crucial importance of the China market for the development of the Japanese economy and shipping industry. They emphasized the importance of keeping the door of trade open in China.[41]

Under the circumstances, it was not surprising that there was little conflict between Japanese and American expansionism in China. The two were basically informal and economically oriented, and their conflict was more potential than actual. The Japanese generally favored the American doctrine of the open door, although they were no less determined than the Americans to expand their interests and influence in China. Japanese commerce had everything to gain from the application of the principle of equal opportunity vis-à-vis railway charges and harbor dues. Japan was entering the first stage of industrialization, and its success was reflected in the continued growth of its exports to China. It should be noted, however, that Japanese trade was expanding in all directions, as was American trade. The volume of bilateral trade between Japan and the United States was always larger than that between either country and China. Despite the gripping myth of the China market, American economic relations were far more deeply involved in Europe and Latin America than in Asia. For all these reasons, few in Japan or the United States were conscious of any tension in their relations in China. Both countries were pursuing economic expansionism beyond the territorial limits of their respective empires, and more often than not Japanese and American expansionists were friendly competitors.

The Asian continent was not what most Japanese had in mind when they considered expansion. The wider Pacific region was more frequently mentioned as an ideal area for undertaking peaceful expansion. Interest in the Philippines did not wane in the years immediately following the Spanish-American War. In 1902, for instance, there were about 1,500 Japanese laborers in the islands, a threefold increase over 1898. But the Philippines were not as promising as Hawaii as a place for the emigration of Japanese manual laborers, where there was a sufficient supply of Filipino workers. What was needed there was the importation of Japanese capital and skills, which was to increase steadily but at first only slowly. Japan's interest in the Philippines lay in their promise as a market. As Moriyama Nobunori wrote in his *Bei-Sei sensō* (The Spanish-American War), probably the only book-length study of the war by a Japanese at that time, now that the United States had acquired the islands its capital was likely to rush in and contribute to the industrialization of the Philippines. Japan should take advantage of their proximity to Taiwan and "should never give up enormous profits that we could obtain in peacetime." The author admitted that American annexation of the Philippines had in effect frustrated Japanese ambitions southward, but this expansion was a historical fact and Japan could not oppose it. The Philippines and Cuba were to the United States what Taiwan and Korea were to Japan. They fell within the respective empires, and the only competition possible between the two was economic.[42]

Hawaii and the West coast of the United States held the greatest interest for Japanese expansionists. The number of passports issued to Japanese laborers going to Hawaii increased from 5,913 in 1897 to 12,952 in 1898 and 27,155 in 1899, reflecting a relaxation in the anti-Japanese movement in the islands after their annexation. But as they came under territorial rule in 1900, the United States law forbidding contract labor was applied to Hawaii, causing Japanese immigration to drop to 4,760 in 1900. Freed from the contract system, Japanese laborers began moving to the continental United States, bringing about a near doubling of the Japanese population between 1899 and 1900. There were about 24,000 Japanese in the United States in 1900, and the number doubled again in the following four years. Not only laborers from Hawaii, but students, merchants, and farmers began arriving directly from Japan. Immigration companies which hitherto had arranged contract emigration to Hawaii now sent out shiploads of Japanese to the West coast of the United States.[43]

Numerically, the presence of Japanese in Hawaii and North America was impressive: on the eve of the Russo-Japanese War, there were over 65,000 in Hawaii and nearly 40,000 on the West coast. Together they comprised more than two-thirds of the Japanese population abroad. Economically speaking, emigration to China and Korea was considered less important than that to the Pacific American continent.[44] The preference for a warmer climate and richer soil, long expressed by Japanese writers, stayed with them as they pondered the more immediate questions of international politics in Manchuria. The urgent need, as they saw it, was still to enrich the nation, and economic expansion could most easily be visualized in connection with trade with and emigration to the territories bordering the Pacific Ocean. This was particularly the time when interest in emigration to America reached unprecedented intensity.

"Hawaii! The new world of North America! How wonderful it is that our farmers, laborers, and merchants, all vigorous and healthy, have been turning their attention more and more to these islands and the new world." [45] Thus ran a typical passage from one of the numerous guides to work abroad, published at the turn of the century.

Reflecting the growing interest in working in the United States and its possessions, a new genre in Japanese journalistic writings emerged: pamphlets on how to prepare for going abroad and conduct oneself overseas. Titles such as *Kaigai dekasegi annai* (A guide to working abroad) and *Kaigai risshin no tebiki* (How to get ahead abroad) began to appear, and most concentrated on emigration to the United States. The first-named was a booklet published by the Emigrants Protection Association, organized in 1902 to assist prospective emigrants. In it the editor pointed out that in Hawaii a Japanese laborer could easily earn over 30 yen a month, and that in San Francisco a domestic servant could make nearly the same amount, whereas in Japan they would not be able to get half as much through harder work. To prepare for overseas emigration, of course, one would need enough initial capital. According to this booklet, about 20 yen would have to be paid as a fee to an emigration company to help a prospective emigrant move to Hawaii. There were twenty-eight emigration companies in existence in 1902, of which nineteen had been founded after 1898, and as many as eight in the year 1902 alone. They made arrangements for the departure of an emigrant, who then had to pay 60 yen for passage, and, upon arrival in Hawaii, had to show the immigration officials that he had at least 91 yen in his possession. Now that the contract labor system had been abolished, the immigrant would be free to engage in any kind of work, and it should be easy for him to recover the investment of 171 yen for his removal. If he desired to go farther, to the West coast of the United States, it would cost more money, but he would have the opportunity of earning more.[46]

"Going to America," wrote the socialist Katayama Sen in 1903, "has now become the ultimate wish of our people. All men from all classes — students, laborers, gentlemen, businessmen — have joined their voices to repeat the wish and put their brains together to study it. . . . At a time when North America's power is rapidly rising and its influence steadily spreading all over the world, it is extreme foolishness not to go there. It is no exaggeration to say that it is a stupid, uncivilized thing not to consider going to America." [47] Katayama had studied in the United States in the 1880's, and at the turn of the century was a recognized authority on American life, especially in connection with Japanese emigration. He mapped out the basic intellectual and practical guideline for this movement, and remained for a number of years the most influential writer on the subject. His first book on emigration, published in 1901, *To-Bei annai* (How to go to the United States), quickly went through several editions, and subsequently he wrote other similar tracts. In *To-Bei annai* Katayama notes that Japan's fundamental concern is the present and future welfare of its increasing population, now approaching 40 million. The obvious solution is to encourage migration overseas, not only to reduce the homeland's population but also, more fundamentally, to promote Japanese industrialization. The Japanese overseas will introduce their country's products to distant lands and make Japan better known to the rest of the world. Unfortunately, he writes, reflecting a prevailing view of that time, the Japanese people are too insular and parochial; even Japanese overseas are not free from provincialism. "If they give up this insular mentality, understand the true meaning of civilization, and engage in business in a spirit of civilization, then their country, Japan, will cease to be a remote island in the Orient and they will be able to expand their influence all over the world." Of all the potential lands for Japanese emigration, Katayama insists that the United States is the most suitable. This is because "the United States is the freest country in the world; it surpasses all other countries in its industrial, commercial, economic and scholastic advancement." Since labor is considered sacred, wages are high; laborers can even afford to spend part of their earnings on education. Moreover, individual Japanese can go there on their own initiative. All they need is some small initial capital and, more important, determination.[48]

There were two ways of reaching the continental United States. The more popular was first to go to Hawaii as a laboring immigrant and then move to the West coast. This involved less difficulty and less initial capital than the second method, going directly to America. The Japanese government was much more strict in the issuing of passports to the continental United States to avoid causing an anti-Japanese movement on the West coast, and as a rule massive emigration solely for the purpose of manual labor was discouraged. As a result, it was the younger people, especially students, who were most likely to be moved by Katayama's plea to go east and settle in the United States. As students, merchants, or visitors, their departure involved fewer bureaucratic difficulties, and only determination and a small sum of money were needed. The young emigrant was likely to procure a passport from his prefectural government if he provided letters endorsing his personal reliability and financial stability. He would then be ready to pack his suitcases — Katayama suggested that the emigrant take at least one new suit, two to three shirts, six handkerchiefs, six pairs of socks, a pair of shoes, a toothbrush and toothpaste, and an English dictionary — and, without much further ado, board the ship, with a strong body and perseverence as his only capital.

The trip to the West coast of the United States took about two weeks. Immigration proceedings were not difficult, and the new arrivals could live among fellow countrymen in such major centers as Seattle and San Francisco. Through Japanese connections they found menial jobs as waiters, "schoolboys," and gardeners. They assuredly would earn enough money to live and, if they had the will, to study. Many of them enrolled in local high schools and colleges, while working morning and evening hours as domestic servants.[49]

Not all Japanese in the United States fitted Katayama's ideal. By 1901 reports abounded of the poor quality of Japanese in America. *To-Bei annai* contained letters written by Japanese student-immigrants in California. One wrote, "the Japanese here are all mediocre types, unable to breathe the air of civilization even though they are in America. They speak of Americans disparagingly and engage in the least enlightening conversations." Another reported that eight or nine out of ten Japanese in California "are simply idlers with whom it is below my dignity to deal." Such reports revealed that many young Japanese who went to America immersed themselves in daily living and lost whatever higher aspirations they might have had before they left home. From another point of view, however, they were in fact quite successful emigrants. They made a living in the new land and expanded Japanese commerce through their purchases and merchandising of Japanese goods. They built enclaves of Japanese settlement in San Francisco, Seattle, and other cities on the West coast. While their number was hardly sufficient to justify a grandiose vision of Japanese expansion, hope persisted that in time they would prove to be the vanguard of the Japanese thrust abroad. At the very least, by being forced to scramble for a living, they would learn to maximize profit and rationalize life. Economic necessity would breed a new attitude toward life and the world. From such a situation new types of men would emerge, Katayama argued.[50] Another writer, long resident in the United States, expressed the same confidence graphically:

Picture yourself boarding a huge ship of over 10,000 tons, crossing the Pacific Ocean in fifteen or sixteen days . . . arriving in America, entering the spacious city lined with stone buildings thirteen or fourteen stories high, walking on clean stone pavements, observing the development of machinery which can build tall buildings with only a handful of men . . . going to a college where men and women engage in education cheerfully and sincerely, riding a train at the speed of fifty or sixty miles an hour through the interior of the country where all you see are vast spaces without a trace of man — and compare this with life in Japan where you will be living on a modest income of thirty or forty yen a month, fighting with your neighbors over a foot or two of land, or involved in lawsuits to obtain water for irrigating a small plot of land. Before you know it your mind will be opened up, your horizon broadened, and your narrow provincialism will melt like a block of ice placed under the sun.[51]

Obviously there was an element of idealism about emigrating to the United States. It appeared as the country from which the Japanese were considered likely to draw the greatest benefits, culturally as well as economically. There was an underlying image of a nation receptive to the coming of people from Japan, especially its youths and educated classes, who would cooperate with Americans in enriching the two countries and contributing to the peace and welfare of the Pacific. Perhaps for this reason, a great deal was written about the need to bring the cultural and life style of Japanese in America up to the level of the Americans themselves. The author of *Kaigai risshin no tebiki* exhorted emigrants to the United States not to strip naked, no matter how hot. "If you behave like African savages," he said, "you can't complain if the whites despise you." [52] It was undesirable, wrote Noma Gozō, a member of the Diet, to send too many ignorant farmers and fishermen to North America before educating them in things Western.[53] Katayama Sen repeatedly urged that the prospective emigrants be equipped with determination, perseverance, and, above all, flexibility so as to adapt themselves to a new environment. He echoed other writers in criticizing Japanese in the United States for failing to learn the customs and institutions of the new land. So long as they behaved as if they were still in Japan, they would bring the scorn of the people down on themselves and would never be able to deal with them on equal footing. As an extreme example, Katayama noted that some Japanese going to the United States from Hawaii still wore Japanese clothes, walked in Japanese slippers, covered their chins with washcloths, hung carrots and white radishes from their shoulders, and otherwise gave the impression that they were going to the next village in Japan. No wonder they were despised by Americans! He implied that, once the Japanese immigrants overcame their uncouth provincialism and tried to understand and adapt themselves to American customs, they would be accepted and treated with respect.[54]

As these authors well recognized, incidents throughout the Pacific coast of the United States revealed anti-Japanese prejudice. On occasion Japanese were denied entry; at least once they were quarantined in San Francisco during a pest epidemic; and in California and Nevada a movement was on foot to apply anti-Chinese restrictions to Japanese.[55] But as yet there was no widespread movement specifically directed against Japanese immigrants in the United States. The government and Congress supported revision of laws to put an end to the long-standing policy of nearly unlimited immigration. The rising concern at this time was not with the coming of Japanese but of many other peoples, especially from south and eastern Europe. There was little indication that Japanese expansion toward the United States would meet with determined opposition from the American people — so long as the Japanese were cultured and behaved themselves. The Tokyo government saw to this by curtailing the number of passports issued to laborers.[56] Otherwise no control was exercised over individual Japanese as they came into increasing contact with Americans.

Although Japanese and Americans regarded one another as imperialists in certain areas of the world, they also pictured their relations as involving a large sphere beyond the limits of their respective empires. In this sphere relations were by and large peaceful. Forces were stirring, however, which were destined to usher in a new stage of Japanese-American confrontation in East Asia.

IV

Japanese Continentalism
and Chinese Nationalism

In January 1904 William Howard Taft stopped by in Tokyo en route from Manila to Washington. He had just been appointed secretary of war, after a term of office as governor-general of the Philippines. Perhaps more than anyone else in his country, Taft personified the spirit as well as the burden of the new American empire. His observation and experience as governor-general of the western Pacific colony had convinced him that the United States was doing the right thing. "Had we followed the counsel of unwisdom, deserted our duty, shrunk from our task, and abandoned the islands after they came into our possession, we should have been guilty of a crime against civilization, and especially a crime against the Philippinos," Taft wrote in a typical letter to a friend.[1] He was equally aware of the islands' ideal location for America's trade in East Asia. He shared the widely held view that the nation's future lay in economic expansion, and that China was a key to it. "One of the greatest commercial prizes of the world is the trade with 400,000,000 Chinese," he said in a speech in June 1905 and on numerous other occasions. Finally, he was mindful of the growing complications of America's security and strategy which meant imperial security and strategy. He was particularly worried about the danger to the Philippines from external threat as well as from internal rebellion, and one of his major concerns as secretary of war was to be to improve the islands' defense system. Taft's visit to Japan just before taking up his new duties in Washington was symbolic. For the next several years he was to play a key role in the tangled relationship with Japan, involving the Philippines as well as China. Even more suggestive was the interest he showed in Japanese emigration to the islands. While in Tokyo he submitted a detailed list of questions on the subject to the Transoceanic Emigration Company, one of the largest such companies in Japan.

Sugiyama Shigemaru, president of the company, responded to Taft's inquiry by asserting that the emigration of Japanese laborers abroad had "proved unqualifiedly successful, as Japanese labor has everywhere met with a friendly reception, and shown itself vastly superior to labor coming from either China or Korea." His firm had sent out about four hundred emigrants monthly but had plans to double the number in the immediate future. It was the sole agent for emigration to Mexico, Chile, and South Africa, but the bulk of the laborers it had handled had gone to Hawaii and the Philippines. It was hoped, Sugiyama said, that more of them would be sent to and admitted by the "fair and vast field of work" in the Philippines, now that the overseas Japanese had exhibited the traits of "sobriety, frugality, and industry." [2] Ironically, even as these thoughts were penned, the Japanese government was reaching a final decision for war against Russia, a war which was to result in adding a new continental dimension to Japanese expansionism.

Hitherto the main thrust of Japan's expansion into China had been southward, and its orientation primarily, though not exclusively, economic and cultural. This "southern expansionism" did not evaporate with the coming of war in the north. As Foreign Minister Komura Jutarō said early in the war, "The Imperial Government while engaging in warlike operation in . . . North China cannot for a moment neglect their important enterprises in . . . Southern China." [3] Though the Russian war was exhausting the treasury, the Tokyo government was determined to make good its rights — which had mostly remained on paper — in Fukien province. It was feared that unless tangible evidence of Japanese claims were constructed, more financially resourceful foreigners might take advantage of Japan's distress to invade the Japanese sphere of interests. Consequently, earnest efforts were made to organize a Sino-Japanese syndicate for constructing a few railways in Fukien and the adjoining provinces. When, just at this time, A. W. Bash appeared in Peking seeking to obtain a concession for constructing a railway between Amoy and Hankow, and Chinese authorities referred him to the Japanese legation, Komura promptly instructed Minister Uchida Yasuya to refuse the request. Furthermore, he was ordered to see Prince Ch'ing, grand councilor and in charge of foreign affairs, and "obtain from him a fresh confirmation of his assurances that no mining or railway concessions in the Province of Fukien should be granted to foreigners without previous consultation with the Japanese Govt." It seemed vital for Japan to continue its economic penetration of south China, so as to foreclose foreigners from taking advantage of the war in Manchuria.[4]

It was, nevertheless, Manchuria that emerged as the key new target of Japanese expansion. This was the most important by-product of the war. From 1904 on, Japanese expansion would be as much continental as maritime, carried out by military as well as economic means. Such a shift was spelled out in a memorandum Komura wrote for Prime Minister Katsura Tarō five months after the outbreak of the war. According to the foreign minister,

Before the war we would have been satisfied with making Korea our sphere of influence and maintaining the existing rights in Manchuria. Now that war has unfortunately begun, due to Russia's refusal to accept these moderate demands, our policies toward Korea and Manchuria must go a step beyond the past policies. Korea should be made virtually our sovereign area; we should establish a virtual protectorate according to the established policies and plans, and we should plan further extension of our rights. Manchuria should to some extent be made our sphere of influence where our rights and interests could be maintained and expanded.

Specifically, Komura suggested that Japan try to obtain the leases of Liaotung peninsula and the Harbin-Port Arthur railway (the southern branch of the Chinese Eastern Railway). He believed that the Russian menace to Japanese rights in Korea could be removed by the withdrawal of Russian troops from Manchuria and by the cession of the Harbin-Port Arthur railway and the Liaotung leasehold to Japan. This was clearly imperialistic expansion, aiming at adding territory and railways to Japan. From Komura's point of view, however, the new continental expansion had other goals as well. It was viewed as part of the expansion of Japan as a whole and the augmentation of Japanese national power, especially economic. As he said, "In recent times the powers have been intent upon extending their rights and interests in East Asia. Each one of them is trying to take advantage of every opportunity to get ahead of others. We should therefore try to expand our national power by extending our rights and interests in Manchuria, Korea, and the Maritime Province. Since we may not be able to obtain indemnities after this war, it becomes all the more important to extend our rights and interests."

Since the main target of the new expansionism was to be Manchuria, it was natural for Komura to stress the importance of opening negotiations with China as soon as the war was over. While the war involved Russia, the Japanese goal was to expand into Chinese territory. Specifically, Komura suggested that Japan demand of China the right to construct railways from a point on the Yalu to the south Manchurian city of Liaoyang, and between Kirin and a point along the Harbin-Port Arthur railway. These two railways, if constructed, would serve to entrench Japanese economic influence firmly in southern Manchuria, and the latter would be integrated with Korea, over which Japan was establishing hegemony. Moreover, Komura suggested that Japan demand the right to cut wood and engage in mining along the Yalu and the Hun rivers. Exploitation of these two rivers, running parallel to the railway between Harbin and Port Arthur, would serve to integrate the whole of the Liaotung region economically. Together with other demands which Komura thought Japan should make, such as the opening of more treaty ports to foreign trade and of the rivers in Manchuria to foreign navigation, these proposals were calculated to entrench Japanese influence in Manchuria, in particular in areas near Korea. It is obvious that the war against Russia was being utilized for the purpose of shifting the thrust of Japanese expansion northward. This was the origin of continental expansionism.[5]

Because expansion into south Manchuria was envisaged as an event accompanying the war to rid the region of Russian power, there was confusion regarding the nature of the new expansionism. Virtually everyone was agreed that Japan's empire, whether formal or informal, was extending its limits to Manchuria. But was south Manchuria to be primarily Japan's defense post against possible Russian counterattack in the future? Or were Japanese interests to be basically economic, to be actualized through private efforts? Was Japan to combine these two approaches? If so, in what way was south Manchuria going to be an exclusive, particularistic domain for Japan's national interests? These were questions that even the ardent advocates of continental expansionism had but scant time to think through.

For the Japanese military, the importance of south Manchuria as part of the new defense system overshadowed all other considerations. During the war countless memoranda and letters pointed out the need to retain control of the region. General Fukushima Yasumasa, a senior staff officer attached to the army in Manchuria, insisted that Japan keep the Russian lease of Liaotung peninsula, obtain a lease of the central Manchurian city of Harbin, build railways from points along the Yalu to Mukden and farther north, and retain troops in such cities as Kirin, Mukden, and Liaoyang.[6] The importance of railway building was constantly stressed as essential to the defense of Korea and the establishment of Japanese control in south Manchuria. As a memorandum written in April 1905 by the army department of the Imperial Headquarters noted, a railway network connecting the southern portion of the Chinese Eastern Railway and the lines in Korea and in north China would "be militarily advantageous and serve to keep Mukden under our control."[7] None of the projected railways was to be built immediately, the Chinese government presenting a stiff opposition, but the war resulted in Japanese military occupation of south Manchuria which lasted until 1907. Most important, at the Portsmouth Peace Conference Japan was awarded the portion of the southern branch of the Chinese Eastern Railway running between Port Arthur and Changchun. Its strategic importance was obvious. As General Kodama Gentarō, chief of staff, said in a memorandum written before the end of the war, under the guise of railway administration Japan should take all necessary measures to strengthen its position militarily vis-à-vis Russia. While the south Manchurian railway should outwardly be an ordinary, profit-making railroad, it would in fact serve as an arm of the Japanese military, carrying out intelligence as well as economic functions.[8]

Expansion into Manchuria, however, was not merely a strategic move. It was also designed as part of the economic expansion of Japan. Hitherto Manchuria had not attracted Japanese settlers, and Japanese trade with that area was not particularly significant. Even before the end of the war with Russia, however, an increasing number of Japanese came to areas under their country's military control. For instance, in December 1904 it was reported that 1,155 Japanese were in Newchwang, whereas before the war the number had not exceeded 100. Some had accompanied the army as it landed and attacked Russian-controlled cities in south Manchuria. They were needed as servants, interpreters, and suppliers of provisions for the army. Others had no such connection; they went to these places to make a profit in conditions of competitive advantage. They had Japanese military protection, and most foreign residents had either left the zones of warfare or been barred from strategic ports, mines, and other sites.[9]

These trickles of emigration to Manchuria were not ignored by Tokyo's officials. They seemed to represent a promising beginning of what would hopefully turn into major continental expansion, and civilian officials were quick to take advantage of the unique opportunity presented by the Japanese military presence in south Manchuria. For instance, the Finance Ministry was impressed by the fact that the port of Dairen (called Dalny while under Russian control), overlooking a beautiful bay at the tip of Liaotung peninsula, would make an ideal window through which Japanese commercial activities could be promoted. Japanese merchants were given permission to go to and reside in the city even before the end of the war. Finance Ministry supervision was envisaged as early as January 1905, when its officials were sent to look after the merchants already there. After a consultation with the War Ministry, it was decided that "only those commodities that are promising in terms of our future trade" should be admitted to Manchuria through Dairen. At the end of May 1905 the city counted 733 Japanese merchants and their families and employees. Their commercial affairs were closely supervised by Finance Ministry representatives who were charged with the task of studying prospects for marketability of specific items, in particular with regard to foreign competition.[10]

The Foreign Ministry, on its part, was intent upon entrenching as much Japanese economic influence in Manchuria as possible, before the end of the war brought a return of Western merchants and goods. As Vice Foreign Minister Chinda Sutemi wrote Vice War Minister Ishimoto Shinroku, shortly after the signing of the Portsmouth peace treaty, the coming of peace was likely to see Manchuria thrown open to foreign economic competition. (The United States would emerge as Japan's chief competitor, Chinda added in his draft letter but omitted from the final version.) Unless Japanese merchants immediately took some decisive steps, the trade of Manchuria would fall into the foreigners' hands. It was imperative to allow some Japanese of means to enter the interior of Manchuria to establish commercial connections with the native population. It was hoped that the army of occupation would aid them by providing railway transportation.[11] In the meantime, the government could take advantage of the military *fait accompli* in Manchuria to force the Chinese to endorse the terms of the Portsmouth peace treaty. In return for Japan's promise to end the military occupation, at the end of 1905 China agreed to the transfer of Russian leases and concessions in south Manchuria to Japan. The most the Chinese negotiators could do was to delay granting the Japanese a right to build feeder-lines to the South Manchuria Railway. Even so, they had to pledge not to build railways running parallel to the south Manchurian line. Komura was right in boasting that as a result of the war "a portion of Manchuria has become our sphere of influence." [12]

Outside military and government circles expansion into Manchuria was welcomed as a continuation of the movement begun earlier. The popular journalist Kayahara Kazan summed up the general sentiment when he wrote, "If Japan is to expand toward the continent, it is natural to start with Korea. . . . If Japanese influence is to continue to expand, it is also natural that it should be directed toward Manchuria." Unless Japan expanded, Russia would again try to expand in the East after the war. The twentieth century, Kayahara wrote shortly after the outbreak of the Russo-Japanese War, "is not a time for individual heroes to vie with one another for fame. It is the time for national expansion and growth. This nationalism which has turned imperialism is now playing an unprecedented role in the drama of world history. Japan stands in the middle of this whirlwind, this ocean current of imperialism." Individual Japanese must become children of the age and dedicate themselves to the task.[13] In a speech he delivered toward the end of the war, Kayahara asserted, "The true progress of mankind can be assured only if those that cannot suffer the struggle for survival retreat, to be replaced by the expansion of those who can persevere in such a struggle." Japan, as such a country, "is destined to create an East Asian economic empire." This was "the ideal of a great people." [14]

This reference to "economic empire" is not surprising in view of the by then well established ideology of economic expansionism in Japan. Hitherto most writers had been stressing Southeast Asia, Hawaii, and the American continent for economic expansion. The war with Russia changed this, and encouraged Japanese to consider Manchuria just as good an area for settlement as these others. As Kayahara said, Japan must look for overseas lands for settling surplus populations, obtaining foodstuffs, selling Japanese products, and investing capital. If possible, these lands should be undeveloped areas rather than advanced countries. Such areas as Korea, Manchuria, and China should be integrated into the Japanese economic system: they must be made Japan's "economic colony." Japan, Korea, and the mainland of Asia were to be integrated into an "economic empire," if Japan was to continue its "growing existence." [15]

An important corollary of the new continentalism was the idea of Japan's mission in Asia. Some had always argued that Japan's destiny lay in Asia, or that Japan's task was to enlighten and reform the decaying empire of China. But the Russo-Japanese War gave an impetus to the vision of Japanese tutelage over China and the rest of Asia. This was not identical with pan-Asianism. The Japanese, as will be seen, were extremely sensitive to the West's fear of Asian unity. They viewed their first war with a Western country less as a racial than as a national conflict, as an occasion to demonstrate that they could beat a country which was ethnically Western but inferior to Japan in many respects. This, instead of boosting Japan's anti-Western, pan-Asianist sentiment, confirmed its sense of superiority in Asia and equality with the West. As Ōkuma Shigenobu asserted during the war, the initial victory over Russia had produced a revolutionary change in the Japanese psychology. The Japanese who for so many years had been accustomed to deferring to everything Western and feeling inferior to white people, now realized that they were equal to any race, any nation in the world. They were finding through experience that men were all equal, that their racial differences were immaterial and what counted was their power, intelligence, and morality. "The war, the Japanese feel, proves that there is nothing that Westerners do which Asians cannot do, or that there is nothing Westerners try that Asians cannot also try." [16]

This confidence underlay the vision of the new Japan playing an active role in the development and progress of postwar Asia. As Ukita Kazutami said, Japan was emerging as a model nation in the East, just as Greece had become the model for Western civilization after defeating Persia. Japan was a teacher to the rest of Asia. The Japanese, therefore, must be prepared to develop a faculty for assisting other peoples in establishing constitutions and making laws.[17] Yano Ryūkei, in his influential *Sekai ni okeru Nihon no shōrai* (Japan's future in the world), published in February 1905, asserted that Japanese influence in Asia should be like the influence of the United States in South America and that of the British in Australia and Africa. The two Anglo-Saxon nations "are known for their respect for human rights, devotion to the principle of freedom, and unceasing progress of ideas and institutions." Japan should work closely with them to bring happiness to future mankind. This meant that in Asia, Japan should "take the initiative and apply the power it has achieved for the welfare of mankind, so as to create a great paradise in the East." [18] As a specific way of accomplishing such a lofty goal, a Buddhist writer stressed the need to send Buddhist missionaries to Korea and Manchuria. Japanese Christian missionaries would not do, since they would be regarded as more or less Western. Only Buddhists would be able to bring Asia to the influence of Japanese civilization.[19]

Japanese officials and people heard themselves reiterating these ideas throughout the war with Russia. The basic theme, as in the past, was expansion. As the new magazine, *Katsudō no Nihon* (Active Japan), whose first issue was published in May 1904, declared, "Japan's inevitable expansion" was going to be the central phenomenon of national life.[20] The country had expanded steadily by means of trade, emigration, and war after the 1880's, but the Russian war was giving it a continental foothold, and Japan would be able to realize what had only remained a dream. Yet continentalism was never the sole goal of expansion. It was one aspect, and the Japanese expected that when the war was over their expansive energy would claim vast reaches of the earth. The sense of outrage they felt at the terms of the Portsmouth peace treaty reveals how seriously they had come to take the rhetoric of unlimited expansion. Accustomed to think of the war as a stage in national expansion, they had expected something more than several specific rights in Manchuria and Korea. The whole island of Sakhalin and an indemnity payment, demands which Russia rejected out of hand, were not considered lightheartedly as Japan's terms for peace. They were linked in Japanese minds to the continued growth of their empire.[21]

Their dream for instant empire was partially frustrated, but not their ideal of universal expansion. Even as policymakers drew up plans for railway development in Manchuria and private merchants were entering the field one after another, voices were calling for expansion in all other directions, and Japanese were setting out eastward across the Pacific as well as westward to the Asian continent. "Now that Japan has achieved world-power status," wrote Ozaki Yukio, mayor of Tokyo, "we must stop being content with crouching in a small corner of the earth. We must broaden our vision and venture out to all parts of the world — Africa, South America, North America, everywhere in east and west — in order to make the whole universe our sphere of action." [22] Kayahara Kazan exhorted Japanese youths to go "to America, to Europe, to China, to Korea, to Siberia, to the South Sea islands, or to Australia. . . . They must expand everywhere in the world." [23] The editorial for *Katsudō no Nihon* declared shortly after the coming of peace: "Peacetime war has already begun. The trumpet has sounded, and the war cry has been heard. Are our people ready to rush to the enemy camp?" Overseas expansion of the nation, the editorial board asserted, should be made the basic motto of the new peacetime war. Those who had capital or labor must not linger about their homes, but go abroad, mingle with foreigners, and show to the world that they could make good the rights acquired in Manchuria and south Sakhalin, or engage with Americans, Germans, and others in peaceful competition.[24]

In 1903 as many as 12,621 passports were issued for Hawaii. The number of Japanese emigrants to the islands had reached a peak in 1899, then declined after their incorporation into the United States. The number, reflected in the passports issued, fell to less than 5,000 in 1900 and less than 3,000 the following year. But the movement picked up momentum again in 1902 and reached the all-time high point in 1906, when 30,393 Japanese reached Hawaii. Obviously they had made plans to migrate just after the Russo-Japanese War, and their coming to the islands, some with the intention of ultimately reaching the West coast, was to create a major crisis in Japanese-American relations. It is interesting that this flow of migrants never abated during the war, and even in 1905 over 7,000 passports were given to prospective emigrants to Hawaii. (This should be contrasted to the Japanese civilian population in south Manchuria at the end of 1905: 5,215.) [25] As a result, the United States and its possessions remained the place with the largest number of overseas Japanese. Around this time there were already over 50,000 Japanese in Taiwan and over 40,000 in Korea; even so they fell short of the 70,000 Japanese in Hawaii. At least 130,000 out of the total of 180,000 Japanese overseas (excluding Korea and Taiwan) were in the United States and its territories. In other words, even while merchants and adventurers were flocking to

China and Manchuria in search of quick profit, there continued an eastward movement of population.[26] What was more, interest in going to America was sustained during the war by the confident psychology of expansionism and by an image of that country as Japan's friend. Neither of these was a new phenomenon, but both attained new meaning because of the successes on the continent of Asia. Expansion at sea and across the Pacific was seen as part of a spectacular growth of the country that was gaining worldwide recognition as a civilized power.

"The Japanese and Americans," Kayahara wrote in March 1905, "are the most progressive peoples in the twentieth century." Both were expanding in the Pacific; their power and influence were such that they were fast coming into direct contact with each other. Their encounter could result in friction, and friction in conflict. However, they were both commercial, not military powers and, Kayahara hoped, unlikely to clash by force of arms. The United States had always "walked the great road of civilization and been guided by the principle of peaceful progress." Japan would surely become America's closest friend so that the two could cooperate to bring harmony in international society.[27] It was natural that, with such an image, Kayahara should have decided to visit the United States and see in what way his fond vision of Japanese-American cooperation and mutual expansion was becoming a reality. He left for San Francisco just after the signing of the peace — doomed to total disappointment.

Interest in going to America was not limited to a few journalists. Shimanuki Hyōdayū, a Christian minister who had founded a small association to aid Japanese students to go to America, writes that more young people came to see him during the Russo-Japanese War to seek advice for going to the United States.[28] A prolific writer and tireless speaker, Shimanuki added fuel to the spreading enthusiasm by writing on the success that awaited Japanese in the new world: "Anybody with a persevering spirit" was assured of success in America. As others before him had done, he exhorted young Japanese to settle and work in the United States, rather than to consider it a transient abode in which to get rich quickly. "If you are determined to become American, to be buried in America . . . then Americans will never detest you but will welcome you." [29] Another association with similar purposes, Kōseisha, lent financial support to worthy Japanese interested in migrating to the United States. In a booklet published in October

1904 it asserted that "America is the freest country in the world, a country that has made the greatest progress in the world in its industrial and commercial development, economic advances, and scholarly achievements. . . . For a healthy Japanese willing to use his hands, America should present no obstacles." [30] Similarly, in a book published a week before the signing of the Portsmouth peace treaty, an author said, "Postwar Japan must not only expand its armament. Its businesses must also expand." But, since opportunities at home were limited, "those who have grand designs for grand business enterprises should migrate to North America." The tremendous boost in national prestige and honor acquired during the war should help the nation undertake vigorous postwar expansionism. National honor could be maintained only if Japanese of all occupations migrated abroad and extended rights and interests. Because of its wealth, North America was the most suitable area for these ends. [31]

By far the best known writer on the subject was Abe Isoo, the noted leader of Japanese socialism. Socialists in Japan had always been interested in the United States, and one of them, Katayama Sen, was among the most influential writers on Japanese emigration to America. Abe was in the same tradition. Katayama was temporarily out of the country during the Russo-Japanese War to attend a conference of world socialists, and it fell to Abe to keep up the tradition of inducing young Japanese to migrate to the United States. In the spring of 1905 he took a Waseda University baseball team to the West coast, and upon his return published a book entitled *Hokubei no shin-Nihon* (The new Japan in North America). This book contained all the essential ideas the Japanese had come to hold toward the question.

Abe notes, as had all other writers, that "The Pacific coast of North America is the most suitable place for Japanese emigration." He estimates, perhaps with a slight exaggeration, that as of 1905 about 60,000 Japanese were there, sending back to their homeland at least 6 million yen annually. They were all saying how carefree life in the United States was: there were jobs for the asking, and no Japanese seemed to regret having migrated. The West coast was so rich in natural resources and mild in climate, and yet so little developed, that it could accommodate many more Japanese. In fact 600,000, or even 6,000,000 Japanese could easily settle and find an occupation there without depriving the whites of their jobs. Compared with the Chinese, who maintained traditional ways of life, the Japanese had proven to be an assimilative people. Those in California really wanted to be American-ized. "It may be difficult now for a majority of them to be completely assimilated to American life spiritually, but the Japanese have cer-tainly demonstrated an ability to assimilate as much as possible." Thus, there was no reason why they could not build a new Japan on the Pacific coast. This was a logical outcome of the "westward move-ment of civilization." America had opened the door of Japan, and it had brought the benefits of civilization to the nation. The Japanese now had a duty to transmit the civilization to the Asian continent. "The Japanese are destined to bring the civilization they have ac-quired through the United States, to China and Korea. Therefore, it is quite natural for them to establish a foothold on the western part of the American continent." The United States was like a teacher to Japan and had rejoiced in Japanese victory over Russia. There was every reason to feel confident that teacher and pupil would further co-operate in the development of the West coast and the dissemination of knowledge to the rest of East Asia. The Pacific coast was a meeting place of East and West. From such a perspective the building of a new Japan in North America must be said to open a chapter in the history of world civilization. North America's West coast was where the opening act in the construction of an ideal world was to be played.[32]

What happened during the Russo-Japanese War, then, was the fur-ther expansion of Japan in all directions, westward as well as eastward, in reality and in imagination. The result was a much closer contact with other peoples than ever before — again in actual practice and in perception. As they undertook to extend the limits of formal empire to the continent of Asia and to continue economic expansion across the Pacific, the Japanese were becoming aware of enormous obstacles in their way and were bracing themselves for the coming storm that would envelop the country as a result of the war. Among the obsta-cles, what concerned them most was the concept of the yellow peril. Shortly after the outbreak of the war, Mori Rintarō, noted doctor and novelist, made public his *Kōkaron kōgai* (An outline of the yellow peril concept). It was based on a lecture he had given the previous No-vember and purported to show "how the whites despise us." With the possible exception of Englishmen and Americans ("who have had a long history of understanding toward us"), the white people "lump to-gether the Japanese and other yellow peoples and look at them with hatred and suspicion." Then Mori summarized a recent German book: Hermann von Samson-Himmelstjerna's *Die gelbe Gefahr als Moralproblem* (The yellow peril as a moral problem), published in 1902. The German author repeated the standard argument that both Chinese and Japanese hated the whites and that if they combined the danger to the West would be formidable. The West, in that event, would be totally ejected from East Asia. The only way to prevent another Mongol invasion, according to Samson-Himmelstjerna, was for the West to befriend the Chinese and help them become strong. Mori, in introducing these ideas to Japanese readers, characterized them as paranoic. At the same time he warned that the prejudice was real and that the yellow peril notion would gain in intensity if Japan defeated Russia.[33]

Japanese officials and writers were familiar with the yellow-peril concept and did what they could to combat it. As Mori's book revealed, however, there were at least two different components of the idea, each of which somehow had to be dealt with. One was the West's fear of Japanese combination with China. As Count Ōkuma said, some Westerners seemed to worry about a coming Asian coalition in which two-thirds of the world's population would participate with a view to repulsing Western power and influence from the non-West. Japanese victory, he explained, was considered by some the opening act in the drama of the yellow domination of the globe, a development that could be prevented only by a united effort of all white peoples. Japan's rise had invoked the memory, long forgotten, of Asia's threat to Europe in ancient and medieval history. He was certain that Westerners feared the Japanese would make themselves heirs to Genghis Khan, a fear that was being encouraged by Russian propaganda. The only way for Japanese to cope with the phenomenon was to trust in the developing cosmopolitanism of the world. In the modern age of civilization and progress, men were divided not by arbitrary distinctions of race and culture, but by different degrees of advancement. The Japanese, Ōkuma suggested, should not be dismayed by the yellow-peril argument but intensify their endeavor to elevate their national cultural life.[34]

The government in Tokyo was not satisfied with such an abstract remedy. In dispatching two special emissaries, Suematsu Kenchō and Kaneko Kentarō, to England and the United States soon after the outbreak of war, the Tokyo government stressed that one of their primary tasks was to influence official and press opinion in these countries and combat any yellow-peril sentiment. This feeling, an instruction given Suematsu noted, was still latent in Europe and America, and was being stirred up by Russian propaganda. Japan was trying to prevent its resurgence by confining military action to Manchuria so as not to disturb peace and commerce in the rest of China. The emissaries were to emphasize that Japan's interest in educating the Chinese, far from being intended to establish exclusive ties between the two countries, was aimed at stabilizing and reforming China, which would rebound to the benefit of Western nations as well as Japan.[35]

The second aspect of the yellow-peril notion stressed the racial and cultural differences between Japanese and Westerners. It was felt that, despite all the progress Japan had made, the West was still not accepting the country as an equal. Westerners seemed to retain a sense of superiority, imagining an unbridgable gap between them and the Japanese. The clearest expression of this was the rising movement against Japanese immigration on the West coast of the United States. As more and more Japanese migrated, they seemed to arouse an intense hostility in Americans. While Japanese were picturing the two peoples on either side of the Pacific as the most progressive in the world, partners in building a better world, Americans apparently were rejecting such talk out of hand.

A number of ideas were presented and proposals made at this time to deal with the situation, but none succeeded in bridging the gap between the image of progressive Japan's worldwide expansion and the actuality of anti-Japanese prejudice. At one extreme was an intellectual exercise to prove that Japanese were essentially no different from Westerners. Taguchi Ukichi, the distinguished economist, sought to demonstrate from history, literature, and phonetics that Japanese were really Western ethnically; far from identical with the Chinese, they were in fact Aryans, and it was the Russians who presented the yellow peril![36] Few took his booklet, published in April 1904, seriously, but many shared his assumption that Japanese were closer to Westerners than to Chinese. The way to combat yellow-perilism, therefore, was not to seek shelter in a little corner of Asia, but to assert the nation's rights boldly, confident of its advancement and its righteousness. Count Ōkuma said he was aware that Japanese laborers were being discriminated against on the Pacific coast of the United States, but he was sure this only demonstrated the superb quality of

Japanese in America. The implication was that nothing could stop the expansion of the Japanese so long as they embodied the best in intellect, ability, and morality. The war with Russia, proving that Japan could fight for justice, should, Ōkuma felt, help the cause of Japanese overseas.[37] Likewise, Abe Isoo asserted that, since Japan was demonstrating through the Russian war how advanced it had become, it could no longer tolerate humiliating treatment of its people abroad. If the United States discriminated against them, the Japanese government should retaliate by taking counter measures against Americans in Korea and Manchuria. Japan's newly won rights in these areas after the war should give the nation freedom to proclaim an Asian Monroe Doctrine if discrimination against Japanese persisted in America. "In order to build a new Japan [on the Pacific coast], the Japanese government must take a firm attitude and protest against every act of discrimination. . . . Taking advantage of the victory [over Russia], our government should deal firmly with the United States government." [38] Japan's "current expansive tendency," a Japanese visitor to America wrote, should not be checked but encouraged by the government at home, which should seek to remove all obstacles in the way.[39] Given such an attitude on the part of Japanese, there was some justification for the feeling on the part of some Americans that their country would be made a postwar target of even more forceful Japanese expansion.

It was one thing to assert in the abstract Japan's right to expand and be treated as an equal nation; the reality of Japanese life in the United States was quite another matter. Awareness of the gap between the image of a victorious and progressive Japan marching across the Pacific and the actual living conditions of Japanese in America provided a serious intellectual challenge to Japanese expansionism. Even Abe Isoo admitted that there were serious defects in their communities such as the tendency to waste hard-earned money on gambling and the lack of friendship associations.[40] The idea that the Chinese in the United States had a much stronger sense of kinship and unity was shared by many observers. A judge from Osaka, who toured the United States in 1904, went so far as to say that the Chinese were much more integrated into American life than Japanese; they seemed far more willing to take the initiative to work hard and make money.[41]

Much of the American agitation against the Japanese was centered in cities such as San Francisco and Seattle. The reason in part was that in cities Japanese merchants, students, and "schoolboys" were more visible, and the newly arrived immigrants were seen there without prior exposure to American life. These Japanese tended to congregate, associate almost exclusively with their countrymen, and perpetuate and accentuate traditional habits. They, rather than agricultural and mining workers, were the initial targets of anti-Japanese sentiment. Abe was critical of students and scholars who went to the United States, but engaged in no serious work. They were utterly valueless compared with those whose skills transcended national boundaries.[42] Another observer declared, "students and youths, who reportedly are a majority of Japanese in San Francisco and Seattle, . . . have no fixed occupations, but spend the day idling away and playing around, conscious only of what to wear. Before they know it they spend five or ten years this way and degenerate into vagabonds, 'American hooligans.' "[43] Perhaps no author gave a more sensitive and less complimentary portrayal of Japanese in the United States than the novelist Nagai Kafū, who was in and around Tacoma at this time. Himself a student, he experienced the humiliation of rejection by American society, inability to communicate with Americans, and alienation from fellow Japanese in the United States. "What a miserable life I led when I was on the West coast of America," he was to write. "All alone, I would just walk amid the pine trees that cover the new continent, feeling lonely and not knowing what else to do." He had hoped to master English by going to school and, if possible, living with an American family. All such dreams were shattered, and he found himself unable to find an intellectual rapport with America and forced to live among Japanese immigrants. They did not impress him, and their plight did not evoke much sympathy in him.[44]

Kafū's collection of short stories, published under the title *Amerika monogatari* (Tales of America) upon his return to Japan (1909), provides a vivid description of life in urban centers. "An Evening in Seattle," printed in May 1904, describes a visit to that city's Japanese section. It is dark, dismal, and stinking. There are little restaurants with store-front signs in Japanese where waitresses play the *samisen*. Other stores sell Japanese foods, catering to the residents. "Most of the passers-by are our countrymen — crooked-legged and short-statured. The only whites around are pipe-smoking laborers." In a small restaurant several Japanese are gaily talking about women and about their experiences in America. They are "schoolboys," becoming discouraged at the slight progress they have made in learning English. But they say they are not impatient; they are going to stay long and study slowly and steadily; in the meantime they will spend the weekend visiting brothels. The disharmony between such an atmosphere and the modern, Western environment was a theme Kafū stressed. His stories were filled with Japanese who, frustrated in their studies and other pursuits in Japan, came to the United States to seek a new life. But here, too, they did not succeed in their ambitions and ended up making money by importing prostitutes or chasing after American equivalents.

Undoubtedly, Kafū's fiction included dramatic caricatures, and he never saw other, nonurban types of Japanese settlers. Nevertheless, he was making a valid point in noting the incongruity of the life led by Japanese in American cities. As he observed them, their life was a far cry from the fond image of an expanding population assimilating itself with American culture and everywhere creating a beachhead for the meeting of East and West. "It is a fantastic illusion to talk of harmonizing the civilizations of East and West," he wrote in July 1905, when he was in New York. The Japanese seemed capable of being accepted abroad only in terms of cherry-blossoms and geisha girls. There was no way in which the two peoples could communicate except at such a superficial level. Life in the West was too deeply rooted in tradition to be easily absorbed by a non-Western people without producing a monstrous incongruity.[45]

Kafū's disdain of simplistic notions relating East to West and his search, continued until his death half a century later, for a more meaningful point of comparison between the two cultures attested to the deepening contact between Japanese and Americans. As the Japanese expanded physically, in Asia and in the Pacific, they came into closer contact with Americans and other foreigners. The responses they provoked could not be dealt with in a conventional, complacent manner. The development of Japanese-American antagonism was thus an inevitable outcome of wartime expansion.

There is little doubt that this antagonism, on the American side, took a yellow-peril form. For some, the war provided the first opportunity to come into direct contact with Japanese. If they did not like the experience, there was even more reason to anticipate with fear the encounter that would follow further Japanese expansion, whether in China or in America.

In Asia during the war a thorough dislike of the Japanese character developed among a number of Western observers. American journalists covering the war were in a strategic position to mold opinion at home, and some of them reacted most negatively to the rise of militant Japan. They were irked by the secretiveness of Japanese military authorities and censorship of news dispatches. The Japanese "want everything for nothing," Willard Straight wrote disgustedly. A former employee of China's Imperial Maritime Customs Administration, Straight worked as a correspondent for Reuters during the war, and his dealings with Japanese in Korea and Manchuria turned him passionately against them. "[They] are absolutely lacking the sense of gratitude in a broad sense, in a business way. . . . Suck the blood and give naught in return. Such are the Japanese — the world's pets," he noted. Japan's Westernization, as revealed in its military victories, the resultant conceit and arrogance, and its behavior toward Westerners as well as other Asians, increased Straight's irritation. He believed that underneath the politeness shown by Japanese to Westerners and despite Japan's veneer of Westernization an unbridgable gap remained, a fatal chasm dividing the two. Because he did not like or understand the Japanese, he was convinced that they hated and despised him. As he confided to a friend in 1904, "For no particular reason, with no real cause for complaint I now find myself hating the Japanese more than anything in the World. It is due I presume to the constant strain of having to be polite and to seek favors from the yellow people. We cannot know them or understand them and they dislike us thoroughly." Japanese soldiers "all hate us, all of them, officers and men," he jotted down in his diary; "God knows the feeling is mutual." The Japanese he actually saw seemed to have little in common with the image of them — progressive, civilized, pro-Western — that was widespread in Western reading circles and encouraged by Japanese propaganda. Straight preferred the Russians. "The Japanese . . . certainly seem very much less human than others," he wrote in 1905, "One cannot feel the individuality of the men themselves. . . . [Russians] are white, and that means much. . . . One recognizes him [a Russian] as a man, and the Japanese will have to change a good deal before they cease to cause one to look for the tail." [46]

"Come to Korea and see . . . the real yellow man," Straight wrote just after the armistice, "Not the pleasant fellow you meet at Harvard, not the very likeable men I knew in Tokyo, in the Foreign Office, but the real Jap, the kind there are pretty nearly thirty million of." Every

Westerner he talked with seemed to have the same story: "Insult, chi-canery, injustice. 'The white man must go.' " [47] Exactly the same reaction was recorded by Stanley Washburn of the *Chicago Daily News.* Having traveled with the Japanese army, he sensed his initially pro-Japanese sentiment melt away and become displaced by an intense dislike of the country. As he confided early in 1905 to George von Lengerke Meyer, ambassador in Russia, the Japanese "at heart do not care for any whites not even for the English or Americans, who are useful to them now and are working them for all they can. They laugh in their sleeves about the open door in Manchuria, for when the time comes they can beat us in manufacturing due to cheap labor and therefore get the trade. They are most untruthful and deceitful as well as tricky in business transactions." Washburn said this was "almost the universal feeling of English and Americans in the East." Foreigners in Asia preferred to employ Chinese, who were more honest than Japanese.[48] When an anti-American boycott broke out in some Chinese cities in 1905 as a protest against Chinese exclusion from the United States the reaction of Western residents in China was that it must have been instigated by Japanese.[49]

The yellow-peril reaction to Japanese expansion on the Asian continent had its counterpart on the Pacific coast of the United States. Just as Westerners in China dreaded the beginning of the end of their power and influence, Americans on the West coast feared a Japanese invasion would turn the region into a zone of alien, nonwhite civilization. In view of the accelerating tempo of Japanese immigration from Hawaii and Japan proper, it was felt that their number would increase even more rapidly as a result of the victory over Russia. Japanese soldiers, in particular, having learned how to demonstrate their prowess, would not want to go back to peaceful life at home but would emigrate to California, transplanting Japanese styles of life and entrenching themselves as a beachhead for the Orientalization of the entire West coast. This fear led newspapers such as the San Francisco *Examiner* and *Chronicle* to champion Japanese exclusion and brought about repeated pleas from the California state legislature to the federal government to restrict future Japanese immigration.[50] The Japanese, representing entirely different ways of life and thought but backed up by a strong government that had fought against mighty Russia, could in a short period of time transform the character of American life on the West coast. One need only have some idea of the incompatibility between Eastern and Western ways of life to become convinced of the need to reject the further inundation of California by Japanese.

A generation of American writers had harped on the theme, but the current and future coming of Japanese served to dramatize it and make anti-Japanese agitation comprehensible intellectually and emotionally. In other words, the coming of Japanese to the United States was seen for what it was: the expansion of Japan eastward, with all its cultural and social implications. Whereas the Japanese, in coming to America, were hoping to bridge the gap between East and West, the Americans, in rejecting them, held to the notion of Western supremacy and of incompatibility between it and the blending of different cultures.[51]

Such views were not limited to the Pacific coast. "Japan is an oriental nation," President Roosevelt wrote in December 1904, "and the individual standard of truthfulness in Japan is low. No one can foretell her future attitude." Similar remarks were sprinkled all over his correspondence. Japan was a civilization, but its "motives and ways of thought . . . are not quite those of the powers of our race." The President held a very low opinion of California agitators against the Japanese. He believed the American people should show every courtesy and respect so that Japan would have no cause to resent the United States. Nor can it be doubted that Roosevelt admired the Japanese during the war. "What nonsense," he wrote John Hay, "it is to speak of the Chinese and Japanese as of the same race!" But fundamentally there was a consistent ideology in Roosevelt's handling of the Japanese question. Even before 1906, when the California crisis came to a head, he had formulated a basic attitude on Japanese-American relations. Japan he regarded as "a power jealous, sensitive and warlike. . . . There can be none more dangerous in all the world." Japan's civilization was "in some important respects not like ours," especially because of its samurai tradition. Roosevelt felt it would be a full generation before the new industrialism could moderate the martial spirit. In the meantime the Japanese would dedicate themselves with fierce intensity to economic as well as military strengthening of their country, and would emerge as "the leading industrial nation of the Pacific." [52]

For a man who had long believed that the twentieth century would see the center of civilization move to the Pacific, such conclusions had obvious implications. Whether Japan and the United States could live peacefully together depended ultimately on whether two such heterogeneous civilizations could learn to do so. It was in the interest of the Anglo-Saxon nations, Roosevelt wrote Cecil Spring Rice at the beginning of the war, to be prepared for the rise of Japan. Their attitude "should be one of ready recognition of the rights of the new comers, of desire to avoid giving them just offense, and at the same time of preparedness in body and in mind to hold our own if our interests are menaced." While his attitude was clear, he had no faith that Japanese-American relations would be anywhere near the relations among nations of Western civilization. The care with which he tried to avoid provoking Japan to unnecessary conflict did not derive from any confidence in the compatibility of such divergent ways of life and thought. He felt it was all but impossible for Westerners to understand Asians and to be understood by them. He shared the suspicion of many that, despite their veneer of Westernization, underneath the Japanese remained anti-Western. "I wish I were certain," he wrote, "that the Japanese down at bottom did not lump Russians, English, Americans, Germans, all of us, simply as white devils inferior to themselves not only in what they regard as the essentials of civilization, but in courage and forethought, and to be treated politely only so long as would enable the Japanese to take advantage of our various national jealousies, and beat us in turn." This was the language of a yellow-perilist imagining the specter of pan-Asian anti-Westernism. As Roosevelt wrote to the historian George Otto Trevelyan, "it is not to be expected that [the Japanese] should be free from prejudice against and distrust of the white race." [53]

Wartime Japanese expansion was thus giving rise to a serious problem in Japanese-American relations, with cultural and racial implications. It would be wrong, however, to consider the period solely from the point of view of Japan's expansion. The United States, too, continued to expand in Asia and the Pacific. And this expansion, like its Japanese counterpart, was as much psychological and intellectual as economic and political.

The Russo-Japanese War provided impetus to America's expanding economic relations with East Asia. For one thing the United States proved to be a crucial war financer for Japan. The Tokyo government's estimates of the cost of war grew steadily as more ships were sunk and more ammunition exhausted than had been expected. Japan's leaders knew that their countrymen could not be counted on to shoulder all the financial burden; in fact, concern with the country's meager financial resources had been one factor which had checked a more belligerent attitude toward Russia.[54] Though the political parties would surely cooperate with the government once the war started, just as happened during the Sino-Japanese War, there was a limit beyond which taxes could not be increased and government bonds could not be sold without destroying the economy. Consequently, obtaining foreign financial assistance was regarded as the only viable solution if the country was to wage war successsfully. Loans could be obtained abroad only if foreigners could be induced to believe Japan had at least an even chance of victory; should victory be achieved, Japan could easily pay back the loans from the war indemnity. In such a chain of reasoning the most difficult task was to arrange the initial loan agreements. Britain curtly discouraged Japan from entertaining such a possibility when Tokyo asked London's views toward the end of 1903. Once the war started the climate in London's financial circles improved as a result of Japan's initial victories. Even so, Takahashi Korekiyo, Japan's envoy to England for the purpose, had difficulty obtaining a loan at no more than 6 percent interest.[55]

Initially no thought was given to turning to the United States for money. American investments had been conspicuous in some Japanese industries, but it had not been believed that the United States would be willing or able to help finance Japan's war. It soon developed, however, that as much as half the amount of money Japan first sought to borrow in London could be raised in America. This was the result of a chance encounter between Takahashi and Jacob Schiff in London. Through the latter's good offices, the Kuhn, Loeb and Company expressed an interest in handling a Japanese loan in the United States. This was a providential break for Japan; America's willingness to lend money strengthened Japan's standing in London financial circles, which thenceforth became more receptive to Japanese requests. Minister Hayashi noted in London that an American loan in addition to a British loan was full of political significance, adding prestige to the Japanese cause. The Tokyo government was quick to grasp the opportunity and authorized Takahashi to go ahead with arrangements with Kuhn, Loeb and Company. Altogether 410 million dollars worth of loans were raised in the United States during the war. Small sums were subscribed by Americans in rural and small-town communities, serving to interest them in economic affairs in the Orient. In purely mathematical terms this was a tremendous expansion of American economic stake in Japan. At 6 percent a year, 410 million dollars would produce an interest payment of over 24 million dollars — more than half the total exports from Japan to the United States.[56]

United States trade with China and Japan (millions of dollars)

Year	China		Japan		Total U.S. trade	
	Exports	Imports	Exports	Imports	Exports	Imports
1900	15	27	29	33	1,394	850
1902	25	21	21	37	1,382	903
1904	13	29	25	46	1,461	991
1905	53	28	52	52	1,518	1,117

Source: *Statistical Abstract of the United States*, ed. Department of Commerce and Labor (Washington, D.C., 1905).

There was a corresponding expansion of American exports to Japan. The table tells the story. The doubling in exports to Japan between 1904 and 1905 cannot all be attributed to the war, but it is noticeable that the overall export trade of the United States increased only by 4 percent between 1904 and 1905. A tremendous demand was created by Japan's war effort, and as the United States supplied it with increasing quantities of cotton, wheat, flour, and machine goods, the American share in Japan's total imports increased from 14.0 percent in 1903 to 15.7 percent in 1904 and 21.3 percent in 1905. There was phenomenal growth in the sale of raw cotton to Japan: in 1904, 37 million pounds were exported to Japan, an amount equivalent to 11.4 percent of the total raw cotton consumed in the country; the following year the volume rose to 124 million pounds and the ratio to 29.4 percent. The amount from the United States was still not as high as that from India or China, nor did Japan account for more than a fraction of the overseas market for American cotton. Nevertheless, a trend had been set, and it was significant that, at a time when Japan needed an increasing quantity of imported materials, both raw and manufactured, the United States supplied as much as 15.7 percent of them in 1904 and 21.3 percent in 1905. Moreover, for the first time in history the United States was selling to Japan as much as it was buying from it. This turned out to be a temporary phenomenon, but as a whole there was a much steeper rate of increase of American exports to Japan than that of imports from Japan.[57]

American export trade with China had not generally been as great as that with Japan. But in 1905 there was an abnormal expansion. This reflected the expectation in the United States that as soon as the war was over more ports would be opened up in the Ch'ing empire, with a corresponding rise in demand. Whereas only 13 million dollars worth of commodities had been sold to China in 1904, the value increased to 53 million in the following year. America's share in China's import trade doubled, from 8.5 percent in 1904 to 17.0 percent in 1905. American exports to Japan and China combined increased by about 67 million dollars between 1904 and 1905, whereas the overall United States exports increased by only 57 million. This helps to explain the great interest shown during the war in further cultivating the markets of East Asia.[58]

Ironically, it was just at this juncture that a crisis in Chinese-American relations developed, threatening to becloud the prospect for further expansion of American economic interests. Some Chinese officials were willing to consider the United States China's friend. Hsü Chüeh, minister to Italy, suggested in December 1904 that China ask the United States to mediate between Russia and Japan to bring the war to an end, pointing out that the treaty of 1868 mentioned America's readiness to offer good offices to help China, and that the United States was the first country to recognize Chinese neutrality in the war.[59] Until the summer of 1905, however, there was surprisingly little official mention of the United States in connection with the war. Actually, America was becoming the main target of the incipient Chinese nationalism, as revealed most graphically in the immigration dispute.

The episode has been studied extensively and need not be detailed here.[60] Two factors are of fundamental importance. One is the emergence of modern public opinion in China at this time. "A public opinion is being developed and practice is being gained in the methods of organizing and directing it," noted the *North China Herald* in August 1905, referring to the widespread activities of political associations and the press in China.[61] The American minister to China, W. W. Rockhill, agreed. "There is now," he reported to President Roosevelt, "coming into existence in China a public opinion and a native press; both crude and usually misinformed, but nevertheless it is a public opinion and the Government knows it and recognizes that it must be counted with. This public opinion and press are at least developing a national spirit in China." [62] In the Chinese context, the emergence of public opinion would mean that the Confucian emperor and his court officials were no longer the sole embodiment of the country, making decisions for the entire state and accountable only to themselves and to "the mandate of Heaven." Not only the gentry, from whose ranks officials came, but also young students, many educated abroad or at foreign schools in the treaty ports, as well as merchants were beginning to voice an interest in and concern for national affairs. They spoke of their views as "public opinion" (Yü-lun). Liang Ch'i-ch'ao, the constitutionalist leader, was reflecting their opinion when he asserted that China must become a nation, that its people must participate actively in national affairs, which could no longer be left to Confucian scholars and officials.[63]

Such a voice reflected the growing concern on the part of increasingly politically conscious segments of the population that something must be done to save the country from foreign domination and enhance its status as a member of the international community. Most typically, these men founded local associations to study national affairs and joined their resources to undertake various enterprises to prevent further foreign encroachment. By the time of the Russo-Japanese War, chambers of commerce and "self-government associations" in many cities and local communities had begun to provide a network of opinion-making bodies. They addressed themselves to various agencies of the Ch'ing government and worked with provincial officials for political reform and economic development. These public opinion leaders were for the most part reformist rather than revolutionary on domestic issues. They urged gradual and peaceful programs of reform, looking ultimately to the establishment of a constitutional government. This, to them, seemed the only viable alternative if the country were to be united and strengthened. If the country were to survive foreign domination and eventually regain independence, it must first be able to speak in one voice. Only a country united and enjoying popular support would command the respect of the powers and could push ahead with native enterprises to prevent further foreign control.[64]

Second, the Russo-Japanese War, erupting just as public opinion was emerging in China, made a profound impact on Chinese officials and the public. The monthly *Tung-fan tsa-chih* (The Eastern miscellany) contained a number of articles on the war's implications for the future of China. According to one author, the Russian-Japanese struggle was about to decide the questions of "the glory or decline of Asia and Europe, the rise or fall of the white and yellow races, and the strength or weakness of despotism and constitutional government." [65] This statement, in the lead article of the first issue of this instantly successful magazine, was quite significant. The article was followed by another in which the author stressed the need to reform China's institutions, extend knowledge, and recover national strength to such an extent that the nation, "allied to Japan in the east, cooperating with Korea in the north, attracting Siam in the south, and inviting Afghanistan, Persia, and others in the west," would be able to deal equally with the West. China had been invaded by Russia, but "our friendly neighbor has come to our assistance and is fighting in our stead." If Japan won, "obstacles in the way of the yellow race would be removed, and the situation in East Asian politics would gradually begin to improve." [66] Racial sentiment was clearly expressed, and for Chinese observers there was little doubt that Japan's victory meant a setback for the white race. The whites, according to another article in *Tung-fan tsa-chih,* had subjugated the red and black races and had been steadily gnawing away at the yellow race. The only solution was for the latter to assert itself.[67] Ultimately this meant China's strengthening, but in the meantime Japan was contributing to the same cause. The Slavs, said *Chung-wai jih-pao,* a daily newspaper, were the last of the white race to try to conquer the world. But the Chinese could take heart now that Japan was fighting against Russia: "We can have some confidence in the regeneration of the yellow race." [68]

These views did not imply pan-Asianism or a sentimental notion of solidarity with other yellow peoples. Rather, the war was understood by an emerging public opinion elite in China as signaling the end of the myth of the invincibility of Western powers and showing possibilities for change even for China. Thus, practically all writers coupled a racial interpretation of the war with a plea for reform and strengthening of China. This was also the way officials viewed the situation. Ts'en Ch'un-hsüan, governor-general of Liangkwang, felt Japan was bound to win the war since Japanese national opinion was united. Because of this, China should do everything possible to see to it that Japan would not claim Manchuria as a result of victory.[69] It was a typical expression of official opinion, combining satisfaction with Japan's probable victory and determination to speed up the strengthening of China.

Given this background, the attitude toward the United States in connection with the immigration dispute was not surprising. The United States had not been excepted from the Western imperialist powers that China's opinion leaders were urging the government and people to combat. Liang Ch'i-ch'ao had asserted as early as in 1900, "The so-called imperialism of today . . . is like what is happening in the Americas; it is expansionism, territorial acquisitionism, and invasionism." The United States had broken the old principle of non-aggression, absorbing Cuba and Samoa and subduing the Philippines by force. The twentieth century, forecast by many as the century of freedom, actually was opening with the suppression of Philippine independence. Thus, Liang said, struggle between independence and imperialism would be the century's main characteristic.[70] Although Russia soon replaced the United States as the main target of Chinese nationalistic opinion, there remained an undercurrent of resentment against America that could surface at the slightest provocation. The immigration dispute, coming to a head as Congress sought to enact a new Chinese exclusion law, provided such an opportunity. China's opinion leaders had been increasingly irritated by the treatment accorded Chinese immigrants and visitors in Hawaii and the United States; they considered it an insult to the country, and supported the government's effort to seek improvement. As a practical weapon some began considering the boycotting of American goods and services. The idea originated in Hawaii, where the editor of *Hsin Chung-kuo pao* (New China daily) had suggested a boycott in 1903. "We resort to a boycott in order to help our government," declared Ch'en I-k'an, a prominent supporter of Liang Ch'i-ch'ao. China, he said, was too weak militarily to resort to force; therefore, its people were the only weapon to see justice done. Hitherto the Chinese had stood patiently by, but the time had come for them to be organized and try systematically to back up the government's negotiations.[71] The idea was seized with enthusiasm not only by Cantonese, who were the bulk of immigrants to the United States, but by students and merchants in general.

The headquarters of the boycott movement were in Shanghai, center of China's foreign trade. The General Chamber of Commerce, under the leadership of Tseng Shao-ch'ing, a constitutional leader, organized plans for a boycott in 1905. The merchants first sought redress on the immigration matter by threatening a boycott; at a May meeting of the guilds' representatives, it was decided to boycott American goods if the United States did not modify its absolute exclusionist stand within two months. When this threat did not produce the desired result — President Roosevelt merely promising to ease restrictions on non-laborers temporarily entering the United States — the boycott was put into effect in July. It spread to other cities, as Shanghai merchants, students, and newspaper editors called on counterparts elsewhere to follow their lead. In Canton a society "to repudiate the [immigration] treaty" was organized, embracing eighty-two commercial establishments, eight schools, and fifteen philanthropic institutions, according to one record. By August the chambers of commerce of more than twenty cities had telegraphed Shanghai, supporting the movement.[72]

Without explicitly saying so, the Chinese were serving notice that foreigners could expand into China only on their sufferance, and only if they reciprocated. As the founder of the constitutionalist movement, K'ang Yu-wei, who was at that time in America, stated, "The Chinese only want fair play. . . . They say: 'We admit all Americans,' why should we not insist that America should admit all physically fit Chinese?" [73] Propaganda material circulated during the boycott stressed the fact that China had opened itself to cheap American goods, while sending out its laborers to build railroads and work in factories in the United States. This was a two-way process, and America should not simply think of selling goods to the Chinese while denying them an outlet for work and visit. Such an argument was given plausibility in part by Japan's success against Russia. To students, who supplied most of the agitators and wrote handbills and posters, the Japanese victory gave confidence in the righteousness of their movement.[74] Like the Japanese, it was argued, the Chinese should extend their own rights, promote their independence and strength, and aim at "making the twentieth century a century for the new China." If the boycott should succeed, it would prove Chinese determination and ability to be united for a common purpose. Foreigners would know that the Chinese could no longer be slighted.[75]

The movement was not extreme. The boycott as a "civilized way" of dealing with the issue was stressed. Mercantile leaders of the movement made the point of distinguishing it from earlier manifestations of xenophobia. They would employ only legal measures; they insisted that an orderly, nonviolent refusal to sell or buy specific foreign goods was not contrary to law or treaty. At the same time, they made sure that no blind attack was made on foreigners, and that the Chinese should not give the impression of using force to prevent individuals from dealing in American goods. "Maltreatment of Chinese laborers derives from American labor's private views, while the boycott of American goods derives from the Chinese people's sense of public justice. Neither is what the two governments really want and has anything to do with friendly relations between the two countries," asserted a letter sent by Shanghai merchants to the Waiwupu (foreign ministry). "The people back up diplomacy through just policy and civilized action," said a lead article in *Tung-fan tsa-chih*. In their memorials the boycotters stressed that they were responsible citizens trying to help the government maintain a just stand. They were not attempting to disrupt order and stability of the country.[76]

Ch'ing officials were nevertheless worried. Yüan Shih-k'ai, the influential viceroy of Chihli, for instance, from the beginning was determined not to allow any agitation within his jurisdiction, which included the major port city of Tientsin. His task was easy, however, as the merchants in that city were generally not enthusiastic about the boycott, fearing market stagnation. Yüan strictly ordered officials in Chihli province to control popular agitation and exhorted merchants not to be swayed by "careless agitation."[77] This expressed his consistent view that matters of policy should be handled by the government and no popular initiative should be allowed. Other officials did not go that far. Chou Fu, one of Yüan's protégés and viceroy of the Liangkiang provinces, admitted that the anti-American boycott resulted from "public indignation" at the mistreatment of Chinese laborers in America. However, he felt the boycott was more harmful to Chinese than to American merchants, and feared that, unless it was brought under control, "ignorant people, not knowing where the merchant associations' true intentions lay, might resort to violent tactics and make warlike speeches, while bandits may take advantage of the situation to confuse and agitate foolish people, create an incident, and complicate international relations." Since by the end of August the United States government had promised to treat merchants, students, and travelers fairly, Viceroy Chou saw no reason why the anti-American movement should continue. He ordered the *taotai* (district officials) under his control to bring the movement to an end, prohibiting the pasting of posters advocating an anti-American boycott. There was no reason why public speeches should be prohibited, he instructed the *taotai,* but they should be peaceful and not aim at destructive purposes.[78] Ts'en Ch'un-hsüan, the Liangkwang governor-general, expressed sympathy with the boycott as a peaceful, civilized, public-spirited demonstration of the Chinese people's anger with the American policy of exclusion. But even he recognized the possibility that the movement might develop out of hand and disturb public order. He concluded that the best way was to urge people to exercise restraint and caution, while the government did its utmost to modify the existing arrangements regarding Chinese emigration to the United States.[79]

Under such official pressure and persuasion, the boycott steadily lost its force. Merchants in Tientsin and other northern cities had not been active participants, and their ranks were joined by the Shanghai cotton guild, which defected late in August. In Canton merchant concern shifted to the financing of the railway between Canton and Hankow. The impact on American imports was minimal, as far as can be seen statistically. The fact that there was relatively little decline in American exports to China in 1906, after the unusually large quantity of exports in 1905, may be taken as evidence that as a whole Chinese importers and consumers failed to penalize systematically commodities from the United States. Nevertheless, China's opinion leaders had gained a valuable experience in organization and propaganda. Most of the ad hoc associations and other local groups that had carried out the campaign were not disbanded but remained intact, even after the death of the boycott. These associations would continue to function as groups, and though their immediate interest after 1905 shifted to constitutionalist agitation, their existence would provide a ready-made organizational network for any future event involving foreign affairs.[80] The subsequent years were to show that Japan rather than the United States would be the major target of their nationalism.

The historical significance of the anti-American boycott lay in the fact that it served as a catharsis, as the American officials and people came to take Chinese nationalism seriously and to adjust their expansionism to it. At a time when Japan was presenting a spectacle of determined continentalism, such a turn of events had important implications for Japanese-American relations. No basic change, to be sure, was brought about in United States immigration laws as a result of the Chinese agitation. Neither the government nor public opinion supported the admission of Chinese laborers as immigrants. It was recognized, for instance, that the construction of the Panama Canal would benefit from the importation of Chinese labor, but the Roosevelt administration decided to use only American and Puerto Rican workers.[81] There was readiness, however, to accord better treatment to Chinese merchants, students, and other visitors to the United States on temporary missions. Secretary of State Hay and Secretary of War Taft, in particular, strongly pressed for modification of rules concerning the admission of Chinese "gentlemen" to the United States. "Our record is simply infamous," Hay wrote Taft at the end of 1904, "and the difficulties in the way of reforming the matter seem almost insurmountable." [82] President Roosevelt nevertheless managed to issue certain instructions to immigration officials in mid-1905 that removed some of the most offensive features of the existing practice—such as thorough inspection and detention of Chinese visitors at ports of entry.

When, in June 1905 in a speech at Oxford, Ohio, Taft charged that the United States had been "unjust" to the Chinese, public response was immediate. The Chinese, Japanese, and Corean Exclusion League of Alameda County (Oakland) resolved: "Whereas . . . the language recently used by Mr. Secretary Taft, which, for want of tact, impartiality, and lack of knowledge of the subject under discussion, is not to the credit of one holding such a position . . . [Resolved] that immediate action of a clear, well defined and energetic character, is expected from all who feel the urgent need of legislation by Congress, having for its object the exclusion of Chinese, Japanese, Coreans, and all other objectionable aliens whose presence would be prejudicial to the best interests of American citizens." [83] A man wrote to Taft in outrage: "This talk about students and merchants; we as a people look upon it as a pretense, a pretext, a subterfuge, why, we all know how easy it is for laborers in China to become students and merchants for the purpose of reaching our shores." [84]

Most response to Taft's speech, however, was overwhelmingly favorable. While none advocated unrestricted Chinese labor immigration, most writers, in print and in private letters, expressed the fear that America's commercial interests would be jeopardized by harsh treatment of Chinese already in this country. A man wrote from Seattle that "a large majority of the people on the Pacific coast are level headed and . . . they appreciate the importance to them of Pacific coast commerce and despise the raving of demagogues." [85] A writer from San Francisco assured Taft that "the people of California are not represented by the ambitious leaders of a few labor unions of this city." [86] Bishop John H. Hamilton of the same city said, "You [Taft] will find the best people in our communities with you in demanding decent respect to be shown the Chinese merchants, professional men and students." [87] "In the light of recent events in the Far East," according to another correspondent, "it would be madness for the people of the United States to imperil their Asiatic trade to satisfy the unreasonable demands of a special organized body, whose membership is largely composed of men whose specific interests run counter to the general interest of the rest of the American people." [88]

Most American observers agreed that there was nothing inherently incompatible between Chinese nationalism and American expansionism; in fact some viewed the former as a product of the latter. It was noted that in 1905, out of a total of 3,776 American Protestant missionaries in the world, 3,107 were in China. The rise of nationalistic public opinion was recognized as a product of modern education, which the missionaries had done so much to develop in China.[89] An American missionary wrote to the Waiwupu, congratulating the Chinese people for their firm stand against the mistreatment of their countrymen in America. If the movement resulted in the modification of regulations, he wrote, it would be to the mutual benefit of Americans and Chinese.[90] Arthur H. Smith, a missionary of long residence in China who was visiting the United States during the boycott, noted that the Americans whom he saw seemed to recognize the justice of the Chinese cause. Many of them told him, "I am glad of it! I would have done the same thing in their place!" It was recognized that the Chinese were at last aroused and behaving as a people, with the sentiments and abilities of a nation.[91]

In discussing the anti-American boycott, writers in the United States doubted that it would do damage to American interests. On the contrary, they saw Chinese nationalism as a further impetus to the expansion of American trade and investment activities. By expressing its sympathy with China's nationalism, the United States, these observers asserted, could continue to cultivate the Chinese market. Business and commercial interests on the East coast and cotton mill owners in the South were almost unanimous in expressing their sympathy with the Chinese movement. A new era of progress was dawning upon China, a group of their representatives told President Roosevelt, and it was imperative for America not to jeopardize the great opportunity for "moral and material participation in that progress." [92] The American press used the phrase "China for the Chinese" to sum up its view of the developments in China. But this seemed synonymous with the Westernization of China, a development to be welcomed for the promotion of American interests. As the *New York Times* said in October 1905, the more the Chinese tried to free their country politically and economically from foreign domination, the more they would need to introduce Western ideas and practices. Thus, in the end, while the Chinese would try to have greater control over their resources and trade, "the tendency of the adoption of Western methods and ideas in political organization, in industry, and in business will be toward the ultimate breaking up of exclusiveness." This would all be to the good of Western interests. They could help, and in turn be helped by, the modernization of China. [93]

American commerce and Chinese modernization were not the only themes developed as Americans discussed the immigration dispute and the boycott. Some went further and began talking of special relations between the two countries to provide a framework for international politics in East Asia after the Russo-Japanese War. American expansion — whether economic or cultural — seemed to call for the consolidation of friendly ties with China as an alternative to acquiescing in the domination by the big imperialist powers. The call for particularistic arrangements between the United States and China was not yet loud, but early signs of it can be found in the movement for educating Chinese youths in the United States. Shortly after the outbreak of war, the Yale Alumni Association of China wrote President Roosevelt that it was imperative to divert the flow of Chinese students from Europe and Japan to the United States. In order to do so, regulations governing their entry to the United States would have to be modified. [94] In July 1905 Professor Jeremiah W. Jenks of Cornell, who had taught in China, suggested that part of the Boxer indemnity funds be utilized for educating Chinese students in the United States. [95] His ideas were strongly supported by A. W. Bash of the China Development Company, who wrote Taft that the time was opportune to befriend the Chinese to prevent their falling under Japanese influence.[96] Francis M. Huntington Wilson, the young diplomat who was leaving his post in the Tokyo embassy to serve as assistant secretary of state, expanded on this theme in a letter to Roosevelt. "I think students and other respectable people from the Far East should be as far as possible encouraged to come to our country, and should be well trusted while there, so that they would go home pro-American. If we could get a lot of students to come to America to be educated it would certainly strengthen our commercial position and our influence in the Far East." [97]

Few questioned that America's "influence" in East Asia would be compatible with Chinese nationalism, or that it would take the form of championing the cause of Chinese-American understanding. It remained to be seen in what way this "influence," should it grow, would affect Japanese continentalism and the framework of Japanese-American relations.

V

Confrontation: The Japanese View

One of the most interesting developments in Japan after the Russo-Japanese War was the self-consciousness about "Japan in the world." The nation, having fought a deadly struggle with a mighty Western nation and obtained the world's acclaim as a brave, energetic country, had emerged as a first-rate military power, secure, for the time being at least, from an immediate threat to national existence. Having pursued single-mindedly the crucial goals of treaty revision, control over Korea, and the achievement of great-power status, and having attained these objectives less than forty years after the Meiji Restoration, the Japanese seemed to have entered a new era in their history. They were to behave as citizens of the world no less than of Japan and to reach out to the outside world as much as it had reached out to them. Above all, now that the nation was released from the costly, if necessary, program of military strengthening as the first priority, there was a renewed need to develop peacefully through economic development and expansion.

Such were the ideas expressed in Japan in the years following the war. Nowhere was the phenomenon more tellingly revealed than in the publication of new journals such as *Kaikoku seinen* (The maritime youth, 1906), *Shinjidai* (The new era, 1906), *Shin Tōyō* (The new Asia, 1909), *Shokumin sekai* (The world of colonialism, 1908), *Sekai no shōnen* (Youth in the world, 1906), *Sekai no Nihon* (Japan in the world, 1911), and *Kaigai no Nihon* (Japan overseas, 1911). Published through the initiative and support, intellectual and financial, of Japan's middle-class leaders — in politics, business, journalism, and the universities — these journals represented the voice of postwar Japan's opinion-making elites. There was a wide overlapping of personnel among them. Ōkuma Shigenobu, for instance, wrote for several, as did scholars like Ukita Kazutami and journalists like Kayahara Kazan. Most of them had written in the same vein before 1905, but they now had an influential medium through which to spread their views. Postwar issues in Japanese relations with other countries, especially the United States and China, cannot be discussed without consideration of this opinion group.

Some of the most influential of these men formed a Social Education Association in June 1906; the magazine *Shinjidai* was its organ. Having as its honarary president Ōkuma Shigenobu and as its officers individuals such as political officials Ozaki Yukio, Gotō Shinpei, and Inukai Ki, scholars Takada Sanae, Ukita Kazutami, and Tomizu Hirohito, economists Fukuda Tokuzō and Horie Kiichi, and writers Noguchi Yonejirō and Kurahara Koreatsu (both of whom had studied in the United States), the association boasted a galaxy of Japan's most distinguished authorities on foreign affairs. The declaration of the association spoke of the need for "creating a new Japanese people." The new people were to be "a great cosmopolitan people . . . who are not satisfied with the reputation of being a warlike nation but who try to be the model of a peaceful people . . . a cosmopolitan, humanitarian people." [1] Reflecting such ideals, the first issue of *Shinjidai,* under the editorship of Kurahara, declared the purpose of the publication to be the making of a new Japan along these principles. Japan, it was asserted, must maintain its prestige and dignity in the competitive world outside, but at the same time contribute to the common goals of mankind: peace and civilization. At the founding of the Social Education Association, Takada Sanae expounded on these points, saying that Japan's foreign policy must now be directed toward measures which would enable the people to act peacefully in the world arena. The Japanese, he said, should be encouraged to engage in peaceful struggles in the world, involving no military clashes. To do so they must be endowed with "internationally recognizable talents and a sense of toleration . . . an ability to engage in worldwide activities through harmonizing internationalist and nationalist tendencies." [2]

These ideas had existed long before the Russo-Japanese War. What was new was the confidence with which these words were spoken, as well as the sense of urgency accompanying them. There was a feeling that the war had been a victory of the forces of progress and civilization over those of reaction and backwardness. Japan, in other words, had won a right to participate in history's progressive march toward an ideal world. According to Kurahara, Japan had joined Britain and the United States as the great powers whose interest it was to bring about peace in the world and welfare to mankind.[3] Inagaki Manjirō, who had written about Japan's commercial opportunities in the Pacific, felt his optimism substantiated. He wrote in *Shinjidai* that the Russo-Japanese War had once and for all demonstrated the costliness of wars and that the nations in the world should more than ever before endeavor to prevent recourse to force. They were determined to employ peaceful methods to protect and extend their interests, and thus Japan's postwar commercial expansionism was completely in line with the trend.[4]

The sense of urgency was derived from the feeling that, despite the unique conjunction of historical forces where Japan's future seemed to parallel that of the world, in reality the Japanese people did not appear to be quite up to the task. Unless they awakened to their historic task, national expansion could take a disastrous course, a writer warned on the pages of another influential journal, *Katsudō no Nihon* (Active Japan). They would have to develop a new outlook on national and international affairs, an outlook that included economic, cultural, and moral as well as military and political considerations. Actually, the writer noted, Japan faced postwar economic dislocation, burdensome taxes, a decline in public morality, and a rising vogue of materialistic pursuits of happiness. Under the circumstances, it was more than ever imperative to educate the people so that they would successfully perform the task of "postwar management," a term frequently used to describe the overall reconstruction of Japan's internal and external affairs.[5]

Given the view that war in the near future was unthinkable and that the world was entering a new stage in the development of civilization, it was not surprising that so much interest was expressed in Japan's economic expansion and in particular overseas settlement and migration. This is another index of postwar Japanese thinking and provides a background to the crisis in Japanese relations with the United States. "Just as England tremendously expanded its foreign trade after victory over Napoleon, so can Japan be expected to take advantage of the [new] situation to expand trade and increase national strength." So wrote Kaneko Kentarō, back from his mission in America. Since, he said, the expansion of trade was the most vital area of national policy, the nation should take steps to import raw materials needed for manufacturing and to export vigorously all items that could compete with foreign products. "If we protect domestic industry and nourish resources for commercial and industrial prosperity, and then go out to the world market to expand the sale of our products in the great battle for markets in the world," Kaneko said, Japanese prosperity would be assured and economic progress secured.[6] The encouragement and expansion of domestic industry was particularly urgent, given the fact that the economy had been devoted to the war effort and was now burdened with foreign debts. Unless the Japanese were prepared to win victory in the coming "peacetime war," warned so many industrialists, Japan's military victory over Russia would have been in vain.[7]

Much of postwar Japan's economic expansion was directed toward the mainland of Asia, especially Manchuria. But it was by no means limited to that area. In an article entitled "The Japanese as an expanding people," an editor for Katsudō no Nihon wrote in 1906 that the basis for Japanese expansion had laid by the two wars, and that apart from Korea, where Japanese influence would naturally be transplanted, "the whole of Asia is offering itself as a suitable field for Japanese action. . . . But our expansive energy, now bursting out after a long period of polishing up and waiting, should not be channeled only in the direction of Asia, but should cover the whole of mankind."[8] Yamaza Enjirō, chief of the political affairs bureau of the Foreign Ministry, agreed. He wrote that while the "management" of Manchuria and Korea would provide a field for postwar Japanese expansion, these were not sufficient "as areas for extending our expanding national strength." Overseas expansion, he suggested, should be promoted in such areas as South America and China.[9] Another writer insisted that Japan's "great expansion in emigration and trade" should be planned in all parts of the world, not just in Korea and Manchuria. He was especially interested in the Dutch East Indies, which seemed to offer an ideal arena for Japanese "management," involving the investment of Japanese capital and technology and the creation of a market for Japanese goods.[10]

Emigration and settlement overseas were clearly part of the postwar expansion envisioned by these writers. War with Russia had not diminished the interest of the Japanese government and the public in peaceful migration. Now that the war was over, there seemed to be just the right opportunity to promote anew the settlement of Japanese in distant lands. Serious, scholarly books and articles on the general subject of emigration and colonialism appeared for the first time. Before the Russo-Japanese War the American-trained Nitobe Inazō had been regarded as the authority on these matters. Although trained as an agricultural economist, he was instrumental, while teaching at the Sapporo Agricultural School (later Hokkaido University) in interesting a number of students in the subject and in establishing his own reputation as a transmitter of European studies to Japan. He left the school in Hokkaido to head the prominent First Higher School in Tokyo, and in 1908 he was also appointed to a chair in colonialism at the Imperial University of Tokyo. Gotō Shinpei, then president of the South Manchuria Railway, was instrumental in establishing this chair. Because of his experiences in Taiwan and Manchuria as a colonial administrator, he was keenly aware of the need to promote the study of colonialism as a serious academic subject and was able to raise funds for the purpose. Nitobe was chosen to fill the first chair, and from this position was able to train a number of scholarly specialists who in subsequent decades were to play prominent roles in Japanese politics and the academic world.[11]

One of the first books on the subject to appear after the war was Ōkawahira Takamitsu's *Nihon imin-ron* (Japanese emigration), published late in 1905. This was followed in 1906 by Tōgō Minoru's *Nihon shokumin-ron* (On Japanese colonization). Both authors were students of Nitobe's, and although their titles reflected a bifurcation between emigration and colonization, the two books in fact talked about the same thing: the expansion of Japan. In a special preface Nitobe wrote for Ōkawahira's work, he reiterated the familiar idea that "Expansion is the great phenomenon of modern history." Japan had no choice but to accept the fact and expand. This need not entail forceful seizures of other lands but simply aimed at "seeking such areas as our people can engage in legitimate labor and such conditions as they can develop their potentialities to the fullest." No matter under whose flag a particular territory lay, Japanese should go out and settle. Hitherto, Nitobe wrote, the Japanese had tended to migrate to white countries and to benefit from contact with a higher civilization, but now they were more likely to expand into areas such as South America, South Asia, Korea, and Manchuria. No place on earth was outside the boundaries of Japanese expansion. Ōkawahira voiced that very sentiment in his book and sought to theorize the need for Japanese emigration. According to him, emigration was the best way to promote industrialization and increase capital in Japan. The emigration of laborers would prevent the lowering of wages and standards of life at home by restoring an equilibrium between the supply and demand of labor, while overseas Japanese would send and bring home the money earned. The money was equivalent to foreign loans at no interest. Once the Japanese overseas established their "social colonies," they would be able to supply needed raw materials for the homeland and develop a market for Japanese products. The result would be the rise and expansion of Japanese commerce and industry. Emigrants were truly "the vanguard of the army of expansion." The establishment of colonies and encouragement of overseas migration were the "trends of the times," and unless Japan followed them, the future of its expansion and its people would indeed be bleak. Since, as a result of the Russian war and the renewal of the British alliance, war was unlikely for at least ten years, Japan should take advantage of the favorable moment and devote its energy to national expansion through peaceful means. It should try to encourage the emigration of at least one million people during the next ten years.[12]

As can readily be seen, the line between emigration and colonization was rather tenuous. Most authors, advocating massive overseas emigration, were visualizing the creation of Japanese communities overseas as centers of economic and social activities closely linked to the mother country. In case they existed in advanced Western countries, they would benefit from the higher living standard and more developed civilization of the host communities. If, on the other hand, Japanese settled in less developed areas abroad, they would be a dominant strain in the local scene, conceivably affecting the coloration of indigenous politics and economic life. Though the outright use of force was not envisaged, such a situation would be much closer to colonization than to mere emigration—like the massive English colonization of the North American continent. Thus, "peaceful expansionism" did not simply mean the passive emigration of individual Japanese, but could imply a government-sponsored, active program of overseas settlement and positive activities to tie distant lands closer to Japan.

Tōgō Minoru's influential *Nihon Shokumin-ron* reflected these considerations. "Imperialism and colonialism," he said, "are the great

currents of the world today, and the nation must develop in accord-
ance with the currents." Japan, because of the shortage of arable land
and because there was no possibility for further expansion of productivity except through overseas emigration, must inevitably undertake a
policy of overseas expansion. The author was convinced that "apart
from the white races the Japanese are the only one with an aptitude
for colonization." They must join the Western imperialists in promoting "natural expansion." Ideally, such expansion could and should be
peaceful rather than aggressive, nationalistic rather than seeking universal dominion, and economically rather than militarily oriented. But
Tōgō admitted that when peaceful migration did not suffice or was
impracticable the nation would have to resort to force to seek territorial aggrandizement. His discussion of colonialism shifted constantly
from emigration and imperialism to expansionism in general, revealing that in Japanese thinking at that time there was no clear dividing
line among them. What provided a focus was a universalistic vision of
expansion:

From the ice-bound northern Siberian plains to the continental expanses of
China, Korea, and East Asia; farther south, to the Philippines, the Australian
continent, and other South Sea islands; then eastward to the western coasts of
North and South America, washed by the waves of the Pacific Ocean — there
is none in these regions which cannot be an object of our nation's expansion.
If our people succeed in constructing new Japans everywhere in these areas
and engage in vigorous activities throughout the Pacific, then our country's
predominance over the Pacific will have been ensured.[13]

Japan's self-perception as an overseas settler and colonizer gave an
ideological impetus to thousands of men to leave the country. Most
of them, it is true, sought the protection of Japanese power by migrating to Korea and Taiwan. The former, in particular, attracted far
more Japanese than any other territory after it became a Japanese protectorate in 1905. But outside these areas the number of Japanese
steadily grew, and in 1907 there were 232,000 of them. Of this number
65,000 were in Hawaii and 60,000 in the United States. While the
Kwantung Leased Territory witnessed an influx of Japanese newcomers, their number, exclusive of military personnel, was still only 38,000
in that year. Actually the immediate postwar years saw the last up-
surge and climax of Japanese migration to Hawaii. In 1906, 30,393
passports were issued in Japan for passengers bound for Hawaii, the

highest number in history. Another 15,757 entered the islands in 1907, the last year of massive Japanese immigration. Despite the influx of over 46,000 people from Japan during 1906–1907, however, the Japanese population of Hawaii increased by only 27,000 between 1905 and 1907. The reason in part was that many thousands of Japanese migrated from Hawaii to the United States, causing a sharp increase in the number of Japanese on the West coast. The result was a series of incidents involving them with Americans, culminating in the prohibition of migration from Hawaii to the continental United States, and of the emigration of Japanese laborers to America.[14]

There is little doubt that here was a serious crisis brought about by Japanese expansion. Studies of the immigration dispute, notably by Thomas A. Bailey and Charles E. Neu, although excellent and well documented, have tended to concentrate on the American side of the crisis and view it in terms of local prejudice and national politics.[15] Historians still consider it primarily a case of American race prejudice and a minor irritant in Japanese-American relations; they fail to see it in the context of Japanese expansionism. Unless one adopts this larger perspective, much of the historical significance of the period will be lost.

The Japanese had known about and often discussed the phenomenon of race prejudice in California and other Western states, but it had not deterred them from advocating massive postwar expansion in the direction of the American continent. The series of events during 1906–1907, beginning with San Francisco's segregation of Oriental children in separate schools and including numerous attacks on and boycotts of Japanese businesses, jolted their optimism and severely questioned the basic assumptions of their postwar expansionism. Nevertheless, few of them gave up the idea entirely.

Most writers were virtually unanimous in stressing the wider implications of the San Francisco crisis, triggered by the school segregation incident of October 1906. Even before it developed into an immigration problem, the incident was viewed in Japan as being of vital significance for the future of Japanese expansion not just in California but throughout the world. As Ōkuma Shigenobu said, the San Francisco problem was in a sense an inevitable product of the expansion of Japanese overseas. It was natural that a people engaged in "global activities" would arouse the jealousy and antagonism of others. But this did not excuse their anti-Japanese attitude. The Japanese people "have entered the stage of global action and are engaged in a peaceful competition in the world." They had every right to be treated the same way as Europeans and Americans. Mankind as a whole would be the loser if the world could not accommodate the peaceful activities of all races in all parts of the world. As a result of wars with China and Russia, Japan had been accorded the status of a great power. The time had come for the people to be given equal status so that they could carry out the ultimate goal of modern Japanese history: to enter the arena of global activities as individuals. From such a perspective the San Francisco problem was not a local incident; it was a test of whether obstacles would continue to exist in the way of the Japanese people's entry into the sphere of worldwide activities.[16]

The Japanese government's handling of the immigration dispute did not mollify the expansionists. The government, too, was interested in expansion and based its postwar foreign policy on the need to extend Japanese interests abroad. The major difference between the government and its critics was that the former stressed the expansion of Japanese commerce and considered emigration just one part of postwar expansionism, whereas for the latter emigration and overseas settlement were of great symbolic importance. Foreign Minister Hayashi Tadasu, the top official dealing with the California crisis, was convinced of the need to encourage Japan's expansion in the direction of what he called the "lines of least resistance." This would involve stressing industrial and commercial expansion and limiting of emigration to the United States so as not to jeopardize trade between the two countries. Because the Japanese would never tolerate having the limits of their expansion prescribed by another government or people, they would have to do so themselves by voluntarily restricting emigration to the United States.[17] Hayashi did not minimize the seriousness of the anti-Japanese movement on the West coast; his solution was not to let it affect other aspects of Japanese-American relations but rather to play down its importance in order to stress ways in which the two nations could remain friendly while they engaged in their respective expansion. Such a policy was supported by his colleagues in the cabinet and provided the basis for the Gentlemen's agreement of 1907 and 1908, which was a series of notes exchanged by the two governments setting forth specific ways of restricting Japanese labor emigration to America.[18]

Hayashi did not go as far as some other officials in advocating ac-

commodation with the United States. Men like Itō Hirobumi and
Ambassador Aoki Shūzō in Washington were so alarmed over the California crisis that they recommended an explicit understanding with
the United States giving the latter a virtual free hand in regulating
Japanese immigrants. In a memorandum to Hayashi dated November
6, 1907, Itō insisted that Japan must take all necessary steps concerning the immigration question so as to prevent a rupture in Japanese-
American relations. To this elder statesman the spectacle of Japan
provoking the resentment and hostility of Western nations was truly
alarming, and he felt the principle of limitless expansion should be
sacrificed to the more political goal of maintaining understanding between the countries.[19] Ambassador Aoki likewise felt that as the two
countries expanded in the Pacific and East Asia the maintenance of
basic understanding was more than ever desirable. Under the circumstances, he thought it best to eliminate the immigration question altogether from relations between the two countries. This could be done
by Japan's taking no formal action regarding the question while endeavoring to maintain the framework of peaceful commercial competition throughout the Pacific and Asia.[20]

Such negativism made some political sense and was adopted in 1908
as official policy when Japan entered into an agreement with the
United States (the Root-Takahira agreement).[21] But it had no appeal
to those who ardently believed in the possibility of limitless expansion. "Our government," asserted *Yorozu chōhō*, "must consider our
national pride, our expansive force, and the difficulties in which fifty
thousand of our countrymen are living." [22] If the Foreign Ministry
should shrink in the face of the anti-Japanese agitation, one writer
said, "the expansion of the Japanese people will be abruptly halted."
Discrimination overseas was a sign that Japanese expansion was suc-
ceeding; otherwise selfish foreigners would not object so hysterically
to the coming of the Japanese. They could maintain the respect and
ultimate acceptance by foreigners only if they persisted in a resolute
stand and desisted from expedient compromise. Diplomacy consisted
of promoting the expansion of national interests and welfare and preventing obstacles in their way. If Japan's diplomats failed in their task,
they must by all means be replaced.[23] It was humiliating, wrote Tōgō
Minoru, to see the government acting in dread of American reaction
and without any positive principle. Such a policy would only stifle the
opportunity for the expansion of the Japanese overseas.[24]

When, in February 1907, the San Francisco issue was tentatively settled through a package of compromises, most important of which was Japan's acquiescence in the new immigration act authorizing the President to restrict immigration, there was widespread disappointment. Even those who usually expressed pro-government views in Japan resented the legitimization of race prejudice. As *Tokyo Nichinichi* said, the Japanese could never accept the position of inferiority compared with European immigrants to the United States. The paper would counsel patience to the people in order to give the two governments time to work out a better solution. But even as moderate a newspaper as *Nichinichi* could not refrain from reiterating the widespread notion that despite discrimination in the United States nothing would deter the expansion of the Japanese race. Japanese would continue their successful expansion to America.[25] Abe Isoo similarly wrote that the Japanese must awaken Americans from race prejudice, just as Perry had awakened Japanese from a policy of seclusion. The Japanese were singularly free of such prejudice, Abe noted; therefore their multiplication on the Pacific coast, to hundreds of thousands and even to a million and more, would be a good thing to break the racial barrier and bring about a new kind of life, an embodiment of racial harmony.[26]

The response of *Yorozu chōhō*, probably the liveliest daily of the time and the most prominent of anti-government papers, typified popular thinking. Because the newspaper was constantly in touch with the California scene through its correspondent, Kayahara Kazan, and because of its traditional association with Japanese socialists, many of whom had been to the United States and retained great interest in emigration, its pages were sprinkled with references to these matters, making it a representative organ for the exposition of views on Japan's overseas expansion. In January 1907 it ran a series of editorials entitled "The need for encouraging emigration." The paper noted that there were over 120,000 Japanese in Hawaii and the Pacific coast of the United States, and that they sent back 12 million yen annually, each immigrant contributing an average of 100 yen (50 dollars). Should the number increase to 1,000,000, they would be sending home as much as 100 million yen, enough to take care of interest payments on wartime loans. Even a million Japanese in North America seemed a small figure, compared with the 12,200,000 Germans and 5,000,000 Irish in the United States. There were 3,500,000 Italians abroad, in America, Brazil, and elsewhere, and they were estimated to send home 75,000,000 dollars annually. During the Russo-Japanese War over a million youths, mostly from farms, were sent to the front, but their absence had no noticeable effect on agricultural productivity. Japan could, therefore, afford to send as many men abroad, and the money they sent back could be used as capital for acquiring better implements and fertilizer and for opening up more lands for cultivation. Japanese immigrants overseas, according to this paper, were not as rough as Italians, not as mercenary as Chinese, and not as expensive as laborers as Germans abroad. For this reason, "in terms of their nature and the amount of their supply, our emigrants are really the best in the world." The only reason why a scant ten or twenty thousand Japanese went abroad each year, while half a million Italians did so, was because the government was not doing enough to encourage emigration. It had neither subsidized shipping for carrying emigrants, nor spent a cent on the education of prospective emigrants. Its surveys overseas had been haphazard and superficial. There was no special office in the Foreign Ministry for dealing with emigration matters, and no budgetary allowance for the purpose. As a beginning, the government should at least undertake a systematic survey of two crucial questions: how best to expand emigration to and settlement in Hawaii, the Pacific coast of the United States, and Canada; and the potentialities for encouraging emigration to Mexico, Peru, and Brazil.[27]

Given such expectations, *Yorozu chōhō*'s reaction to the compromise solution of the California crisis was not surprising. To stop the immigration of Japanese laborers completely, as the United States government seemed to be intending, would have devastating economic consequences for Japan. "It is a great loss not to be able to export our surplus labor force and use it abroad; it is a great humiliation to have our laborers treated like Chinese," declared an editorial of February 20. America's measures to prohibit the immigration of Japanese labor, and the Japanese government's seeming acquiescence in them, "are a humiliation to our people, and will seriously injure the friendly relations between the two peoples." "The path of expansion of our people, victorious in the recent war, is about to be closed. Their rights overseas are about to be curtailed." The government must resolutely protest to the United States. If the government could not protect citizens abroad, there was no point in its existing; the essence of foreign policy was to care for Japanese overseas so as to help their expansion. But in reality Japan's diplomats and political leaders seemed to be succumbing to America's injustice. Unless the government was prepared to support overseas enterprises by citizens, there could be no real economic progress for the nation. Once Japanese were discriminated against with impunity in the United States, other nations might follow suit, thus excluding them from all areas of the earth. This was tantamount to sealing off the globe to Japanese expansion.[28]

There were ideological ties between such views and those of the Japanese in California and elsewhere on the Pacific coast as they faced the rising sentiment of Japanese exclusion. The rhetoric of Japanese expansion, accepted by all groups in Japan, was faithfully echoed by Japanese in America. Most of them were poorly educated and not quite the embodiment of the cosmopolitan spirit that Japanese observers fondly pictured, but they were far more in touch with currents of thought in the mother country than historians have assumed; they were much more part of the phenomenon of Japanese expansion than mere victims of American persecution, as described by many writers.

The self-image of Japanese in America was almost identical with that in the homeland. *Shinsekai* (The new world), a daily published by and in Japanese in San Francisco (and Oakland during the aftermath of the earthquake of 1906), gives a good indication of thinking among those who sought to articulate the meaning of their experience. On November 3, 1906, the Emperor's birthday, the newspaper talked of Japan's phenomenal expansion since the war—in commerce, agriculture, industry, trade, and shipping. Japanese overseas were part of the picture. Those on the Pacific coast represented the Yamato race, the editorial continued, and their increasing development in the face of prejudice and persecution by ignorant whites must be their constant goal in order to repay the Emperor's mercy and kindness. The anti-Japanese agitation, according to a correspondent for *Shinsekai,* was rooted in the jealousy and competitiveness Americans felt toward Japan's amazing economic expansion.[29]

Direct communication between Japanese in America and in the homeland was provided by that remarkable reporter, Kayahara Kazan, who was sent to San Francisco as a correspondent for *Yorozu chōhō* in the fall of 1905. Given the mental baggage with which he arrived in America, the shock of rude awakening was inevitable. He had fondly believed in the "westward migration of civilization" and in Japan's mission to transmit the civilization of the West to Asia. He had thought of the United States and Japan as the two most advanced countries of the twentieth century, a fact which he thought was being demonstrated by the migration of Japanese to America where they would be creating a new frontier for Japanese expansion and for the building of an even higher level of civilization. By coincidence, he arrived in California just as the anti-Japanese movement was getting under way. As an editorial writer for *Shinsekai* his literary talents were put to good use in capturing the spirit of Japanese sentiment toward the movement.

"From the day I arrived in the United States till the day of my departure, I was simply overwhelmed with what I saw," Kayahara was to remark of his life in America.[30] For a thirty-four-year-old journalist, who had accepted all the clichés about enlightened Japan and peaceful expansionism, what he saw on the West coast was nothing short of incredible. It forced him to examine every idea he held, and the result at times was extreme reaction. This was particularly true at first, as he tried to comprehend the meaning of the anti-Japanese agitation in a way that would not damage his complacent nationalism. Given the faith he shared with his fellow countrymen that Japan must expand, the portion of his ideology that had stressed the enlightened, peaceful aspect of expansionism had to be reemphasized. In a November 11, 1906, editorial for *Shinsekai,* entitled "The coming war," he accepted the "expansion of the newly risen Japan" as the basic axiom. Obstacles in the path of expansion had been and must still be removed. Japan had found it necessary to fight China in order to demonstrate that Japan was the strongest civilized country in Asia, and then to defeat Russia to show that Japan was stronger and more civilized than Europe's strongest and least civilized nation. "China now knows better and looks to Japan as its teacher. Europe, too, understands, and no European nation today wants to hurt Japanese feelings or injure Japanese interests. The only country that does not yet understand is the United States." Americans, Kayahara wrote, did not recognize that Japanese expansion must be directed, at least in part, toward the United States. They tended to underemphasize Japan's expansive energy and continued to regard the Japanese as children. While the nation needed ten more years of peace, if war should come it was bound to be with the United States, to determine which country was the strongest and most civilized in the world.

Such an emotional outburst revealed the depth of the dismay felt by Kayahara and so many others whose faith in Japanese expansion was being shaken by frankly anti-Japanese prejudice in the United States, hitherto believed to be the most enlightened of Western countries. Since he could not so easily give up his faith in progress and in cosmopolitanism, the mainstay of postwar expansionism, Kayahara developed additional themes that were also taken up by others. For example, he noted that it was not the American people as a whole that were expressing anti-Japanese prejudice, but certain of the ethnic groups; the Greeks, Italians, Slavs, Latins, Irish, and Spanish Americans were responsible. The list left out "Teutons," whom Kayahara admired as the founders of the American republic. Actually the Teutons and Japanese were the only great races in the world! The Japanese by implication should not be deterred by the agitation in California but act together with the "Teutons" in further developing such principles of civilization as individual liberty and determination to obtain set goals. Another theme, contradicting the ethnic interpretation, was the view of the Pacific slope as a theater of racial confrontation as a result of the expansion of the white and yellow races. It was inevitable, Kayahara wrote, that as Japan expanded it would seek to extend its influence not only on the Asian continent but also across the Pacific. The white race, however, had been expanding steadily westward, making it unavoidable that the two races would meet somewhere west of the Rockies. The San Francisco crisis was a serious issue precisely because it had this historic meaning. It would determine how far the two races would expand. "The Japanese in San Francisco and the Pacific coast are the spearhead of the nation as it collided with another race. They shoulder the historic responsibility of determining whether the future world is still to be dominated by the white race, or whether the latter is to be replaced by the Japanese race." The Japanese had as much right to assert that the whites restrict their expansion to east of the Rockies, as the whites to refuse the coming of Japanese to California. Kayahara concluded using one of the most belligerent expressions of the whole episode:

Struggle. Struggle like men. Endeavor. Endeavor like men. Japan is not China. Behind you stand the navy of five hundred thousand tons and the army of one million men. Above all you have the support of forty-five million countrymen. Struggle, endeavor, and overwhelm the white race. Never use cunning means as the whites do. The struggle between races is not only a problem involving interests but is a problem of life and death.[31]

Kayahara's belligerency was extreme, but his faith in Japanese expansion was not. Optimism in the face of the crisis in San Francisco was shared by other writers on the pages of *Shinsekai*. An editorial on December 13, 1906, noted that the Russo-Japanese War had revealed the historical trend of the spread of Western civilization eastward. Japan had proved that civilization and power were not the monopoly of the Caucasian race. Japanese soldiers and officers, having won the truly historic fight, henceforth should engage in another kind of battle by migrating en masse to the United States. "It is quite natural," it was pointed out, "for the soldiers who had enhanced their glory in the Eastern hemisphere to establish a reputation as businessmen in the Western hemisphere." They would be soldiers in a peaceful, commercial war. As *Shinsekai* put it on another occasion, if war should come between Japan and the United States, it would be decided in commerce rather than in actual fighting. Its fate hinged on the commercial activities of Japanese on both sides of the Pacific. Through massive emigration and shipping Japan could establish beachheads on the Pacific coast, and its business enterprises could dominate the whole West coast.[32]

Such rhetoric was never translated into specific action. There was no expectation that the Japanese government would protect its citizens in America by force. Nor was there much hope that the Japanese community on the West coast would in the foreseeable future come to dominate the Pacific states. The relation between the Japanese in the United States and their home government was rather tenuous, the sole direct point of contact being the consulate in San Francisco. The consul was in touch with various Japanese groups, but he himself did not represent their interests in dealing with the local authorities. From the beginning the embassy in Washington took the matter up with the United States government, which in turn had to deal with the municipal and state officials on the West coast. But Ambassador Aoki did not bother to travel to California until after his resignation was announced, and the highest Japanese official sent to San Francisco was the chief of the commerce bureau of the Foreign Ministry. While the consul in San Francisco became a member of an ad hoc committee organized to discuss the school board incident, his function as representative of Japan was limited to reporting to the home government.[33]

Under the circumstances it was not surprising that all the Japanese community could do was to hope for the best by trusting in the good sense of the federal government under President Roosevelt, and by cultivating the good will of Americans so as to isolate the prejudiced few. There was much rejoicing over the message to Congress submitted by the President on December 4, 1906. As he condemned the anti-Japanese agitation and called for the naturalization of Japanese already in the United States, *Shinsekai* expressed pleasure at the prospect that the Japanese would henceforth be treated equally with whites, thus opening the way for "our people's real expansion." [34] From this time on the acquisition of the right to naturalize became a cardinal point of principle for the Japanese on the West coast. Once they became citizens, their rights and property would be legally protected, but without citizenship everything was subject to the whims of Americans. Because American citizenship, constitutionally, was accorded only to Caucasians and descendants of American Indians and Africans, and since people of Mongolian origin had been specifically denied the right of naturalization, the Japanese quite naturally sought to portray themselves as different from Chinese, Koreans, and other members of the Mongolian race.[35]

Ironically, at such moments, when Japanese in California tried to depict themselves as different from other Asians, they often had to admit candidly that their ways of life and behavior in America were such that from the American point of view they could not be totally distinguished. Pages of *Shinsekai* were filled with stories of petty crimes among and by Japanese. When there were no reports of robberies, rapes, or breaches of contract, the newspaper featured articles on the general behavior of Japanese immigrants. The picture was far from the complimentary one that some editorial writers presented. "There is not a day," reported a writer in March 1907, "when in the Japanese section of the city [San Francisco] there are no shouts and noises very late at night. If the situation continues, all Japanese, even those who are civilized, will be looked down upon as barbarians." It was to be regretted, the newspaper wrote on another occasion, that the Japanese in San Francisco were more interested in idling away their time than in working hard. Many Japanese idlers and bullies had been expelled from the city before the great earthquake, but since then they seemed to have come back like floods. "To speak very frankly," said another, "there are too many Japanese who come to America that are barbaric. To watch them land from the ship, their appearance and clothes are really very hideous and give the impression as if they were slaves. . . . Unless some improvement is made, the reputation of Japanese will fall, and the hatred of the white community will increase." When Secretary of Commerce Victor H. Metcalf was dispatched by President Roosevelt to observe the Japanese scene at first hand, *Shinsekai* did its utmost to remind its readers to give him a favorable impression, and not confirm him in the caricaturized image of the lowly, Oriental immigrant. Japanese were admonished to get haircuts, shine their shoes, and otherwise make sure their "shortcomings" would not show. "Let us hope," the paper added, "that there won't be too many Japanese, grouped in threes and fives, clad in dirty clothes, standing and laughing loudly like so many primitive men." After Metcalf's visit, the Japanese consul was quoted as expressing his satisfaction that the Japanese residents as a whole had given him no cause to blush. But *Shinsekai* continued to admonish its readers to avoid "barbaric" acts so as not to alienate Americans.[36]

Interestingly enough, this was also the position that Kayahara Kazan was coming to take. He left for London in May 1907; by then his views of Japanese in America had become less belligerent and more crystallized. He still believed in Japan's peaceful expansionism, and became probably its most persistent advocate. But his observations of Japanese life in America, and the rejection of Japanese by Americans led him to revise the earlier, optimistic forecast of Japanese progress and Westernization. On the contrary, the longer he stayed and the more he saw of his countrymen living in the new environment, the less certain he became about the immediate prospect of successful expansion. He was more and more convinced of the fundamental differences which he believed existed between the two peoples, and he was not yet certain how they could be reconciled. Soon after he went to London, Kayahara summed up his observations of life in America by saying that Western civilization was the product of mobility, of emigrants, while Asian civilization was stationary, developed by those who never moved. From such a distinction followed the undoubted contrast between the West's individualism and cosmopolitanism, and Japan's familism and nationalism. Kayahara was not yet saying, as he would in a few years, that this distinction made Japan that much inferior to the West. Nevertheless, he was coming to grips with facts as he saw them among Japanese in America, facts far from what he had earlier perceived.[37]

Such reflective views would imply that Japanese discrimination could not all be blamed on crude American racism. The Japanese themselves, from this point of view, needed improvement. But none advocated the suspension, however temporary, of emigration just because the people were not up to the standards of Westerners. Expansion was a given factor, and everything else was geared to obtaining that goal. If Japanese in America must mend their ways in order to establish their rights, they would do so. They would seek naturalization as a way to be accepted as American citizens. They would continue to work closely with Japanese authorities to have the backing of the home government. They would do anything except give up expansionism.[38]

The belief that expansion, at least in the direction of the United States, was to be peaceful, involving no military conquest or territorial aggrandizement at the expense of others, was reflected in the general Japanese view at this time that the San Francisco crisis and Japan's adamant reaction did not really indicate a fundamental difference between the two countries. A few, to be sure, talked of war. American-educated Kurahara Koreatsu said, "the future of the Japanese people, just beginning to expand in the world," was in danger of being stifled as a result of Tokyo's meek attitude. The government and people of Japan must unite and speak in one voice of the righteousness of their cause. The American people, lovers of liberty and humanism, would surely awaken. Nevertheless, if peaceful, diplomatic means were to no avail, Japan would be forced to resort to guns. "Fifty years ago Commodore Perry brought his battleships to Uraga. It was for the purpose of spreading civilization in the world. Now, fifty years later, Japan's fleet should enter the Golden Gate. It is for the sake of world humanism." [39] Likewise, an unsigned editorial for the *Tōyō keizai shinpō* (Oriental economist), generally a conservative and antimilitaristic business journal, declared in June 1907 that the patience of the Japanese people was being exhausted. They had done no wrong to Americans in Japan, but a portion of the American people were subjecting Japan to humiliation and regarding it with open animosity. "Race prejudice and the various kinds of antagonism that accompany it have exceeded rational limits and cannot be reconciled with our national dignity. So long as the Americans behave without reason and perse-cute our countrymen, the only solution is to resort to gunfire." [40] From an opposite standpoint, *Heimin shinbun* (People's daily), the socialist organ, expressed fear that war was fast approaching. Because of American race prejudice and the oppression of Japanese laborers in the United States, a writer for the paper noted, the inevitable eco-nomic competition between the two capitalist countries across the Pacific was becoming more and more fierce. American prejudice would surely drive the Japanese ruling class to retaliate in kind and use the crisis as an excuse for military augmentation. The coming war would be on a far greater scale than the Russo-Japanese War. The Japanese socialists must, therefore, persist in their pacifist stand and awaken the people to the approaching danger. The writer, however, was unable to say how war could be avoided in view of the fact that it was American labor that had the strongest anti-Japanese sentiment.[41]

On the whole the California episode did not produce the type of war hysteria felt in the United States in 1907 and afterward. The over-whelming reaction of Japanese leaders — government, military, busi-ness, and press — was one of dismay at the first serious crisis between the two peoples and of disbelief that it should lead to anything more grave. Little thought was given to the possibility of armed conflict as a consequence of the immigration dispute. Although planning for post-war strategy got under way in 1906 and a war plan was adopted in 1907, military strategists paid scant attention to the situation in Cali-fornia. The overriding concern was still with Russia, although the Jap-anese army and navy had divergent notions about the future of na-tional defense. The army's thinking was most clearly expressed in the famous memorandum written by Lieutenant-Colonel Tanaka Giichi of the General Staff in 1906. Most of his ideas, after going through several revisions, were incorporated into the 1907 war plan. Tanaka did not rule out the possibility of armed collision with the United States, but he saw it as a result of the two countries' clash of interests in south China, the region most likely to be the next object of their re-spective expansionism. In the event of war, Tanaka argued that nei-ther Japan nor the United States had sufficient troop strength to in-vade each other's home territory. The best strategy for Japan, therefore, was to attack the Philippines. This was the only mention of the United States in his lengthy memorandum, and interestingly enough it was totally expunged from the final "draft war plan" which

Marshal Yamagata Aritomo presented to the throne in October 1906. At the end of the year Chief of Staff Oku Yasutaka was instructed further to deliberate on national strategy, and another paper was drafted by the General Staff. In it the army defined its brand of expansionism by noting that the basic goals of national policy were the extension of national interests abroad and the acquisition of overseas lands for settling surplus populations. The former objective could be pursued commercially and peacefully, but the latter might necessitate the use of force. The most desirable objects of Japanese expansion were: first, Siberia, Manchuria, and Mongolia; second, the Philippines, the Dutch East Indies, and the South Sea Islands; and third, Central and South America. Nothing was said here about the California dispute, and it seems reasonable to conclude that for the Japanese army war with the United States was among the least likely of possibilities in the near future.[42]

The navy was different. It considered the United States a likely enemy, and its views were coupled with the army's in the 1907 war plan, which pointed to Russia, the United States, and France as Japan's imaginary enemies in that order. However, as Tsunoda Jun and Hata Ikuhiko have noted, the navy's primary concern at this time was with naval expansion to keep pace both with other powers and with the Japanese army, and there was no detailed study or plan of war with the United States.[43] Documentation is exceedingly meager, but some idea of naval thinking can be detected in the writings of Satō Tetsutarō, an officer often called the Mahan of Japan. He wrote volumes on naval and maritime matters, including the influential *Teikoku kokubō shiron* (History of Japan's national defense), published in 1908. He starts with the premise that Japan is an insular country, a sea power whose security depends on an adequate navy. The nation was unique as a Pacific as well as an East Asian power, and Japanese home waters were the shield against aggression. To strengthen this shield must be the basic national strategy. Since Japan had no intention of forcefully expanding into the continent of Asia, Satō wrote, there was no need for an increase in army strength. It would provoke Russia but have no effect whatsoever on the sea powers' attitude toward Japan; these nations would take Japan seriously only if the latter built up its naval strength. At a time when the major powers of the world were developing their navies, with inevitable implications for

Japanese security, it was an extreme folly to concentrate on the army and on the continent.

The Japanese navy's view of Japanese-American relations was derived from such thinking. Given America's economic wealth, Japan was considered no match for the United States in a serious armament competition. It was felt, however, that Japan should try to strengthen its navy, diverting resources from the army if necessary, in order to balance American supremacy in the Pacific. This seemed to be the only basis for maintaining stability in the ocean. Satō expressed his view that the two nations on opposite sides of the Pacific were destined to share responsibilities for peace in the ocean; there was no thought that one had to predominate over the other. He and his colleagues, nevertheless, were disturbed by the immigration dispute which they feared might result in hostilities between the two countries. He wrote, "Americans seem excessively nervous; it is said that they tend to have a not very pacific sentiment toward us. It is difficult to know what puppet-players among them are influencing their views." It was imperative to avoid actual war, lest the result be calamitous.[44]

Japan's navalists were overwhelmed by what they took to be America's determination to impress Japan by sending its fleet on a cruise across the Pacific. The "great white fleet" sailed into Yokohama in October 1908. The naval attaché in Washington wrote that the world cruise was obviously meant as a demonstration to impress American naval power on Japan. Under the circumstances the best Japanese tactic should be to show the Americans Japan's sincere interest in peace so the American people would have no reason to suspect Japan's intentions. Actually, he wrote, the ships' visit to Japan was a great opportunity for the Japanese to try to counter American misunderstanding of their country. If American sailors and admirals were "intoxicated by our friendship," they would return home with memories of Japanese goodwill and dissolve all remaining feeling of mistrust their countrymen had of Japan.[45] The naval leaders in Japan agreed and did all they could to impress their friendly and peaceful sentiment on the American visitors. Satō, writing shortly after the event, chose to believe that the two nations must maintain peace, and that Japan must try to realize this goal. He would, he said, insist only that Japan maintain a system of adequate defense in case of emergency and to win the respect of its Pacific neighbor.[46]

Though the United States was added to the list of hypothetical enemies in 1907, Japanese naval authorities seem to have assumed that
there were no fixed patterns of international relations to designate a
particular country Japan's enemy. In a memorandum written that year
for the officials sent to London to discuss naval cooperation with Britain under the terms of the second Anglo-Japanese alliance (1905), the
Navy Ministry pointed out that the Russian war had broken the balance among the powers; international politics were in a state of flux,
and it was difficult to foresee the shape the next war would take. At
least it seemed obvious, the memorandum noted, that the war would
be fought by more than two nations; the enemy would be a combined
force of several powers. One possibility was that of Russia, Germany,
and France aligned against Britain and Japan, with the United States
and Italy remaining neutral. The assumption of a multiple enemy
force was accepted at the naval representatives' conference in London, and the allied strategists agreed to make broad plans to anticipate such a force. It was decided that the two navies should be maintained at a level higher than that of any possible combination of
imaginary enemies. Thus, there was no assumption that conflict with
the United States was imminent. Despite the immigration crisis which
was causing American writers to forecast trouble, there was no similar
development in Japan. Naval officers kept publicly disclaiming any designs on American territories in the Pacific.[47]

The refusal to believe that the two Pacific nations were fated to collide was shared by influential Japanese writers. They expressed dismay
at the appearance of such fatalism in the United States. These writers,
virtually without exception, agreed about Japan's need to undertake
expansion and were chagrined at the anti-Japanese sentiment on the
West coast, but in their opinion these had nothing to do with the
continued relationship of amity and understanding between the two
countries. They could not understand why some Americans should be
agitated about alleged Japanese designs on the Philippines, Hawaii,
and the West coast. As *Tokyo Asahi* said, "we are revolted at the idea
that Japan is a bellicose nation and is waiting for an opportune moment to start war with the United States. Japan is probably the country where war is most hated by the people. . . . To say that Japan
today has designs on Hawaii and the Philippines is like saying the
United States has designs on Taiwan and Kyūshū. Such ideas are
nothing but extreme foolishness. Japanese-American relations are nat-

urally relations involving mutuality, but the mutuality consists of civilized, moral mutuality, not the barbaric relationship of mutual aggression." [48] The Japanese, believers in peaceful migration to the American possessions, were shocked when Americans suspected them of secret designs on the Philippines. A *Nichinichi* editorial of April 28, 1907, pointed out that the Philippines were the East Asian base for American civilization. "It perfectly suits our policy that the United States, a nation noted for its fair-minded foreign policy, should have a base in East Asia and concern itself with Asian problems." Only those who sought to divide Japan and the United States would attribute to Japan aggressive designs on American possessions.

Talk of war which began to be heard in the United States in 1907 gave the Japanese an opportunity to reformulate national principles and ponder the future of their relations with America.[49] "Suspicious nations often look at us as an aggressive people," the influential *Tōyō keizai shinpō* wrote, but "they completely misunderstand us. Where can one find an instance in the two thousand years of our history when Japan started an aggressive war with another country? During the past fifty years Japan's diplomatic posture has always been defensive. It is beyond contention that the recent two wars have been forced upon us and were motivated by self-defense." [50] This did not mean, many writers hastened to add, that Japan was not an expansive nation. An editorial in *Tokyo Nichinichi* noted that "imperialism" had been a national policy since 1868; but the term implied merely the building of a strong nation. "We have had an opportunity to expand our influence in recent years," it was noted, "but the powers know that what our country intends is not territorial aggrandizement but the extension of intellectual and economic influence." [51] Such being the case, it was exceedingly difficult to understand why Americans viewed peaceful Japanese immigrants like an invading army, an editor of *Tōyō keizai shinpō* wrote. The eastward migration of the expanding Japanese population was a peaceful, humanitarian, natural phenomenon, and it was incomprehensible why they must be regarded like so many enemy soldiers.[52]

Such expressions delineate the continuing dichotomy between peaceful expansionism and military conquest, and consequently the view that Japanese migration to the United States should pose no threat to the traditional friendship between the two countries, unless the American people wanted to make it a *casus belli*. Since the Japanese intended no hostility, there could not conceivably be any chance for serious conflict. Thus, the Japanese press on the whole took a calm attitude when the American plan to send its fleet on a world cruise became known. It was the Americans and not the Japanese, *Nichinichi* pointed out, who talked about the serious implications of the cruise and worried about a possible clash between the fleet and the Japanese navy. The Japanese would regard the cruise as a strictly routine exercise by the United States navy, in no way related to the dispute over immigration. Japanese commentators expressed disbelief that the United States should want to use its fleet to demonstrate against and overawe Japan, since the latter had no intention of menacing American interests. *Nichinichi* summed up the generally held view by noting, in October 1907, that not a single Japanese statesman believed in the possibility of war with the United States. "We only regret," it pointed out, "that a portion of the American people tend to drive a wedge between Japan and the United States." On another occasion the paper accused some Americans of confusing reality with "illusions in their own minds" when they viewed Japan. Americans seemed to have an unjustifiable fear and suspicion of Japan, while the Japanese knew they had nothing but peaceful sentiment. Such a confession of failure to communicate indicated the coming of a new epoch in Japanese-American relations.[53]

VI

Confrontation: The American View

Just as the immigration dispute was considered by the Japanese a hindrance to their postwar expansion, Americans responded to it in all seriousness. Whereas the Japanese regarded the United States and its possessions primarily as spheres for peaceful, economic activity, Americans believed with equal firmness in the likelihood of military confrontation. All factors — political, economic, racial, cultural — combined to create a particular attitude toward Japanese expansion, which was never to leave American consciousness until the end of World War II.

President Theodore Roosevelt's response was typical. He had no sympathy with violent attacks on individuals already in the United States; they served no purpose whatsoever other than humiliating the Japanese and making them more hostile toward America. However, he strongly believed that the white and the Asian races could not coexist peacefully anywhere in the world, least of all in the United States. The Japanese question in California must be related ultimately to the issue of the living together of Japanese and Americans, representatives of two different cultures. "I have to recognize facts," he wrote to John Strachey in December 1906, "one fact being governmental conditions as they actually exist in a democracy, and the other being, what so many sentimentalists tend to forget, the great fact of difference of race. . . . [If the Japanese] began to come by the hundred thousands it would be a very, very bad thing indeed, and it would then be too late to have a peaceful, or at least a non-irritating, solution."

Roosevelt would have welcomed the immigration and naturalization of a few cultured Japanese. In his annual message to Congress in December 1905, he gave expression to a melting-pot philosophy: "If the man who seeks to come here is from the moral and social standpoint of such a character as to bid fair to add value to the community he should be heartily welcomed. . . . We cannot afford to consider whether he is Catholic or Protestant, Jew or Gentile; whether he is Englishman or Irishman, Frenchman or German, Japanese, Italian, Scandinavian, Slav, or Magyar." Such an idea was the foundation of the Rooseveltian nationalism that recognized no divisive factors within American culture and society and visualized the worth of all Americans as equal members of a national identity. But this identity was clearly Western in origin and orientation. As he wrote, "We Americans are a separate people. We are separated from, although akin to, many European peoples." The principles on which the nation was founded, the ways of life which the American people followed, were recognizable only with reference to standards in Europe. Roosevelt was a cultural integrationist at home but a relativist with respect to the world at large. He saw many levels of civilization and various types of culture in the world. He never advocated the mixture of all of them, nor did he believe such a thing was possible. For this reason he was as opposed to the immigration of Asians as were the exclusionists on the West coast. The argument was not primarily economic but rather cultural, derived from the often unstated belief that two such divergent cultures as Asian and Western could never mingle.[1]

These views were not very different from the more frankly stated public positions taken by the exclusionist press of the West coast. Subscribing to the notion of incompatibility of races, the *San Francisco Chronicle* wrote, "We desire to continue on friendly terms with Japan both for sentimental and commercial reasons. There is but one way to do it, and that is to keep Japanese manual laborers out of the country. Our workingmen will never bother Japan. As for giving up our civilization for that of Japan, which must follow the free admission of Japanese coolies, we won't do it, and the Japanese and United States governments combined can not make us do this."[2] *The Sacramento Union* said, "Our contention is that when Congress again legislates in relation to exclusion it should so broaden that legislation as to keep out the objectionable of all nations, even if it shall go so far as to say . . . this is to be a white man's country, in order that we may have here no more race question than we have." The *San Francisco*

Call cited the temper of postwar Japan, ready to assert its right to expand. The Japanese, it noted, "are disposed to be troublesome and cocky. The less we have to do with a nation that carries a chip on its shoulder the better. As long as the Japanese are permitted to come here in considerable numbers they will be a cause of international friction and danger. Nor are they desirable in any way. As laborers they are inferior, unreliable and tricky. We can very well spare the lot." In an editorial entitled "A conflict of civilizations," the same newspaper insisted that the "irreconcilable conflict between occidental and oriental civilizations" was the root cause of the California crisis. "Their ways are not and never will be our ways." [3]

Among intellectuals, Archibald Cary Coolidge's influential *The United States as a World Power* is another example of the same type of thinking, showing that even a highly respected man could share many preconceptions and attitudes of the "ignorant" exclusionists on the West coast. Coolidge admitted that "the Japanese have entered so whole-heartedly into European civilization, and have proved themselves such adepts at it, that we can imagine their being regarded as one of the white peoples." This was precisely the problem, for such developments all the more highlighted racial differences. Japan's success in Westernization had not, in Coolidge's view, altered the fact that they belonged to a separate race. The two could not be mixed without doing violence not only to white men's prejudice but also to science. As was the case with hybrid dogs, "if kinds that are too alien to one another are bred together, the product is a worthless mongrel." Admixture of different types of the white race had produced the modern West, Coolidge admitted, but this "does not prove it to be desirable that the American people of the future should be a compound of whites, negroes, and Chinese." He was convinced that Asian immigrants in the United States "form the vanguard of an army of hundreds of millions, who, far from retreating before the white man, thrive and multiply in competition with him." It was the white man, not the Asian, that must lose out in such a contest, since "All evidence we have . . . goes to prove that white men, as a working class, cannot maintain themselves in the long run against the competition of Chinese, Japanese, Hindus, and perhaps others." If "the countless millions of their teeming native lands" followed the few thousand Asians already in America, the outcome was predictable.

The anti-Chinese and anti-Japanese agitation on the West coast, according to Coolidge, was related to a far larger question: "Is the future population of the Pacific coast to be white or is to be Oriental?" To him it was absolutely clear that the American people "will go to any extreme before they will allow their Pacific coast to become the domain of the yellow race or of any but the white." He went on to say, "Such action need not be a reflection upon the Chinese and the Japanese. It simply means that, if white men and Mongolians cannot live side by side in the same land, the Americans, being white themselves, will reserve territory for the people of their own blood." Because of racial differences between Japanese and Americans, in particular, Coolidge favored complete restriction on the immigration of Japanese, since they would mean an "addition to the American population of another ethnic element, which, whatever may be its own virtues, would not, in the opinion of many, blend well with the rest." Hence the explicit declaration: "we may accept it as beyond doubt that, if Japanese immigration to the United States were to keep on growing at its recent rate, some means would be found to stop it, treaty or no treaty, peacefully or by force, at any risk and at all cost." [4]

In another widely read book, John H. Latané's *America as a World Power,* published in 1907, the theme of American expansion in the Pacific and the Orient was coupled with apprehension over Japan's expansive thrust in the same areas. Strained relations between the two countries had resulted, the author wrote, from the clash of their respective expansions, and Japanese migration in the Pacific was giving rise to serious concern over the future control of that part of the world. While not as extreme as Coolidge in delineating the racial tension involved, Latané concluded with a plea for Anglo-Saxon solidarity. The course of world politics, he said, "is destined to lead to the further reknitting together of the two great branches of the Anglo-Saxon race in bonds of peace and international sympathy, in a union not cemented by any formal alliance, but based on community of interests and of aims, a union that will constitute the highest guarantee of the political stability and moral progress of the world." [5] Such platitudes, widely held since the 1890's, were being seriously challenged by the Japanese question, but they still provided the intellectual framework in which the immigration dispute was viewed.

Published opinions as well as private communications to the government make it clear that the Roosevelt administration's handling of the dispute had widespread support. Officials considered the influx of Japanese immigrants to be the root cause of the West coast's hostility toward them, and felt that there would be no amicable relations with Japan unless the tide was checked or, preferably, completely stopped. F. M. Huntington Wilson, third assistant secretary of state and the official most directly involved in drafting policy toward Japan in 1906–7, had served in that country and believed he knew something of its politics and mentality. Since the Japanese were "a proud and senti- mental people," he wrote a few days after the San Francisco school board crisis began, it would be best for the two countries if no more Japanese laborers were admitted to the United States, as they would only give rise to more incidents. Wilson would support a general law to "exclude not only Orientals but several other of the less desirable races while still admitting the most desirable." [6] As Charles E. Neu has shown, American policy was gentle but firm in holding Japan ac- countable for the number of its people coming to the United States. Even a small increase of immigrants resulted in urgent telegraphic dis- patches to Tokyo to remonstrate with the government, and every month detailed reports on incoming Japanese were compiled by the Department of Commerce and Labor to give ammunition to the State Department. Since the bulk of Japanese newcomers had first gone to Hawaii and then moved to the Pacific coast, Roosevelt sought summarily to end the flow by an executive order forbidding such mi- gration. When he found out, in March 1908, that a hundred and fifty Japanese laborers had arrived during the previous month, he at once sent a note to Secretary of State Elihu Root, complaining that it was "certainly regretted that as large a number came in. Even without them, there are more Japanese coming to America than I like to see." [7]

Administration officials persuaded themselves that the United States could take some restrictive measures without hurting Japanese sensitivity because the American government fully conceded Japan's right to forbid American immigration to that country. Huntington Wilson noted that there was nothing unusual about Japanese exclu- sion, since Japan would surely do the same should its streets and facto- ries swarm with American laborers.[8] This was a feeble argument in view of the wage differential between the two countries, and Secretary Root, not satisfied with such an unsophisticated justification, was genuinely perturbed by the implications of restricting peaceful migration of peoples. In a letter written to Oliver Wendell Holmes in March 1907 he said,

The subject of the exclusion of laborers is acquiring a new interest in my mind. The struggle of the laborer to protect himself against the labor competition of an alien race, which he is unable to meet successfully, is to be classified with the struggle of the Boers to protect themselves against the political encroachment and predominance of the more alert outlanders, and with an effort which is now going on in Haiti on the part of the citizens of the Black Republic to protect themselves against the business competition of foreign traders whom they are at this moment trying to exclude. The whole subject of peaceful invasion by which the people of a country may have their country taken away from them, and the analogy and contrast between the swarming of peaceful immigration and business enterprise and the popular invasions by force of arms in former times, such, for instance, as those overrunning the Roman Empire, are most interesting.[9]

Root must have been aware that "peaceful invasion" was what American merchants and bankers were attempting in Central America, and that Japanese exclusion, at least philosophically, seriously challenged his own country's peaceful expansionism.

There were of course men who attacked Japanese exclusion as bigoted and harmful to American trade. "The Japanese and Chinese in California are a quite necessary element in our population," wrote one correspondent to the State Department.[10] They were "far and away a better class than most of the foreigners in our midst," another said.[11] A handwritten letter to President Roosevelt asked, "Do we want war with the Orient which will cost hundreds of millions and a continual hatred for years to come? [The Japanese] is a sober, industrious citizen and we make nothing by antagonizing him. If we do, we will have Asia to fight, commercially and otherwise." [12] The board of directors of the San Francisco Merchants Exchange resolved to oppose anti-Japanese discrimination, which would only damage "the most friendly trade relations between the two countries." [13] Likewise, the Tacoma Chamber of Commerce told Roosevelt and Root that any discriminatory treaty with Japan "would curtail the market for our wheat and flour and have a direct and damaging effect upon the farming interests of the entire west." [14]

These were reiterations of arguments used against Chinese exclusion in 1905. In both instances concerned Americans expressed dismay that prejudiced labor leaders and local politicians should present themselves as the opinion leaders of the West coast, and urged that commercial interests not be subordinated to such irresponsible racism. There was, however, one important difference between the Chinese dispute and the Japanese crisis. Even among those opposed to Japanese exclusion there was a near-unanimous consensus that war with Japan was a possibility. Secretary of State Root stated as early as October 27, 1906: "Owing to their recent admission to recognized equality with the other civilized nations, they [Japanese] are particularly sensitive about everything which questions that equality; one-tenth of the insults which have been visited upon Chinese by the people of the United States would lead to immediate war." Japan, he cautioned, "is ready for war, with probably the most effective equipment and personnel now existing in the world." Whether one supported or opposed stringent restrictions on Japanese immigration, one had to agree with Root that there was far more likelihood of war with Japan than with China. Japan's image was that of a martial state, more a military camp than an ordinary nation. As Root wrote, "The Japanese Government always conducts its affairs like a military commander planning a campaign and it has extraordinary capacity for prompt and sudden action. If they see that the tendency of events is going to lead to war, they will not hesitate an instant to bring it on at the time most favorable to them." [15]

It was only a step from such a view to a belief in the inevitability of conflict between the two countries, and from there to a picture of Japanese immigrants not simply as an army of peaceful invasion but a vanguard of military conquest. Japanese immigrants, unlike their Chinese counterpart, were linked to the home country's war machine and expansive foreign policy. This perception accounts for the much wider geographical distribution of strongly alarmist views vis-à-vis Japan, compared with opinions expressed during the Chinese crisis. It was as though Americans in all parts of the country, becoming aware of Japanese power, saw signals in their encounter with Japanese that became suddenly very meaningful. This was the state of mind that constituted the first war scare across the Pacific.

For instance, in a letter dated December 31, 1906, an interpreter with the United States immigration service at El Paso reported that a Japanese working as a servant in the vicinity was in fact a military officer.[16] In February 1907 the mayor of Portland, Oregon, wrote tell-ing of Japanese making surveys and drawing up maps of the coastal area.[17] Another correspondent told President Roosevelt that Japanese were in charge of every mile of railroad west of the Missouri, with the implication that in the event of trouble they could control land communication to the West coast.[18] In July, Secretary of War Taft received a hand-written note from a man in Howe Brook, Maine, saying, "I was in Bucksport, Maine yesterday and learned that a strange Japanese without any apparent business has been a guest at the Robinson House several days. It is common talk that he is spying on Fort Knox." [19] From Lamar, Colorado, a correspondent reported, "there are some Japanese spies in this vicinity. One in particular, a tall, well built, and educated one has attracted my attention lately; his very demeanor, speech and general deportment, bears him out to be an officer." [20] At the end of the year a man wrote President Roosevelt from Los Angeles, summing up all the arguments that had become common features of the alarmist literature. The Japanese, he said, "are and have been seeking employment in every public and semi-public building. They are employed on all railroads and most of the avenues of approach." The result was that they were acquainted with necessary strategic information for making war. Their intelligence work was aided by their group discipline and cohesiveness. "They are silent, sly, inquisitive, and toward Americans inclined to be sullen. . . . They are educated observers of every 'foot of ground' so to speak, from Alaska to South Dakota." [21]

This suspicion of Japanese military designs added a new and startling dimension to the more traditional argument derived from racial and economic considerations. Always present, these would not have been sufficient to create an atmosphere of war hysteria as early as 1906–7. It was only when the perennial immigration dispute was viewed as part of Japanese expansionism that American-Japanese relations were seen as heading for a showdown. Not unnaturally, Americans overseas were among the first to accept the fatalist view. In December 1906 an American resident in Mexico wrote Taft saying Japanese expansion "spelled disaster for the white race." He was convinced that war would come within ten years: "it will be hard, but decisive." American citizens all over the world, he wrote, "are anxiously waiting for our Government to sit up and take notice." [22] An old navy officer, now a pensioner in Melbourne, reminded President Roosevelt a year later, "As there is a large number of Pensioners in this country,

I would suggest that an offer be made to them, to return to the United States and become enrolled in a Veterans' Reserve Corps, to assist in any trouble, that may arise with Japan." [23] A man from Newark who had lived in Japan told Roosevelt that "these deceitful and spying tricky people" were prying into military secrets and that the only way to prepare for war was to stop having Japanese servants on United States battleships.[24] Charles Denby, on his way to Shanghai to take up his duties as consul general, wrote a personal letter to Root in July 1907, expressing his agreement with what he said was the prevailing sentiment in Europe that "Japan has definitely decided on war with the United States within the next few years." This, he asserted, was "the logical development of Japan's national ambitions." [25] Charlemagne Tower, United States ambassador in Berlin, assured the State Department that, "in a war between the United States and Japan, the moral support and the public sympathy of the German people would be unequivocally upon our side." [26]

From California to Delaware, from Ohio to New Jersey and Pennsylvania, Americans suggested how best to prepare for and win the expected war. Spanish-American War veterans offered their services to the army, and others suggested how Japanese already in the country should be handled.[27] It was not surprising that not a few expressed concern with Japanese collusion with American blacks. A man wrote from Los Angeles that a secret move was under way among the Negroes in the South and West to encourage the Japanese to go to war with the United States. "They have a committee now negotiating with Japan and if the Negroes of this country [succeed] in forming a secret alliance with Japan it might mean trouble for the U.S." [28] Another letter from Dexter, Missouri, suggested, "In view of the approach of troubles between our country and Japan, and recognizing the fact that Japan has introduced night fighting . . . that the colored regiments in the United States Army be put on night service to meet the emergency that may arise should hostilities begin between us and Japan." Negro troops, it was pointed out, "are of the proper color." [29]

The United States army was sensitive to these communications and did what it could to ascertain the truths of the rumors and obtain other pertinent information. The military intelligence division of the general staff periodically compiled data on the Japanese army. One such compilation was made in February 1906 "from confidential information in the possession of MID," and another, over a year later, showed the number of Japanese in Taiwan, Hawaii, the Philippines, and the United States.[30] In February 1907 Secretary Taft approved the sending of Major Samuel Reber and Captain William Chamberlaine of the general staff to Japan, the Philippines, and Hawaii on a confidential mission to obtain relevant facts.[31] Their findings were fairly innocuous. On May 31, 1907, Reber forwarded a report on his observations in Japan, including the country's financial conditions, shipbuilding, and arsenals. He found no present sentiment for war with the United States, but he recommended that a sufficient number of officers conversant with the Japanese language be kept in Japan to watch developments.[32] In Hawaii, Captain Chamberlaine found a feeling of apprehension caused by the presence of Japanese, many of whom were "ex-soldiers of low intelligence." From Japan he reported on the defensive system of Tokyo Bay, including a list of batteries and armament. But he found no anti-American feeling and no signs of unusual activity at naval bases.[33] The military attaché himself wrote from Tokyo in May that no preparation for war against the United States was apparent.[34] On the other hand, Major Eben Swift, sent on a confidential mission to China and Japan with a special fund of $500 authorized by Secretary Taft, on his return reported without hesitation that "Japan contemplates war with the United States." He based his conclusion on the recent increases in Japan's armed forces, the fortification of Taiwan, rumors that discharged soldiers were going to Hawaii and arms were being sent to the Philippines, and the observations of prominent foreigners in East Asia that war was inevitable.[35]

In the meantime, Captain R. H. Van Deman of the general staff was instructed by the chief of staff to write a memorandum on Japanese activities in Hawaii and the Philippines. The seven-page report, dated April 3, 1907, was typical of army sensitiveness to the Japanese question. The writer asserted, "Knowing . . . the character of the Japanese and their well known policy of preparation, from a military point of view, for eventualities in any direction, I think we may accept it as a fact that they are and have been for a considerable period paying considerable attention to this country in the way of getting military information, topographical and otherwise." In Hawaii there appeared to be a plan to "push into the islands . . . a rather large number of men who are not of the coolie class but who are posing as such." But Van Deman's greatest concern was with the Philippines, where it was feared Japanese agents were closely in touch with the insurgents. "I think there is good reason to believe," he concluded, "that Japanese individuals now in the Philippines are engaged, not only in increased efforts to gain military information . . . but that they are endeavoring, for some purpose, to create in the minds of the Filipinos an idea that Japan would be glad to see them independent and that she stands ready to establish a protectorate over the islands. It may be that these individuals have no connection with the Japanese Government . . . but this seems hardly probable to say the least." [36]

In April 1907 the commanders of twenty-two army forts (mostly on the West coast and the Mexican border) were instructed by the military intelligence division to determine in complete secrecy what intelligence activity, if any, Japanese were engaged in, and to investigate rumors that they were entering from Mexico and purchasing large tracts of land for colonizing the border states. The reports from the forts were as a whole negative. The commander at Fort McIntire, Texas, said he had been able to learn of no land purchase by Japanese in his area. "The officials here," he added, "are fully alive to the situation, the border is being carefully guarded, and I believe it would be difficult for any Japanese to get in, and remain long without detection." [37] An army engineer in Colorado denied that Japanese were engaged in any extensive map work in Mexico along the United States boundary. No American, he said, "had noticed Japanese doing anything but legitimate work or passing between towns in search of work." [38] Fort Clark, Texas, reported that a large number of Japanese along the Rio Grande sought entry to the United States, but that no military significance could be attached to them.[39] The commander of Fort Liscum in Alaska wrote he had been unable to find any information "which would lead me to believe that Japanese Agents have been engaged in charting any part of the Alaskan coast." [40] On the other hand, Fort Columbia, Washington, informed the War Department that two Japanese had been seen with some maps; the commander had tried unsuccessfully to have them shadowed.[41] When, in July 1907, the commander of the San Diego district, California, telegraphed that a young Japanese had been caught with a sketch pad and that, although no sketches had been found, he had been interrogated and ordered off the area, the acting secretary of war immediately instructed him to verify the statements made by the Japanese concerning his identity. They were corroborated upon investigation, but the exchange of telegrams and writing of numerous memoranda on such a trivial matter revealed the seriousness with which the army, even its highest authorities, viewed the Japanese crisis.[42] Major W. G. Haan, of the coast artillery corps, was so worried about the safety of the fortifications in the Pacific states that he suggested that, in case of trouble with Japan, "one of our most serious problems will at the very beginning be to corral all Japanese now on this coast in the United States, a thing which I consider absolutely essential to the safety of some of our fortifications on the coast." He was convinced that ten to twenty thousand Japanese on the West Coast were ex-soldiers and possessed at least ten thousand rifles. Because of their tight discipline and organization, "much damage could be done if they were to take us unawares at any of our harbors." [43]

The United States navy seems to have been less given to alarmist views and sensitiveness toward alleged Japanese designs. As William R. Braisted's authoritative study shows, during 1906–7 naval authorities as a whole remained calm and continued their emphasis on the Atlantic Ocean. That Japan would attack the Philippines in the event of war was not disputed, but the navy was much more concerned with evolving a global strategy and much more interested in the developing rivalry between Germany and Great Britain.[44] A memorandum, written in February 1907 by Admiral Charles S. Sperry for Secretary of Commerce and Labor Oscar Straus, is a good example. Sperry did not believe that "incidental differences" arising between the two countries were unique. So long as these were not magnified out of proportion by sensational journalism, there would be no rupture in Japanese-American relations — a situation which would prove most embarrassing to Britain, trying to maintain friendly ties with both countries. Sperry argued that Japanese expansionism, derived from the nation's increasing population and limited resources, had been given temporary relief as a result of the war, as it had "acquired the rich, sparsely populated, and undeveloped Korea." It was unlikely, therefore, that Japan would want to disturb the world status quo by force. "Japan needs to economize in order to meet her war debts and to provide capital for the development of Korea, and apart from any sentiment of traditional friendship it seems impossible that any responsible Japanese statesman should contemplate a rupture with this country. Even if in a measure successful, Japan would have to bear the expense of preparedness for a counterstroke from the United States as well as from Russia." [45]

The navy, nevertheless, began a study of military strategy against Japan which, combined with similar planning by the army, became the basis of the 1907 war plan against "Orange" (code name for Japan). On June 14, 1907, President Roosevelt asked "what plans had been made by the Joint [army-navy] Board, the War Department and the Navy Department, in case of trouble arising between the United States and Japan." Four days later the joint board was convened and adopted a basic strategy: "owing to the preponderance of naval and military power possessed by Japan in the Pacific Ocean, the United States would be compelled, whilst preparing for the offensive by the assembly of its fleet in the Atlantic, to take a defensive attitude in the Pacific and maintain that attitude until reinforcements could be sent from the Atlantic to the waters of the Pacific." In the event of an emergency, it was recommended that certain preliminary steps be taken at the beginning of hostilities, such as the accumulation of a large supply of coal at the naval base in Subic Bay, the shipment of a quantity of army mines to the Philippines, the dispatch of the battle fleet for the Orient, the concentration of land forces in Subic Bay and Manila, and the strengthening of the defense of the Pacific coast forts. When representatives of the War and Navy Departments saw the President on June 27, he instructed that some of these steps be taken in the immediate future. The most important one was to "arrange to have the entire fleet of battleships transferred from the Atlantic to the Pacific Coast some time in October of this year." This was the origin of the world cruise of the United States fleet, undertaken in 1907–1909. There is little doubt that it was designed as part of preparedness against war with Japan. As Roosevelt told Colonel W. W. Wotherspoon of the Army War College, "whilst he had no idea or belief that there would be a war between the two countries, he was satisfied with the report of the Joint Board and concurred in its conclusions. [He] wanted the movement of the fleet . . . to partake of the character of a practice march. . . . [Such] a movement would have a strong tendency to maintain peace." For the same reason, he strongly urged that the defenses of Subic Bay be stepped up.[46]

Senator Henry Cabot Lodge must have been acquainted with some of these plans when he assured William Sturgis Bigelow at this time that "the Administration is entirely alive to the situation and although it does not apprehend war or any danger of war it will not be caught unready or unprepared." Bigelow expressed fear that Japan might present some demands upon the United States in connection with the immigration dispute, which would be too insulting to accept, with the result that Japan would "hoist their flag in Hawaii overnight." Lodge agreed that there "is nothing to prevent their seizing the Philippines or possibly Hawaii," but assured his friend that the United States navy could take on the Japanese. Moreover, "a wanton attack . . . upon the United States would rouse the American people, who have one marked quality, as they have shown in the past, of not staying beaten. We have plenty of obstenacy [sic] and we should hold on." At that time Lodge did not believe war with Japan was an immediate possibility, but, like Roosevelt, he felt preparedness ought to be stepped up because the Japanese were "very sensitive and very much disposed to attack anybody." [47]

One reason Lodge did not think war was likely was that in his opinion Japan could not afford it. It could not possibly borrow money for an American war from other nations, least of all from Britain, which had done much to finance the Russian war. Although the Anglo-Japanese alliance was still in effect, Lodge saw no likelihood that it would work to America's detriment in the event of war. He did not believe, for instance, that the British navy would be at the disposal of an invading army of Japan. Administration officials were nevertheless concerned with the implications of the alliance for American security, and did what they could to try to emasculate it.[48] In doing so, President Roosevelt and others of his administration were confident that the Anglo-American countries could take a common stand toward the Japanese immigration question. Assistant Secretary of State Huntington Wilson said the United States and Britain must be kept in close confidential relations, "for our mutual benefit in dealing with the great question." With this in mind, in early 1908 Roosevelt told McKenzie King, who came to Washington to discuss the matter: "What I would like to accomplish is some kind of a convention between the English speaking peoples, whereby . . . it would be understood on all sides that the Asiatic peoples were not to come to the English speaking countries to settle, and that our people were not to go to theirs." [49] Quite propitiously, from such a point of view, there occurred attacks on Japanese in British Columbia throughout 1907, similar in character to those in California. The incidents served to strengthen the belief that, despite the Anglo-Japanese alliance, there was more in common between America and Britain than between the allies. Secretary of War Taft, while on his Asian tour in the fall, tele-graphed Roosevelt from Nagasaki that Japan's immigration dispute with the Commonwealth countries "helps us and we can be sure that they will treat us as well as they do England in respect to immi-grants." [50] Henry White expressed "joy" at an anti-Japanese outburst at Vancouver which, he said, "was a fortunate one for us and seems to have put a guillotine upon the whole business." [51]

While British policy was still one of honoring the Japanese alliance in East Asia, there was little doubt that on the immigration question Britain stood with the United States. In a candid letter to James Bryce, then in the United States, Foreign Secretary Edward Grey noted in March 1908 that the situation concerning Japanese in Can-ada was critical. He did not think there would be war even if a Japa-nese exclusion law was passed in Canada or the United States. But the Pacific slope, he wrote, "is in a state of high fever, and what I fear is that a suspicion may arise among the people that, when the pinch comes, we shall not support them in resisting Japanese immigration. Should such a suspicion get hold of them, there would be no limit to the untoward political consequences which might ensue." Conse-quently, Grey assured the Canadians of London's full support in the matter. This did not mean that Grey would actually coordinate action with Roosevelt on the immigration question; but coming from one who sought to base his foreign policy upon solid understanding with the United States, such a statement ensured that, at least theoreti-cally, the Anglo-Japanese alliance would be not only inoperative but even nullified in the event of an immigration dispute leading to war across the Pacific.[52]

With America's leaders, writers, and the general public so preoccu-pied with the possibility of war with Japan, it is easy to see that the war scare of 1907 and afterward was not an isolated instance of local-ized hysteria but an expression of a national sentiment. The rising vogue of fictious writings, treating an imaginary war between the United States and Japan, was a product of this phenomenon. Homer Lea's *Valor of Ignorance*, for instance, had few ideas that had not al-ready been expressed publicly or privately by scores of Americans. Though not published till 1909, this book contained all the ingredi-ents of the new crisis literature that became prominent after the Russo-Japanese War. Lea argued, "At present, and for some time to come, there are only two powers, that can . . . enter into a war for the supremacy of the Pacific." This was because the two, the United States and Japan, were rapidly expanding into the region and eliminating competitors, the former through the acquisition of new territories, and the latter through its "predetermined march to the Empire of the Pacific." Lea characterized Japanese expansionism in a military way: "Japan has directed her undivided attention to that conflict which — should it end in victory — will give half the world over to the imperious barony of her daimios and samurai." The United States was the only power which, through its own expansionism, stood in the way of Japanese domination. The two expanding empires could possibly avoid conflict only if they were related racially, "with concomitant similarities in religious, ethical, and sociological conditions." But this was impossible because "to make the Japanese racial character in order to conform with that of the Occident would require, even were it possible, a longer period of time than we can conceive." If the two nations came closer, it would be only to "accentuate their racial ambitions, their perverse activities, their hates and their cries." Because of these inherent conflicts, the California immigration incidents were inevitable and could easily be turned into a *casus belli* by Japan. Unless the American people were alive to the danger, Lea warned, they would find Japanese forces conquering not only the Pacific possessions but also the West coast of the United States. Should it occur, "Japan would be placed in a naval and military position so invulnerable that no nation or coalition of them could attack her. Calmly, from this vast Gibraltar of the ocean, she could look down upon the world and smile at its rage and trepidation — this island tribe that owns no heaven and annoys no god." [53]

Homer Lea, despite his latter-day reputation as a sensational yellow-perilist, was essentially a detached observer of Japanese-American relations. He tended to be hysterical about the presence of Japanese on the West coast not because he disparaged them racially but because he thought Americans were blind to the danger of mistreating them. In a remarkably prescient passage he wrote, "To expect the Japanese to submit to indignities is to be pitifully incomprehensible of their national character. And the American people should realize that it is this cumulative memoranda of wrongs that they must, on some certain, sombre day, make answer to." [54]

Other writers were not so temperate. It was easy for them to picture the Japanese already in the United States as advance regiments of the army of invasion. Here Japanese immigration could be viewed as a vital part of Japan's military and territorial expansionism. Such was the imaginary novel written by Ernest Hugh Fitzpatrick, *The Coming Conflict of Nations, or The Japanese-American War*. Published in 1909 in Springfield, Illinois, the book depicts the deathly struggle of the two nations over control of the Pacific. As soon as war started from a small incident in San Francisco involving an American sailor and a Japanese attendant, the story goes, "whole regiments of Japanese sprang, as it were, out of the ground in the Pacific states, fully accoutered and equipped for war. The Japanese Government, foreseeing the possibility of such a rupture taking place, had previously sent over an army of fifty thousand soldiers disguised as coolies." According to the narrator, "With that secrecy so characteristic of the nation, they clouded their actions with a mystery so profound as to deceive the best informed, and at a timely moment they had thrown off their mysterious garb and exhibited themselves panoplied a giant for war." The Japanese, according to the story, won the initial naval victory and "insolently" demanded from the United States the cession of the Pacific states. The American people, however, were determined "never to yield to the Asiatics," since the war was seen as a struggle between "the western civilization of Europe and the ancient civilization of Asia." At that critical moment the British came to the aid of their kinsmen, who were but an "expansion of Anglo-Saxon civilization." As other Western nations maintained neutrality, the Anglo-American countries in the end won a decisive victory and delivered the world "from the yoke of an oriental civilization." When the war was over, the Anglo-Saxon army of occupation was welcomed with open arms by the Japanese, and the friendship was reciprocated! The postwar settlement was, moreover, far from unfavorable to the vanquished. The victors noted that "Japan's natural expansion lay in Asia, and that being an Asiatic power, it would be unjust to prevent her from expanding along her natural lines." This is a remarkable denouement on the part of the author, well aware of the different directions Japanese expansion was taking. Thus, the victorious nations concluded that "it would be unjust to Japan, after she had been prevented from exploiting the American Continent, to debar her entirely from her natural sphere, the Continent of Asia, where she could be engaged and her energies absorbed for centuries to come." [55]

Within but a handful of years Americans, from the President down to a semiliterate citizen, had discovered a Japanese menace. While not all agreed that armed conflict was inevitable, the view of Japan as a potential enemy rather than a friend of the United States was already widely held. All this was extremely disconcerting to at least one American who had been a symbol of close Japanese-American ties: D. W. Stevens, adviser to the Foreign Ministry in Tokyo. Writing to Rear Admiral Willard H. Brownson, chief of the Navy Department's bureau of navigation, at the end of 1907, Stevens poured out his sadness at the recent turn of events. The "genuine cordial friendship of Japan," he wrote, had been one of the most valuable assets of the United States. This friendly sentiment was still so strong that the Japanese would never dream of going to war over the immigration question. However, if stringent restrictions were put into effect, "it would be self deception to expect that the Japanese people will continue to entertain for us the same cordial friendship and belief in our good will which at present exist." Even then, Stevens was confident that there would be no war, and "the Philippines and Hawaiian Islands will be as safe from attack then as they always have been." The United States would not lose the islands, but it would forfeit the warm respect the Japanese had entertained for it. It was a pity, he concluded, that anti-Japanese measures should be taken and ideas expressed in response to a belief in "dangers largely illusory." [56]

If there was illusion in the apprehension about Japanese invasion, the fact remained that the changed relationship between the two peoples reflected their greater contact as a result of mutual expansion. Both were expanding nations, and unless they could peacefully interact and live together where they met, distrust and suspicion were bound to arise. No wonder, then, that some were convinced that the only way to maintain amicable relations was to divert Japanese expansion away from the Pacific to the continent of Asia. Such was the solution of Fitzpatrick's imaginary war, which ended when Japan was guaranteed suzerainty over Manchuria, eastern Siberia, and Kamchatka, and when the United States joined with other English-speaking nations to form a gigantic Anglo-Saxon federation. The only problem was that certain Americans wanted to expand into the continent of Asia.

VII

The Role of China

Japan's eyes "for some time to come will be directed toward Korea and southern Manchuria." So wrote President Roosevelt to Leonard Wood, governor-general of the Philippines, early in 1906. The inference was that Japan would have no interest in moving southward or eastward.[1] The California crisis later in the year severely tested the President's optimism, but throughout the remainder of his administration he held to the conviction that recognizing Japan's special interests in East Asia would provide that country with sufficient reason to abstain from threatening the West coast and American possessions in the Pacific. The idea was not limited to Roosevelt. In July 1907 Assistant Secretary of State Huntington Wilson expressed confidence that "the Japanese Government would prefer that its people should migrate to Korea, where Japan has such a great work to do, and [would not be] averse to the cessation of the immigration of laborers and petty tradesmen into this country."[2] With a similar end in mind Ambassador Thomas J. O'Brien in Tokyo confided to Foreign Minister Hayashi Tadasu that "it could hardly be for the interest of Japan to allow the young adventurous men of the country to emigrate, and that the logical policy . . . would be to keep them within the country's own domain by sending them to Manchuria, Formosa, Korea, etc."[3]

Being a universalistic expansionist, in theory at least, Hayashi rejected this argument, saying the Japanese "much preferred to go to the United States on account of the better wages." Public opinion generally supported him. His successor, however, came around to accepting the American view. Komura Jutarō, who returned to the Foreign Ministry in July 1908, had observed the evolution of postwar international relations as ambassador to the Court of St. James's. Shortly after assuming office, he penned his thoughts on the immediate needs of Japanese foreign policy. He defined the two cardinal goals of policy as "the maintenance of peace" and "the expansion of national strength." The former concerned alliances, ententes, and other kinds of traditional diplomacy, through an adroit handling of which he thought peace could be maintained and security preserved. The second was the core of his concern, and one in which he obviously felt sufficient progress had not been achieved since the war. On a scrap of paper which probably served as an outline for his larger memorandum, he jotted down six areas in which Japan had to establish basic policies to promote its expansion: trade, navigation, emigration restriction, joint ventures, fishing, and the communications industry. Clearly, Komura was not an enthusiastic advocate of emigration overseas if it involved political risks and undermined commercial relations. According to him, the expansion of trade and industry had a long way to go, and the nation needed to concentrate its effort on preserving and developing existing markets, encouraging the growth of shipping, introducing advanced Western technology, and otherwise maintaining friendly relations with the countries that were tied commercially to Japan. Under the circumstances, to force Japanese immigrants on unwilling hosts such as the United States, Canada, and Australia was not wise; it could undermine the much more important trade relationship among them. Moreover, the continent of Asia was beckoning, and the Japanese should settle there first rather than dispersing to the four corners of the earth.[4]

Such thinking, which became official policy when Komura's memorandum was adopted *in toto* by the cabinet of Katsura Tarō in September, fitted well with the United States government's desire to see Japanese expansion turn westward. With his characteristic frankness and clarity Komura told Ambassador O'Brien that "there was ample territory under the jurisdiction of Japan where [laborers] could find employment, and that it would be for the interest of the country to develop its own resources and not allow their most ambitious, capable adventurous young people to go elsewhere; that Japan had no interest in populating the United States, and desired only to continue and to increase international trade." [5] This was the policy of "concentrating on Manchuria and Korea," later the subject of much criticism in Japan.

By 1908 continentalism had become a prominent feature of Japan's postwar foreign relations, and the Japanese did not have to be reminded that Asia offered an inviting opportunity for expansion. But continental expansionism took on new meaning when it became more and more evident that there were limits to the peaceful migration of Japanese eastward. In frustration over the spread of anti-Japanese sentiment in the West, some writers in Japan were reacting with a pan-Asianist response. Tōgō Minoru argued in his *Nihon shokumin-ron* (On Japanese colonization) that, while Japanese emigration and overseas settlement should not be based on racial considerations, the fact could not be ignored that Japanese expansion into white countries was being thwarted by yellow-perilist and white-supremacist talk; should it persist, the Japanese as a last resort would have to be prepared to champion the yellow race and compete with white peoples. "At a time when only the whites seem to be predominant in the world, our Japanese nation should be ready to exhibit its genius at colonization and struggle for supremacy in the world." Japan could stand on its own as an Asian nation that had been Westernized. "Our country embodies all the virtues of East and West, and it is destined to coalesce and harmonize them in order to create a great Asian civilization." Japan would ultimately be the victor in the world struggle, as it would naturally expand into and control the Asian continent, the area where a new civilization, born of the assimilation of East and West, was to be created. The Japanese, therefore, must be prepared to start with Korea, expand to Manchuria, and eventually establish a dominant position in the rest of Asia.[6]

Such an exclusively pan-Asianist, particularistic response, however, was rather rare in the years immediately following the Russo-Japanese War. While Japanese self-consciously talked of their continental thrust, this was by no means considered the sole goal of postwar expansion. Also, continentalism was more often an ideal than an achievement, and the Japanese learned there were as many obstacles as opportunities in East Asia, just as there were in the Pacific. To complicate matters further, one of the obstacles was the growing American interest in China, an interest that could collide with Japanese expansionism just as the latter was being frustrated on the American continent.

To understand the magnitude of the Japanese-American crisis in all of its dimensions, it is necessary to recall that not enough had been achieved by the Japanese in China and Manchuria to justify faith in continentalism as the basic goal of expansion. "In 1905," *Tokyo Nichinichi* recalled in its editorial of January 1, 1906, "Japan accomplished unprecedented deeds, emerging victorious in an Asian struggle and joining the ranks of the great world powers. . . . The nation's status rose rapidly, the powers' respect for it increased, and Japan came to be viewed as endowed with both quality and quantity to become the leader of Asia." The nation was emerging as a predominant continental power, with a special position of influence in Korea, Manchuria, and China.[7] In actuality, however, it was only in Korea that Japanese control was undisputed and the objectives of its power well defined. Korea after 1905 was, for all practical purposes, a Japanese colony, maintained by force in the interests of Japanese security and economy. The army and police force maintained law and order, while great numbers of merchants, profiteers, and laborers flocked to the peninsula. The Japanese population in Korea soon outstripped that in the United States, reaching 210,000 in 1911. The United States did nothing to counter the trend, pleased that at least in one area of the world American policy could support Japanese ambitions.[8]

In Manchuria the basis of Japanese prerogatives was of course the presence of its armed forces. The role of the army of occupation was described in the "Principles for Carrying out Military Government," issued by the Kwantung military government in April 1906. This military regime was in control of administration within areas leased to Japan after the war — primarily Kwantung Leased Territory and the areas on both sides of the South Manchuria Railway. The "Principles" declared the aims of military government to be the protection of existing rights and promotion of "the residents' expansion." Whenever there developed a favorable opportunity for extending rights and interests, the military government was to lend its support. More specifically, the military force under its jurisdiction was to help maintain roads, bridges, and the sanitary system in the areas covered by the territorial government, and to "control the affairs of the residents, encourage their system of credit, and remove monopolistic practices." It was provided that the military regime should establish a system of justice to regulate commercial and social affairs of the Japanese residents. All in all, the occupation of Manchuria was designed to aim at extending Japanese interests. According to the "Principles," Manchuria was not Japanese territory, "but in administering it we should consider it a Japanese domain." [9]

This frankly colonialist policy toward Manchuria was not long maintained. It was opposed by the civilian government in Tokyo as too militaristic. As a result the military government was abolished in October 1906, and Japanese troops withdrawn by April 1907, leaving only forces necessary to protect the South Manchuria Railway. [10]

Since the primarily military phase of postwar continentalism was destined to be short-lived, plans were under way to entrench Japanese interests in Manchuria on a more permanent basis. By everyone's reckoning, the most crucial instrument was the railway, in particular the South Manchuria Railway, that portion of the southern branch of the Chinese Eastern Railway between Changchun and Port Arthur that had been ceded by Russia. Gotō Shinpei, the first president of the South Manchuria Railway, typified the economic expansionist approach. He objected to the emphasis on military government in Manchuria and felt Japan's continental expansionism, just like expansion in other parts of the world, should be founded on economic considerations and on much firmer grounds than exigencies of preparedness for another war. In numerous writings and speeches at this time he reiterated the widespread thesis that the foundation of national power was economic, not military, and that economic strengthening was the surest guarantee for national security and expansion. According to his "economic strategy," which resembled the thinking of many other postwar expansionists, Japan must "promote industry, train people in commerce and trade, and obtain peaceful technological knowledge from abroad." Such a proposition was based on his interpretation of the postwar world. He shared the perception held by so many of his countrymen that physical warfare was being replaced by economic competition and that the world powers were spending more and more on commercial expansion and less and less on armament. Japan excelled in the art of war, but was unprepared for the "peaceful warfare" in which other peoples seemed to be engaged. Thus, he would oppose the perpetuation of military government in Manchuria and establish an integrated civilian-military colonial office with a view to making the region a gigantic sphere for economic enterprises. He would invite foreign business and trade, which would enrich the region and increase foreigners' confidence in Japan. He would even make Port Arthur into a commercial port and demolish naval installations there.[11]

The South Manchuria Railway, in the thinking of Gotō and of those who appointed him to its presidency in 1906, was to be the mainstay of Japanese expansionism in Manchuria. Through Japan's control over the major trunk line of south Manchuria, it was expected that the nation's commercial interests would be expanded, the Manchurian economy developed, and Japanese manpower and capital entrench themselves in the region, thus making the area an integral economic part of the homeland. Gotō was hopeful that as many as a million Japanese would migrate to Manchuria and engage in agriculture and mining. Their presence would perpetuate Japan's hold on Manchuria, which would become part of an extended Japanese empire. Since capital was scarce, Gotō welcomed foreign investment to foster economic development of the area. He encouraged foreign travelers and businessmen to come to Manchuria, built modern hotels for their comfort, obtained British loans for rebuilding and expanding the operation of the South Manchuria Railway, and purchased rolling stock and locomotives from the United States.[12] This did not mean, however, that all foreign enterprise was welcome. The South Manchuria Railway, backed by the Japanese government, adamantly opposed Chinese or foreign construction of railways that could seriously compete with the Japanese railway.

One of the first issues in Japan's new railway imperialism was the Chinese plan for the construction of a railway between Hsinmintun and Fakumen. These were cities to the west and north of Mukden, on the other side of the Liao, a major river in south Manchuria. The railway, if constructed, would have traversed less than one hundred kilometers, but since Hsinmintun was already linked to the major Chinese port of Tientsin by railway and to the Manchurian port of Yingkou (Newchwang) by river, the new railway could bring the rich agricultural area around Fakumen closer to these central cities. Furthermore, if extended further northward, the line could reach central and northern Manchurian cities and bring the commerce of these regions within reach of north China. Obviously, such a railway, running almost exactly parallel to the South Manchuria Railway, would compete with it. Future projects by the South Manchuria Railway in western Manchuria and, beyond, Inner Mongolia, could be jeopardized. The Japanese government, in close touch with the South Manchuria Railway, repeatedly protested to China against the premeditated construction.[13]

According to a study made by the South Manchuria Railway in 1908, about 1,300,000 tons of soybeans, the major agricultural export product of Manchuria, were shipped to the southern ports of Dairen and Yingkou. Of this volume it was estimated that 850,000 tons were carried by the South Manchuria Railway, and the rest by horse-driven cart or by junk on the Liao River. About 80 percent of the entire amount was produced in areas north of Tieling, a city north of Mukden on the South Manchuria Railway. Assuming that the soybeans produced in the area around Tieling were in part diverted to Fakumen, which was only thirty miles west of Tieling, it could be estimated that about 30 percent of the 850,000 tons shipped via the South Manchuria Railway in 1908 would now be sent south on the new Chinese railway. Other products would likewise be diverted to the Hsinmintun-Fakumen line, as well as goods imported into Manchuria. Most Chinese laborers, who came seasonally from Shantung province to work on land in Manchuria and who provided the bulk of passengers for the South Manchuria Railway, could be expected to patronize the proposed Chinese railway. For all these reasons, it was concluded that the loss to the Japanese railway in the event of the construction of the Hsinmintun-Fakumen line would exceed 6,600,000 yen annually. What was most feared, however, was the possibility that the continued expansion of Japanese interests would be stifled by the presence of the Chinese railway to the west of the South Manchuria Railway. Western and northern Manchuria, Jehol Special District, and beyond it Inner Mongolia were considered areas full of economic potentialities. This business would be lost to the South Manchuria Railway if the Chinese started building their own railways.[14]

The railway question revealed several vital issues connected with postwar Japanese continentalism. It showed the tendency of Japan's expansionists to think in terms of the future rather than the immediate present. For instance, the loss of 3 million dollars of revenue to the South Manchuria Railway was in itself not very serious. In terms of the immediate damage to the carrying business of the railway in south Manchuria, Chinese construction of a parallel line did not seem excessively alarming.[15] But the Japanese wanted to make sure that they could continue to expand in Manchuria. Ironically, the future was, if anything, more uncertain because of the rising sentiment of Chinese nationalism. Intent on redeeming railway concessions from foreigners, the Chinese were in no mood to give up their own railway development just because it would undermine Japanese profits. Finally, whether they looked to the present or to the future, the Japanese had to admit that they lacked sufficient capital to promote their interests single-handedly. They needed foreign capital, but in such a way as to further promote Japanese enterprises. Foreign capitalists, however, were showing a great deal of interest in helping Chinese construction of railways, and a British firm was backing the Hsinmintun-Fakumen scheme.[16] It was imperative not to antagonize foreigners and yet at the same time to make sure they would not stifle Japan's own expansion.

All in all, there was a serious gap between continentalism as an expectation and as an achievement. Policy was geared to the vision of the future, but Chinese nationalism and the lack of domestic capital were realities, and it was no accident that much postwar Japanese writing about continental expansion addressed itself to these questions. There was a serious division of opinion. In view of the shortage of capital, some advocated retrenchment, not of continentalism itself, but of the political and military structure that accompanied it. *Tokyo Nichinichi* called for curtailment of the personnel of the Kwantung territorial government and questioned the wisdom of postwar tax increases and public loans to pay for enlarged military establishments. The assumption was that without such a superstructure Japanese interests could expand economically and peacefully under the condition of free and fair competition. Japanese merchants were urged to "abide by commercial ethics, refrain from seeking immediate profits, think of future and long-standing benefits, and carry on large-scale enterprises." Japanese expansion could and should be undertaken without undue governmental protection and particularistic arrangements, so that it would not be irreconcilable with the policy of obtaining foreign capital and goodwill. The important thing was not governmental supervision and intervention on behalf of private interests, but the ability of individual Japanese to engage successfully in peaceful competition.[17] *Tōyō keizai shinpō*, reflecting business opinion, persistently called for reduction of armament. According to it, Japanese interests could be promoted without enlarged military establishments in view of the absence of an immediate threat to national security. Increased armed forces would only burden the national economy when the limited resources of the nation required that they be concentrated on the development of industry and trade.[18]

Others more frankly called for continued and increased government supervision of Japanese interests. Typical views were expressed in the pages of a monthly, *Jitsugyō sekai Taiheiyō* (The Pacific Ocean: the business world). For instance, Kaneko Kentarō noted that only through protectionism could Japan hope to foster the growth of domestic industry and expand trade.[19] Another writer called for business combines, which could pool resources and provide sufficient capital for commercial and industrial expansion.[20] A third article talked of the need for the government to step in vigorously so as to enable Japanese merchants in Manchuria to compete successfully with the Chinese. This involved facilitating credit arrangements and granting rebates to Japanese merchants shipping goods on Japanese ships and railways.[21]

Whether advocates of governmental supervision or retrenchment, all were agreed that the actual achievements in the years immediately after the war were less than spectacular. Statistically, it is true, Japanese trade with Manchuria showed impressive gains. In 1905 Japan sold only 2 million tael worth of cotton cloth to China, mostly Manchuria, but after the war the amount steadily increased until it reached over 18 million tael in 1913, equivalent to 18.1 percent of the total Chinese purchase of cotton cloth. Japanese cotton manufacturers and trade companies actively cooperated to extend the export trade. In 1906 they organized a cotton cloth export union to pool their resources. The Yokohama Specie Bank undertook the financing of the union's activities, and the South Manchuria Railway gave rebates on the goods shipped on its cars. Because military occupation lasted until September 1906, Japanese merchants could take advantage of the temporary absence of foreign merchants. Most wartime restrictions on foreign commerce were removed after the fall of 1906, but the initial impetus given to Japanese commerce served to expand that trade in Manchuria.[22]

There was little evidence, however, that Manchuria would be turned into a preserve for Japan's economic expansion. The number of Japanese did not grow rapidly, and obstacles to their activities were legion. As in America, one problem was the nature of the Japanese who migrated. Another was the local situation inhibiting Japanese enterprise. Merchants and servants had gone to Manchuria with the army during the war, and many of them stayed on, forming the core of the initial Japanese population. They were followed by a postwar influx of others in search of quick returns and large profits out of meager investments. "Those with money and resources don't seem to go," wrote Uchida Yasuya, former minister to China, lamenting the fact that "not a few people have gone to China who are simply speculating on gaining immediate riches out of nothing, or who are ambitious adventurers." [23] Yamaza Enjirō, the powerful and popular chief of the political affairs bureau of the Foreign Ministry, agreed. Too many Japanese went to Manchuria with only labor and ambitions and little capital; they were not likely to find success, he warned.[24] These impressions were corroborated by evidence gathered by official agencies. One of the strongest indictments of Japanese in Manchuria at this time was a report submitted by the South Manchuria Railway to the Foreign Ministry in the fall of 1907. It talked of cases of corruption and inefficiency, contributing to maladministration of the newly acquired rights and ill feeling between Japanese and Chinese residents. Japanese officials in the Wusun mines, which the Japanese army had taken over from the Russian management but which the Chinese had not formally granted the right to Japan to mine, were reported to be corrupt and incompetent. Together with the Yentai mines, Wusun was a major coal-producing mine in south Manchuria, and its use was considered essential by the Japanese. As of 1907, however, production was at a standstill.[25]

The report by the South Manchuria Railway noted with disgust the presence of Japanese without stable occupations or incomes. These "hangers-on" were the first of the notorious "Manshū rōnin" (idlers in Manchuria) who came to characterize the Japanese rule of south Manchuria. Some were former interpreters. As many as 3,000 interpreters had accompanied the army during the war, and most of them remained in Manchuria after 1905. There were known cases of bribery; some interpreters working for the military establishment would solicit and receive bribes from Chinese, spend the quickly obtained wealth, and wander to another place to seek a fortune. "The most contemptible of the lot," the report said, were former politicians and merchants who had been employed in Manchuria during the war and had found no jobs in Japan after the war. They were back, but since they were not trusted by their fellow countrymen in Manchuria they approached the Chinese and engaged in illegal practices under the guise of joint enterprises. They often cheated Chinese capitalists of their money, and they ran brothels and pawnshops. Their presence had damaged Japan's reputation in China, but Japanese authorities, the report complained, had not dealt rigorously enough with them. Then there were Japanese from Taiwan, Korea, and north China who claimed some expertise and found themselves jobs as advisers and counselors for the newly established Kwantung Territorial government.

Apart from these transients, the South Manchuria Railway was a major employer of Japanese. Several thousand officials recruited to operate and administer the railway had come from similar positions in Japan. There were also lesser functionaries such as conductors, station attendants, and those in charge of shipment of goods. They could wield tremendous influence by taking advantage of postwar confusion in Manchuria. They stole goods from cars, demanded squeezes in return for their services such as the renting of locomotives and sale of Wusun coal, and arbitrarily refused shipment of merchandise. There was also cutthroat competition among shipping agencies engaged in transporting goods to and from the railway stations.[26]

Many of the problems facing Japanese in Manchuria, however, were derived from local conditions. Chinese labor was cheap and abundant, and the only advantage the Japanese enjoyed, unless they brought with them substantial sums of money, was their connection with the semicolonial establishments of the South Manchuria Railway, the Kwantung Leased Territory, and the Japanese army. But, unlike Korea, opportunities in Manchuria were limited because Japan had no legal control over territories outside the Kwantung leasehold and the areas along the South Manchuria Railway. Even here the problem of land ownership was extremely involved, and no clear treaty right defined land ownership or leasehold by Japanese. Local Chinese merchants already had a well-developed system of credits and marketing, which could not be easily mastered by foreigners. Japanese merchants could sell goods to other Japanese, but this did not result in any expansion of the indigenous market. The Chinese in Manchuria, a Japanese observer pointed out, "are alert, patient, well versed in conditions in Manchuria, and their standards of living are low. They are physically adjusted to the climate, and in many other ways they are superior to Japanese merchants, who find it extremely difficult to com-

pete with them." As for manual laborers, each year hundreds of thousands of Chinese, especially from Shantung, came north to work in
Manchuria. There was little opportunity for laborers from Japan who,
if anything, demanded higher wages.[27]

The situation in China proper was even less promising for speedy
Japanese expansion. The anticipated growth of the China market
never materialized. But Japanese writers and businessmen never tired
of pointing out the importance of the opening up of China as a fabu-
lous market, especially as it went through what appeared to be institu-
tional reforms and economic modernization. In an editorial entitled
"The future of China as seen from an economic standpoint," *Tōyō
keizai shinpō* asserted in June 1907 that the Chinese market was on
the verge of phenomenal expansion, as railways were being built and
all areas of the interior of China became accessible to foreign goods.
"This great expansion of the Chinese economy will be a boon not
only to the Chinese but also to mankind as a whole, and the Japanese,
in particular, stand to benefit from it in view of their geographical
proximity and economic closeness to China." It was hoped that they
would lead the way in the rejuvenation of China so that the two peoples could closely cooperate and consolidate their economic partner-
ship.[28] Another writer, describing "an economic alliance between
Japan and China," alluded to the opening of China's riches to the
world as a result of the removal of Russian control. If the two peoples
could pool their resources, however insignificant an individual's capital accumulation, there would be a huge amount of money that could
be invested in Chinese industry, trade, and transportation.[29]

Chinese imports (thousands of tael)

Year	Total	From Japan	Percentage of total
1905	447,100	61,315	13.7
1906	410,270	61,052	14.9
1907	416,501	57,461	13.8
1908	394,505	52,500	13.3
1909	418,158	59,975	14.3

Source: *Shina kindai no seiji keizai* (Modern China's politics and economy),
Nikka Jitsugyō Kyōkai, ed. (Tokyo, 1931), pp. 198–209.

Unfortunately, there was no great expansion of China's import trade after the Russo-Japanese War. In fact there had been greater expansion before the war. Between 1894 and 1904 the value of imports in tael had more than doubled. But after the war the rate of increase was much more moderate. The table shows the story. Between 1906, a lean year, and 1909, the value of imports in tael remained stationary, even registering a decline in 1908. With the overall size of the market stationary, it was not surprising that there was actually a steady decline in Japanese sales to China in the immediate postwar years in the tael value of trade. This did not mean that the export trade dropped in terms of the yen, which was linked to gold. Trade transactions in China were carried out in silver, rather than in gold, so that the value of trade did not necessarily reflect fluctuations in the volume of trade. For instance, if the price of silver vis-à-vis gold rose, the same item imported from Japan would be worth less in terms of the tael. At any rate, there was no increase in Japan's share of the China market at this time.[30]

The forecast that, as China changed, its demand for foreign capital would grow did not prove true at this time. If anything, the forces of change within China tended to be economically nationalistic. Merchants, gentry, and intellectuals stressed "rights recovery" and the need to develop China's own industry and railways. Province after province enacted laws and regulations severely restricting the right of foreigners to engage in mining and other kinds of enterprises. The anti-American boycott of 1905 had shown that the Chinese had the will as well as organizational framework to refuse to buy from foreigners. Foreign loans were still resorted to — especially in order to buy back the concessions that had been given out earlier — but there was growing opposition to loans as infringements on China's freedom and sovereignty. At a time when tension was developing between the court circles in Peking and the provincial leaders, and between various political factions at both levels, negotiations for foreign loans were looked upon with suspicion, as they could be diverted to political and military use.[31]

For all these reasons, the much heralded coming of a new period of Japanese expansion into China never materialized. If the Japanese were not aware of the depth of nationalistic and antiforeign sentiment in China, they were soon forced to the realization through such incidents as the Buddhist missionary controversy and the *Tatsu Maru* incident. In the case of Japanese Buddhist missionaries, Chinese official and public opinion seems to have exaggerated Japan's ambitions. According to a 1908 survey conducted by Japanese consuls throughout China, there were only about thirty-five Buddhist preachers from Japan engaged in proselytization in China. They lacked numerical strength and financial resources to undertake any project of long-lasting nature. Yet from the Tokyo government's point of view, even such a beginning was significant as a symbol of expansion. The missionaries, Consul General Segawa Asanoshin in Canton wrote, could serve important functions as gatherers of information on local conditions, guides to Japanese travelers, teachers of Chinese youths, transmitters of Japan's influence, and otherwise as intermediaries between the two countries.[32] At a time when Western Christian missionary activities were being vigorously promoted, the Japanese could not give up their right to do likewise, just because it was Buddhism, not Christianity, that they wanted to proselytize among Chinese.[33] But Chinese authorities and local leaders continued to discourage and often obstruct by force the building of schools and temples by Japanese Buddhists. After the abolition of the traditional examination system in 1905, the Chinese were establishing a new system of education, and were prone to object to any action by foreigners that seemed to interfere with the process. The lack of compromise and understanding on this issue, which involved no use or threat of use of force by Japan, revealed the hollowness of the talk about postwar cooperation between Japan and China.[34]

The threat of force, however, became an issue in 1908 with the *Tatsu Maru* incident. The *Tatsu Maru*, a Japanese freighter, had left Kobe with a consignment of arms, equipped with legal papers but probably intended for smuggling into China via Macao. These arms could find their way to anti-Manchu revolutionaries in South China. To stop the flow of arms to these revolutionaries, Chinese officials seized the ship off Macao, at a location which Japanese and Portuguese both claimed was Portuguese territory. The Japanese flag was hauled down and the arms were confiscated. The Japanese government protested strongly, on the grounds that the ship was engaged in legal traffic and was not even in Chinese waters. The basic principle involved was that of treaty rights, and the Chinese action seemed to infringe upon Japan's right to engage in legal trade. Using strong

pressure and intimating the threat of force, Japan compelled the Waiwupu to agree to humiliating terms: apology, punishment of responsible officials, reparations for damages done to the ship, and payment
for the confiscated arms (which were to be transferred to the Chinese
government).[35]

Such developments aroused Chinese nationalistic reaction. Public
opinion in Canton was immediately mobilized with a view to retaliation. The Self-government Association, founded in 1907, served as a
useful apparatus as the merchants once again discussed reprisal. In-
censed by the terms of the *Tatsu Maru* settlement, the association resolved in late March to boycott Japanese goods and services. As in the
case of the anti-American boycott of 1905, Canton's leaders had
strong political views; one of them, Hsü Ch'in, was a member of the
Political Culture Association, founded in 1907 by the constitutional-
ists. Under the leadership of the Self-government Association mass
rallies were organized to protest against the "national disgrace," and
handbills were distributed to enjoin the people to support the boycott. Again as in 1905 the boycotters attempted to keep the movement within reasonable bounds; they stressed that it was a civilized
method of protest and cautioned people not to resort to "uncivilized
tactics." However, the Chinese merchants did not simply seek to modify the terms of the *Tatsu Maru* settlement, although it was naturally
humiliating that foreigners should smuggle arms into their country,
contributing to disturbances and disorder, and that their government
should consent to punish officials under foreign pressure. But the boycotters also talked of rights recovery. A "song of national disgrace" exhorted the people to stir themselves, assert their rights, enhance the
national reputation, and reach the level attained by civilized
countries.[36]

In Japan, just before the outbreak of the *Tatsu Maru* incident, the
opposition party, Shinpotō, held a national congress and resolved to
push the government toward realization of postwar expansionism.
Ōishi Masami, now the party's senior member, accused the government of having failed in the objective of promoting the extension of
Japanese rights and interests in China. This, and the passive response
to America's infringement on Japanese rights in California indicated,
he said, that the Saionji cabinet had not carried out the tasks assigned
to it by public opinion.[37] The expansion of rights and interests in

China of course had been attempted by the government, but it had not achieved the desired end because there was as yet no overall strategy and no clear thinking to cope with changing events in China.

"The way to deal with China," Foreign Minister Hayashi had written, "is for the Powers to combine and insist on what they want and to go on insisting until they get it." He showed little understanding of the currents of nationalism in that country. He believed that the Chinese had always been and remained essentially an antiforeign people, confident of their superiority. "It is impossible to obtain anything from the Chinese merely by argument or through mollifying them; one has to add pressure and threats." He hastened to add that there was no point in unnecessarily irritating them; humanitarian considerations alone dictated that Japan deal politely and compassionately. But there was no point in appealing to their sentimentality or to their reason. The foreign minister did not change his views even after the *Tatsu Maru* incident. He was at a loss to understand why the Chinese should boycott Japanese goods just on account of an insignificant incident.[38]

Somewhat in contrast was Minister Hayashi Gonsuke in Peking, who served in the post between 1906 and 1908. He reflected the thinking of Japanese diplomats in China, who as a whole took developments there more seriously than their superiors in Tokyo. Minister Hayashi believed that Japan should pay the utmost attention to China's nationalism and critical political conditions. Specifically, he felt Japan should present itself as China's friend, in sympathy with Chinese national aspirations and with the central government in trying to realize them. The rights-recovery movement was "a natural sentiment accompanying the rise of national self-awareness," he wrote, and it was futile to suppress it. Japan should rather seek to take advantage of it by respecting this sentiment and "guiding" the expression of Chinese nationalism. "The consolidation and expansion of the rights we gained in Manchuria after the war must depend on the friendship of the Chinese government and people." Japan should give up insisting on minor rights and avoid giving the impression of avariciously exploiting China. Rather, only the most vital rights should be pushed, again in the spirit of cooperative undertaking with the Chinese. Regarding China's domestic politics, Japan should maintain close relations with Chinese leaders in Peking and in the provinces, so as to win their confidence in case some critical developments should occur.[39]

Minister Hayashi's ideas showed an approach different in emphasis from that of Foreign Minister Hayashi who stressed standing on treaty rights and acting together with other powers. Both were interested in expansion, but the former would do so through working with the Chinese, whereas the latter was more inclined to unilateralism as well as to imperialist collaboration. The trouble was that Minister Hayashi's approach was more easily advocated than carried out. As a way to practice the policy of working together with the Chinese, he suggested the establishment of close ties with high Chinese officials, especially Yüan Shih-k'ai, but events proved the futility of this idea. Not only did top Chinese leaders fight among themselves, but most of them found it increasingly difficult to retain power. Wider and wider circles of men were asserting their right to participate in politics and power. Still, Minister Hayashi showed greater appreciation of the force of nationalism in China than his superiors, and believed Japan should impress the Chinese with its readiness to be reasonable concerning the protection and extension of rights. Essentially, such an approach came down to stressing the economic aspect of Japanese expansionism and de-emphasizing political and military aspects.[40]

Most of Japan's postwar expansionists could not have agreed more with such emphasis on the peaceful, economic character of Japanese interests. But because the result of postwar economic expansion was meager, and there was as yet little to show by way of the entrenchment of Japanese interests in China and Manchuria, it was not surprising that voices should now be heard calling for a more vigorous policy. However, there was also a new factor: deliberate American opposition to Japan's expansion on the Asian continent. The postwar era was marked by the rise in America of a view of Asia that emphasized Chinese-American intimacy and implied a change in Japanese-American relations. The image of Japanese-American competition and conflict in China for the first time emerged clearly. Recognition of this rivalry clarified for observers in the United States the basic issues involved in its expansion in the East, while the resulting tension placed another obstacle in the way of Japanese expansion.

Perhaps the clearest expression of the belief in a fundamental conflict between Japan and the United States in China after the Russo-Japanese War was Thomas F. Millard's influential book, *America and the Far Eastern Question*, published in 1909. Having been a correspondent in China and close observer of the East Asian scene during and after the war, Millard became a spokesman for the group of Americans who were calling for a vigorous governmental policy to counter what they saw as the danger of Japanese hegemony over the Asian mainland. In this book he asserts that the United States "has reached a crisis of its industrial development. . . . [We] have come to a point when we must seek an outlet in new markets or soon see industrial conditions in America arrive at a state of arrested progress." If such an argument for economic expansion sounds dated, the panacea he offers is even more so: trade with Asia. He reiterates the familiar argument that, "in scanning the world for the commercial opportunity necessary for [economic expansion], the eyes of our statesmen cannot fail to turn to the East." These time-worn ideas, however, are given new meaning when Millard juxtaposes them with another idea, that "Japan's goal is commercial supremacy in the whole East." This means competing with and defeating Western enterprises and establishing industrial hegemony over China. "Industrial domination of China" is called "an objective of Japan's economic policy," and to compete with Western influence Japan is pictured as employing unfair practices such as secret remissions of taxes and customs duties to Japanese merchants, rebates of transportation charges, the exercise of military and political authority to handicap competitors, and the imitation and counterfeiting of competing articles. Millard further argues that the Japanese regard America "as Japan's most formidable future competitor among western nations." This is because the United States "produces at home the greater part of raw materials needed for extensive industrial organization, and has cheap and convenient access to eastern Asia; benefits not possessed in the same degree by any European nation."

Such being the case, Millard continues, the Japanese know that they cannot possibly compete with American economic power under conditions of free and fair competition; hence the need to use all military and diplomatic means to gain an upper hand. As evidence he cites the alleged policy pursued by the military authorities in Manchuria to exclude foreign merchants and commerce from the occupied areas. "I am convinced," he writes, "that almost from the moment a locality [in Manchuria] was occupied by Japanese armies it was the deliberate and calculated effort of Japan to use her possession of these territories to establish and advance her commercial interests." The result has been the impairment of Chinese sovereignty and the violation of the principle of the open door. Under the circumstances, the West may well consider "whether further extension of Japan's trade policy, as expressed by its prevailing commercial ethics, can be reconciled to western interests in the East." The United States in particular is in a crucial position because of its great economic strength. "If American diplomacy actively interests itself in preserving the integrity of China and the 'open door,' it will be very difficult for Japan's policy to continue to make headway."

This last assertion is worth noting. Unless the United States government bestirred itself on behalf of the open door, American commerce would lose to Japan, inasmuch as that country was willing to use all means to promote its own interests. Millard implies that the United States must make an effort to counter Japan because the two nations' interests were diametrically opposed in East Asia. Japanese-American amity, he says, would never be restored to its previous condition even if the vexing immigration dispute were somehow solved. Because of Japanese continentalism, relations between the two countries had entered a wholly new phase. "It is perhaps not going too far to say that relations of America and Japan are only now becoming serious, in the sense that they directly include propositions about which modern nations, upon due provocation, go to war." Here Millard's diagnosis reaches a philosophical level, and he sees conflict as existing even before Japanese continentalism. The two nations were in conflict, and Japan demonstrated the fact by its acts on the Asian continent. Such a view could not have been arrived at without corresponding images about events in China and about America's role in East Asia.[41]

To what extent there was "rivalry" between Japanese and American expansionism on the Asian continent is a moot question. Writers then and since, in the United States and Japan as well as in China and other countries, have repeated the argument that Japan's policy of aggressive economic penetration of Manchuria and China conflicted with American business activities and the policy of the open door. Soviet historians of American-East Asian relations such as A. Dobrov, G. Sevostianov, and L. N. Zubok have stressed that American-Russian rivalry in China and Manchuria was replaced by Japanese-American competition after the Russo-Japanese War. This was because, in their view, American business interests that had sought expansion in Asia by supporting Japanese resistance to Tsarist Russian imperialism were confronted with a new situation: the attack on the open door doctrine by Japanese imperialism. The United States was not ready to go to war, but it did everything to step up its expansionist activities in China. The implication is that the Japanese-American war of 1941 was an inevitable outcome of the two nations' contradictory policies and interests in China, a conclusion which is widely held even by those who do not share the Soviet authors' Marxist premises.[42]

United States trade with China and Japan (millions of dollars)

Year	China		Japan		Total U.S. trade	
	Exports	Imports	Exports	Imports	Exports	Imports
1905	53	28	52	52	1,518	1,117
1906	44	28	38	52	1,744	1,226
1907	26	33	39	69	1,881	1,434
1908	22	26	41	68	1,861	1,194
1909	19	29	27	70	1,663	1,312

Source: *Statistical Abstract of the United States*, ed. Department of Commerce and Labor (Washington, D.C., 1909).

There is little doubt that both the United States and Japan were engaged in expansionist policies and activities in China. But in the immediate postwar years their interests collided more in the realm of imagination than reality. For one thing, in terms both of trade and investment, the United States continued to have closer ties with Japan than with China, as Robert McClellan and others have shown.[43] The two countries of course accounted for only a fraction of the overall American trade. In 1906, for instance, American exports to China comprised a mere 2.5 percent of the total United States exports; in 1908 it was down to 1.2 percent. The corresponding figures for exports to Japan were 2.2. percent for both 1906 and 1908. China and Japan occupied a larger share of the American import market. Even so, again in 1906 and 1908, American imports from China amounted to 2.3 and 2.2 percent of the total, respectively, and those from Japan 4.2 and 5.7 percent. American exports to Japan consisted mainly of agricultural produce such as wheat, flour, and raw cotton. Machine goods amounted to only a little over 10 percent of Japanese purchases from the United States. Of crucial importance was the American export of raw cotton. In 1907, for example, 111 million pounds of cotton were sold to Japan, worth 14 million dollars; this was equivalent to 21.4 percent of the total cotton imported to Japan that year, and 24.2 percent of the total cotton used for manufacturing. Japan, it is true, usually obtained more than half of its needed raw cotton from India, but American and Chinese cotton supplied the rest, and these two countries were of equal importance. It is also true that the United States exported most of its raw cotton to European countries, especially Britain and Germany. At this time more than 60 percent of the raw cotton produced in the United States was sold overseas, and, in 1907, this amounted to 481 million dollars, or 25.6 percent of the total American exports. Japan's share in the cotton export was only 2.9 percent. Nevertheless, though this was not clearly perceived, raw cotton remained the single most important item of export from America to Japan; and 10 or 20 million dollars, while by no means decisive in the overall American picture, did make a substantial difference to cotton growers in the South.

If the United States sold raw cotton to Japan, it specialized in cotton goods for China. Cotton yarn, cloth, and manufactures such as shirts, coats, and sheets comprised an infinitesimal part of the total American export trade. In the decade before 1912 the value of cotton goods export for any single year never exceeded 50 million dollars, compared to overall exports amounting to more than one billion dollars annually and to raw cotton exports which brought in 400 and sometimes even over 500 million dollars a year. To China, specifically, the United States annually sold 5 or 6 million dollars worth of cotton goods, comprising 10 to 30 percent of the total American exports to that country. What was important was that most of the cottons were sold in Manchuria. American cotton cloth was usually coarse material, suitable for winter wear. It had found its way to Manchuria since the late 1890's, and for a number of years American cotton goods divided the market with British products. Numerous Southern mills had come to depend on the Manchurian market for their continued and expanding operation.

All these factors serve to put the American-Japanese trade "rivalry" in China, to the extent that such existed, in perspective. American exports to China steadily declined from the high point of 1905, both in terms of the dollar and of the tael value. In 1908 the exports amounted to only 40 percent of those in 1905, when measured in dollars, and less than 60 percent measured in tael. Could the decline in any way be related to Japanese policy and expansionism? Japanese exports to China also declined after 1905, though not as drastically as the American. The only articles in which both countries specialized as export commodities to China were cotton piece goods, and here they did tend to be potential rivals. In 1905 the United States sold over 42 million tael worth of cotton cloth to China — more than 36 percent of the total Chinese import of the commodity that year. From this peak America's share steadily declined, until in 1913 the amount was a mere 8 million tael, or 7.8 percent of the total value of cotton cloth imported to China. For Japan the trends were the opposite. Until after the Russo-Japanese War its cotton cloth exports to China were quite insignificant. But after 1906 they grew rapidly, and only four years later they surpassed American imports.

There is little doubt that the expansion of Japanese cotton cloth export to Manchuria was achieved at the expense of American trade. Given the fact that the two countries both manufactured the same types of coarse cotton cloth, known as sheeting and drill, it was to be expected that Japan would undersell American cloth. Labor was cheaper in Japan, the country was geographically much closer to China, and Japanese officials and businessmen were determined to entrench their country's economic influence in Manchuria by taking advantage of the war and immediate postwar years. Some of Millard's accusations were undoubtedly true: the South Manchuria Railway did give rebates on the Japanese goods shipped on its cars, and, at least until the end of the military occupation in 1906, Japanese authorities did exclude foreign merchants from ports and cities in Manchuria. However, it can be debated whether these practices and the resulting expansion of Japanese trade were such as to justify the fear of a serious struggle with the United States. Japan's sale of cotton yarn, cloth, and piece goods to China altogether amounted to only 24 million dollars in 1905, and the value increased to 26 million dollars in 1907 and 27 million dollars in 1909. These figures hardly reflected phenomenal expansion. Japanese-American rivalry in cotton cloth export was an affair of only a few million dollars. The gradual loss of the Manchurian market was a concern to America's Southern cotton mills, but China did not account for the bulk of cotton exports. Despite the shrinking of sales to China, the American export of cotton goods continued to expand, finding outlets elsewhere in the world. Furthermore, the raw cotton used by the Japanese in the manufacture of yarn and cloth for export to China came in part from the United States. It is suggestive that by and large the American sale of raw cotton to Japan far exceeded the sale of cotton goods to China. In 1907, for instance, 14 million dollars worth of raw cotton was exported to Japan, in contrast to 8 million dollars of cotton goods sold to China. The figures fluctuated from year to year, but the sale of raw cotton to Japan was never smaller in amount than that of cotton goods to China.

In 1906 Minister W. W. Rockhill in Peking noted that the American business community in China was indifferent to Manchuria. American commodities were shipped to that area by Japanese and other foreigners. There was not sufficient vigor on the part of Americans to compete with Japanese business in Manchuria.[44] Exactly the same view was expressed by Consul General Willard Straight, the archenemy of Japanese expansionism. In a memorandum written in Mukden, he said, "A great deal has been said about Japanese control of the Manchurian market. Certain privileges certainly were acquired during the war, but I believe that, should they ultimately secure such a control as has been described, it will be not because they have benefited by preferential treatment, but because foreign firms have not been willing to adopt the aggressive tactics which alone will secure success in this field." [45] In a private letter to William Phillips, Straight confessed it was "a rather thankless task, this endeavor to increase the American export trade. Our merchants, at least those who have addressed inquiries to this office [the consulate-general in Mukden], are not prepared to expend either time or trouble in introducing their wares abroad." [46] To another old China hand, Edwin Denby, he confided at the end of 1907: "I feel quite sure that we could meet and easily overcome Japanese competition were we willing to take the trouble to do so. They are not a commercial race. They are soldiers, first, bureaucrats, and shopkeepers. . . . I do not believe that the Japanese are strong enough to carry on their imperialistic programme in the face of our opposition." [47] These observations buttress the statistical fact that there was no concerted American effort to enter the field to compete with Japanese interests in Manchuria.

If Japanese-American trade relations were more significant than Chinese-American relations, at least statistically, the same was also true of American investments and loans. More American capital flowed to Japan and overseas Japanese territories, in part financing postwar Japanese expansionism, than to China to help expand American interests. Since the Russo-Japanese War did not bring indemnity payments of any kind to Japan, it had to continue to borrow abroad not only for postwar expansion and reconstruction but also to repay debts already accumulated. By the end of the Meiji era, Japan's foreign debts had reached the half-billion dollar figure. Most foreign borrowing, it is true, was done in Europe, especially Britain, but the United States remained a source of money. It is not known what proportion of the South Manchuria Railway's debentures floated abroad, amounting to 70 million dollars before 1911, was held by Americans, but undoubtedly the railroad was providing lucrative opportunities to American investors and manufacturers alike. The postwar period also saw the beginning of direct and indirect American investments in Japan proper, and several firms were organized partially through American financing. For example, in 1905 the General Electric Company pooled its resources with the Tokyo Electric Company for business in Japan, and five years later the International General Electric Company provided capital for the Shibaura Manufacturing Company. By 1914 there were about 58 million dollars of direct American investment in Japan.[48]

Compared with Japan, China was as yet an undeveloped area for American capital investment. It was only after 1909 that American financiers began to interest themselves in lending money to the Chinese government; before the founding of the Chinese Republic in 1912, total American loans to Peking amounted to only a little over 7 million dollars. For direct investments, statistics indicated that between 1900 to 1914 the amount increased from 17 to 42 million dollars, corresponding to the increase in the number of American business firms in China from 81 to 131 in these fourteen years. There is of course a question as to whether there might not have been more extensive American investment in China had there been no international obstacles. Certain circles in the United States were convinced that foreign powers, especially Japan, put obstacles in the way of American capital expansion in China. Certainly the Japanese tended to object to direct investments in Manchuria by Americans and other foreigners — although not to indirect investments. It would be extremely difficult to speculate how far American investments might have been expanded in the absence of Japanese hindrances. The United States was still a debtor nation, and while hundreds of millions of dollars were currently sent abroad, most of the money for direct investments went to the more lucrative markets of the Western Hemisphere, especially Canada and Mexico. After all, in 1905 the J. P. Morgan Company relinquished its franchise to build the Canton-Hankow railway for lack of real interest among investors, and in 1907 E. H. Harriman decided against a project to finance a railway in Manchuria on account of adverse financial conditions at home.[49]

Japanese views of their relations with the United States in China were on the whole in accord with these statistical facts. Before 1909 Japan's leaders and opinion makers did not seriously question the compatibility of the country's continental expansionism and its close economic ties to the United States. The two seemed to go hand in hand. While the postwar confusion in south Manchuria was recognized as a source of irritation to America, the Japanese were confident that once a more stable form of territorial government was established, smooth economic relations would be restored among China, Japan, and the other nations. There was no anticipation that Japan and the United States were fated to clash in China. On the contrary, it was felt that they could cooperate economically to develop Manchuria; the pouring in of American capital would enrich China and raise its purchasing power, and American goods would incline the Chinese toward foreign imports. Even if some American exports competed with Japanese goods, the Japanese were confident that they were so situated geographically that they need not fear such competition. The best official expression on this point is a memorandum written by Foreign Minister Hayashi toward the end of 1907. Japan was favored by geography and diplomacy, he wrote, to occupy a dominant position in Manchuria's commerce. Therefore, "even if we practice rigorously the principles of equal opportunity and the open door, we will need fear no serious competition." Hayashi recognized that there was some justification for foreigners' criticism of the Japanese commercial ethic; Japanese merchants in China were notorious for pirating copyrights, and many, swelled by the sense of victory, had resorted to unfair tactics to undermine Westerners' business positions. American and English complaints were not groundless, and Hayashi thought the government should take heed. He was confident that Japan need not resort to such practices. "The expansion of our commerce and industry in China," he wrote, "is a natural development as a result of the extension of our national power. We should not therefore worry about foreigners' complaints and jealousies so long as we engage in competition by fair tactics. However, we should never tolerate immoral plots and unjust machinations to cheat others and profit ourselves. Such practices will only invite loss of confidence in the Japanese as a whole." [50]

If the actual "rivalry" between the United States and Japan over the China market was minimal, and if the Japanese professed their faith in maintaining good relations between the two countries in China, such confidence was waning in the United States; many Americans were beginning to describe the future of Asia in terms that implied some serious conflict between Japan and the United States. This resulted basically from an emerging view of China and of America's relation to it.

"The history of our relations with China," Willard Straight wrote in 1907, "is much in our favor . . . we alone are regarded as fair and disinterested. This is so much capital to our credit and it seems to me that we should now reap what we have sown." [51] Straight was echoing the growing sentiment among his countrymen that there was something special about American-Chinese relations. This idea was not new. Almost from the beginning, various American officials, traders, and writers had spoken of the differences between the policies of the powers toward China and that pursued by the United States. What was striking in the post-1905 years was the simultaneous emergence of the image of a new and vigorous China reciprocating American friendship. China, it is true, had often "awakened" in the American imagination, but this time observers could point to many concrete instances of that country's regeneration. Very special ties seemed to urge the two countries to join in building a new day for Asia. This was America's task, a logical outcome of its expansion in East Asia, and it was to be welcomed by the Chinese as they set upon the task of regeneration and independence. "The more I see of Manchurian affairs," Straight wrote, "the more am I convinced that we, the Americans, are favored above all others and that ours is the opportunity to befriend China in this her time of need and to aid her in straightening out her affairs here." [52]

The realization that China was awakening could already be seen in American reactions to the anti-American boycott of 1905. But quite apart from the episode, the picture of a new, aroused China became more and more widely accepted. William Jennings Bryan, who toured East Asia in 1905, proclaimed upon his return: "The sleeping giantess, whose drowsy eyes have so long shut out the rays of the morning sun, is showing unmistakable signs of awakening. There was a vitality among her people which even 2,000 years of political apathy could not exhaust." [53] This sounded strikingly similar to observations made by Arthur H. Smith, a missionary long resident in China, who was temporarily back in the United States and published his influential *China and America Today* in 1907. The Chinese, he wrote, were "beginning to show that they have a reserve fund of physical, mental, and moral energy which is not only not exhausted, but is practically inexhaustible." Such an assertion was tantamount to recasting a whole range of clichés that had accumulated about China. Smith was saying not only that the Chinese had always been potentially capable of reform, but even that their traditional institutions and practices were not all that inferior to those of the West. He suggested that the Chinese system of government was "the more theoretically well-balanced the more it is considered," that "democratic local government exhibits the phenomenon of endless variety with substantial unity, and essential indestructibility," and that the Chinese had "for law, and for all the symbols of law and of government, an innate and ineradicable reverence." Moreover, they had a thorough respect for reason and moral ideas, were hard workers, and were characterized by steadiness and sobriety. The Chinese were "a great race with a great inheritance." As might have been expected, Smith rated the Chinese higher than the Japanese in crucial points: "morally, and especially in truthfulness and in commercial integrity, the Japanese are greatly the inferior." Implications for America's role in East Asia were all but self-evident.[54]

Another aspect of the new image was the gradual acceptance of the view that the West had wronged China in many ways and that some of the troubles and antiforeign tendencies were at least partially products of Western intrusion. Very few, if any, spoke for restructuring the whole treaty system on which foreign expansionism had been based; but virtually everyone shared Arthur H. Smith's observation that after the Opium War foreigners in China had been "autocratic, dictatorial, and openly contemptuous of the rights of the Chinese." In his words, "Western Powers had sent to China far too many men of the type of Sir Harry Parkes . . . who mistrusted all Chinese and who would put up with no 'nonsense' from the obstructive officials, and far too few of the Lord Elgin variety, whose simple rule was never to make an unjust demand, and never to retreat from a demand once made." The *Hous-*

ton Daily Post declared, "If in the fullness of time she [China] shall avenge her many wrongs and recover her empire, the world can only regard the achievement as a long step toward justice and right." [55]

It was clear to observers how the United States was, and should be, related to this new China. The idea of America as a true friend, often the only friend of the Chinese, emerged strongly at this time. It was not surprising that this view had as its counterpart the assumption that other powers, notably Japan, were less sympathetic. The sense of rivalry with Japan neatly fitted into the total picture. Practically every writer on Chinese-American relations mentioned as a matter of fact that the two countries had enjoyed historical friendship and that China needed the United States in its hour of regeneration and reform. President Edmund J. James of the University of Illinois wrote, in a letter to President Roosevelt recommending the sending of an educational commission to China, "We are the natural friends of the Chinese. We have been their real political friends." Reasons for this were derived from his version of American policy toward China. "We have stood between the Chinese Empire and dismemberment; we have come more nearly giving them the square deal in all our relations in the East than any other nation." It followed that the Chinese "are consequently less suspicious of us, as far as our politics are concerned, than of any other people." It was true, James conceded, that the Chinese resented the discriminatory treatment meted out to them in the United States, but he felt confident that "fair and decent conduct on our part" toward "Chinese gentlemen" would soothe Chinese sensitivity. As is evident in such a statement, once one accepted as axiomatic the image of a China awakening to its potentialities, one could easily draw the conclusion that here was America's great opportunity. [56]

Some writers at this time began openly speaking of Japan and America as alternative friends of China. Referring to the increasing number of Chinese students going to study in Japan, Smith asked rhetorically, "is it not the part of wisdom for us to put forth our best exertions to deflect this stream of students to our own shores, not for the good of China alone, but also for the welfare of America and of the world?" He believed that the United States could educate the Chinese youths better than Japan, and wrote of the demoralizing, corrupting atmosphere of Tokyo. For those with faith in these special ties it was hard to believe that the Chinese really wanted to study in any country other than the United States. As James wrote, "the Chinese are in many points jealous of the Japanese, and, other things being equal, would often prefer to send their young people to other countries. Among all these countries the United States would be the most natural one to choose." Other writers were convinced that China needed America's help against the encroachment of Japan. In his influential *The United States as a World Power*, Archibald C. Coolidge asserted that China did not "intend to allow the Japanese to take her in hand and direct her footsteps as they have dreamed of doing." The Chinese viewed Japan with "distrust not unmixed with fear." However, they could not singlehandedly repulse Japanese power and influence. They must turn to foreign help, and "there is but one country to which they can well turn." Only the United States could help, since its policy had been and still was "to maintain the integrity of the Chinese Empire, including Manchuria, and to uphold the policy of the 'open door.'" Aid from others entailed risks and perils, while the United States had "a remarkably clean record in the Far East: it alone of all the powers . . . has never taken, or tried to take, one foot of Chinese soil." The Chinese, Coolidge was confident, knew this and were eager for American support, which must be given, since the United States could not afford to lose the opportunity to expand its trade in Asia.[57]

The immigration dispute, for Coolidge as for other writers, did not fit the picture, and had to be somehow reconciled to the general view of America's friendship for the Chinese. He resolved the contradiction by saying that the United States should try to persuade the Chinese that "no hostility is intended against them; that exclusion does not imply a condemnation of their character." It only resulted from "the inability of white and yellow men to meet in large masses, on terms that are satisfactory to both." Coolidge and other writers had no difficulty distinguishing between their country's anti-Chinese legislation and the pro-Chinese feeling that underlay their confidence about American expansion in China. Japan supplied the missing logical link. In a widespread view, China had to choose between Japan and the United States, countries representing divergent policies toward China and engaged in a rivalry in Asia. Whatever America gained in thanks from China, wrote Coolidge, "it will assuredly lose in good-will from Japan." The possibility that China would befriend Japan was not taken seriously, despite the fact that some Chinese reformers were known to be eager to learn from and imitate Japan. Chinese-Japanese friendship could not be entertained as a serious possibility because it would have undercut the vision of Chinese-American ties. Writers generally assumed that relations between China and Japan would not be completely equal and that the latter would always seek to dominate the former. "Chinese are as averse to being ruled by Japanese as by westerners," wrote Thomas F. Millard, "indeed, it may be that brought to a choice between these alternatives China would choose a western master." In his view, since China had an abundance of cheap labor, it would naturally prefer to carry out its own industrialization rather than be dependent on Japan. This was the "natural course," and only Japan's policy of dominance was preventing the realization of the Chinese dream.[58]

Since, according to Millard, the Chinese, in distress over Japanese encroachment, were "instinctively" turning to the United States for help, the question now faced by Americans was, "What will America do?" An answer was provided by a speech Secretary of War Taft gave in Shanghai on October 8, 1907. Taft, probably the most pro-Chinese member of Roosevelt's second administration, reflected the growing sentiment in the United States for closer ties with China. Writing to Roosevelt from Nagasaki, three days before delivering his Shanghai speech, he said that the Chinese "turn to us as the only country that is really unselfish in the matter of obtaining territory and monopolies, [and] I think it therefore worth while to cultivate them and accept courtesies at their hands." [59] Taft represented the voice of America's economic expansionism at that juncture, rejoicing in Chinese development as a great opportunity for expanding American trade, and therefore calling on America's assistance to Chinese modernization. "I am not one of those," he declared, "who view with alarm the effect of the growth of China with her teeming millions into a great industrial empire." He was in total sympathy with the slogan of "China for the Chinese," which to him simply meant "that China should devote her energies to the development of her immense resources, to her industrious people and to the enlargement of her trade and to the administrative reform of the Empire as a great national Government. Changes of this kind could only increase our trade with her." Taft was so impressed with Chinese friendliness during his Shanghai visit that he wrote to President Roosevelt, "there never was a time when the Chinese were more friendly than today." He attributed this sentiment to "the suspicion and fear that they entertain toward Japan and Russia and possibly England." Taft was convinced that the Chinese knew "we do not wish to take any of their territory and that we don't ask any exclusive privilege." As he said in the Shanghai speech, "it is a pleasure to know and to say that in every improvement which she [China] aims at, she has the deep sympathy of America, and that there never can be any jealousy or fear on the part of the United States due to China's industrial or political development, provided always that it is directed along the lines of peaceful prosperity and the maintenance of law and order and the rights of the individual, native or foreign." [60]

Taft's speech was welcomed warmly by the American community in China. The speech, wrote H. B. Morse, president of the American Association of China which sponsored the banquet at which Taft spoke, "was one of those which change the course of history, and was especially significant coming from one of the men who make history." The historic significance seemed to lie in the fact that an important Cabinet member, one generally regarded as the next President of the United States, had asserted America's role in Asia in very clear terms: to continue to expand trade and to aid China's modernization, goals considered totally compatible and complementary. Thomas F. Millard, following Taft to the rostrum, asked rhetorically, "Am I going too far to declare that China and America need each other, that in some important matters their futures are inseparably linked?" His concluding remarks exactly echoed Taft's: "If at this moment I have any deep conviction, it is that the American people will insist upon taking a proportionate part in the development of China, extending such encouragement and aid as may be fitting and acceptable, and what the American people insist upon the Government of the United States will be compelled to undertake." Willard Straight, enthusiastic about the Taft speech, believed that it had frightened the Japanese and "encouraged their continental cousins." The growing self-assertiveness of the Chinese he attributed in part to the speech.[61]

Whether American expansion really competed with and undermined Japanese expansion in China, and whether the United States, by expanding more vigorously into China, was assisting that country's regeneration, were questions that ultimately hinged on the reaction of the Chinese. It is difficult to see that the reality of Chinese policy and opinion had much to do with the image created of them by American speakers and writers. Chinese opinion was synonymous with nationalism, and the rights-recovery movement was gaining greater and greater influence among merchants, students, and some gentry members. Officials were fully aware of and sympathized with such a sentiment, although those at Peking tended to seek nationalistic goals through political centralization, whereas provincial leaders were apt to emphasize provincial autonomy as a way to achieve national rights. There was at this time no strong sentiment for favoring one foreign power over another. The United States in particular was not given a special place in Chinese policy and thinking. Before 1908 it is difficult to note much evidence that the Chinese government consciously differentiated America from the rest of the powers. A handful of officials, it is true, were interested in obtaining American assistance as a counterweight against Japanese influence in Manchuria, thinking that the United States was the most available nation to check Japan because other nations were aligned on the Japanese side. Even this degree of interest in an American alliance was limited to a small circle of men, mostly returned students from the United States. These younger officials, reported Consul General Straight, were "gradually but surely increasing their influence and power. Many of them with whom I have talked are anxious to develop their country with American aid." [62] Thomas F. Millard also reported that Yüan Shih-k'ai told him that the American-educated Chinese showed better results than those trained in other countries and that he surrounded himself with men who had studied in the United States.[63] At this time, however, the only prominent official with decidedly pro-American inclinations was T'ang Shao-yi, governor of Fengtien province, Manchuria. From his headquarters in Mukden he worked closely with Straight to counter Japanese expansion. T'ang told Straight that "he was particularly desirous that American capital should obtain a foothold in Manchuria." No such investment was forthcoming, however, because of the financial crisis in the United States; without hesitation T'ang went to British financiers to obtain funds for the building of a railway between Hsinmintun and Fakumen. "The pity of it all is," Straight wrote in chagrin, "that we cannot induce our own people to accept the opportunities that await them." [64] Before 1908 little on the Chinese side seemed to reciprocate the outpouring of friendly sentiment in the United States.

If, as seems likely, there was no solid foundation to the much heralded coming of a new era in Chinese-American relations, and the actual "rivalry" between the United States and Japan was minimal, the new emphasis on friendship with China and the implied estrangement from Japan served to justify continued American expansion in Asia while denying Japanese expansion in America. There was a fear, as Archibald C. Coolidge recognized, that the Japanese, as a result of their exclusion from white territories, might react by creating a pan-Asian empire.[65] The image of Chinese-American friendship and cooperation justified attacks upon such an empire; it would legitimize continued involvement and expansion of the United States in East Asia while at the same time denying Japanese immigration to America. It was in this subtle, psychological sense that American policy and opinion after the Russo-Japanese War created a crisis in Japanese-American relations. Japanese expansion, promoted by limitless ambitions and sustained by an ideology that was no less genuine because it was superficial, was encountering opposition that could not readily be overcome. It was running into difficulties in America and in China. If Japan was to expand, ways had to be sought to ameliorate this situation. And yet, any new development of Japanese expansionism could not help but involve — and further complicate relations with — the United States and China.

VIII

The United States and Japan
in the World Arena

For ten years after the Spanish-American War the United States and Japan had expanded in Asia and the Pacific. They had emerged as world powers and engaged in world politics. This had brought about closer contact between the two peoples, and the result had been estrangement and misunderstanding that were often bewildering. Theoretically, there should have been no conflict; there should have been no reason why these expanding countries could not have competed amicably and maintained friendly relations. Unfortunately, the more Americans and Japanese professed their commitment to expansion, the greater they found the conflict between them. Overseas Japanese did not impress Americans as exponents of peaceful migration, while American behavior at home and abroad appeared to Japanese more and more as a hindrance to their expansive activities. Because both peoples shared a commitment to expansionism, small differences could become magnified and take on ideological significance. In fact Japanese-American differences came to assume characteristics of an ideological confrontation. Ideological differences are longer-lasting than military and economic rivalries and often determine the way in which these rivalries are defined. The years after 1908 showed how difficult it was to develop a plausible image of trans-Pacific relations that allowed room for disputes without presupposing a basic conflict and the inevitability of war.

Japanese-American estrangement was not lessened when Japan, under the leadership of Prime Minister Katsura and Foreign Minister

The United States and Japan in the World Arena

Komura, adopted a policy stressing continental expansion. The second Katsura ministry, which came to power in July 1908, was determined to make good some of the rights Japan had obtained in Manchuria that had remained largely on paper. Taking advantage of the temporary disarray of Chinese leadership following the deaths of the Empress Dowager and the Kuang-hsü Emperor toward the end of 1908, Komura compelled the Peking government to sign a series of new agreements in mid-1909, which remained a basic legal framework for subsequent Japanese continentalism. China agreed to consult Japan before undertaking construction of a railway between Hsinmintun and Fakumen, and to grant to Japan the right to mine coal at the two important mines of southern Manchuria: Wusun and Yentai. These were among the demands the Japanese had put forth after the Russo-Japanese War. Together with some others, such as improving railway connections between Korea and south Manchuria, these rights ensured Japanese control of the area and established Japan as the predominant foreign power in that part of China.[1]

Under such determined governmental initiative there was renewed interest in migrating to and engaging in business in Korea and Manchuria. The areas replaced Hawaii and the United States as locales for Japanese emigration and settlement, and the agreements of 1909 assured that Japan's hold on south Manchuria would not be relinquished. Whereas in 1906 there were only 16,000 Japanese, exclusive of military personnel, in Manchuria, by 1910 the number had increased to 76,000. Of these, 62,000 were in Kwantung Leased Territory and in areas belonging to the South Manchuria Railway, in other words, Japanese-controlled territory. According to a survey made that year, only a fraction, fewer than 200, were engaged in farming, but over 11,000 were employed in commerce, industry, and transportation. Japan's presence in Manchuria consisted not of agricultural settlements but a colonial superstructure, linking the Manchurian economy to the outside world. Here some 62,000 Japanese presided over a Chinese population of over 430,000 whose number continued to increase in the following decades.[2]

Japan's economic penetration of Manchuria began to manifest itself about 1908. As postwar confusion and uncertainty gave way to clearer policy and improved financial conditions, both at home and abroad, Japanese trade and investment in Manchuria registered phenomenal growth. In 1907, for instance, the South Manchuria Railway handled 1,512,000 passengers and 1,348,000 tons of goods. Three years later, although the railway had not been extended, 2,349,000 passengers and 3,558,000 tons of commodities were shipped by its cars. The railroad's operating budget increased from 14 million yen in 1907 to 115 million in 1911. (Already in 1909 it was making a profit of over 5 million yen.) The treaty port of Antung, once a major port of entry for American imports, began handling such a quantity of Japanese cotton fabrics that by 1910 Japanese imports exceeded American. Japan's role in Manchuria's export trade expanded after 1908 as the Mitsui Bussan Company succeeded in initiating massive sales of soybeans overseas.[3]

The year 1908 also saw the publication of a new magazine, *Shokumin sekai* (The world of colonialism), which was designed, according to its editor, to assist the Japanese to enrich their country through the "peacetime war" of overseas settlement and colonization. "Look around you," the reader was exhorted, "and see if Manchuria, Korea, South America, and our new territories, Sakhalin and Taiwan, are not eagerly waiting for your coming. Other countries, such as China proper, the South Sea islands, and Australia, are all desirous of the coming of Japanese to engage in trade." He pointedly refrained from mentioning the United States and Canada, and there was little doubt that when he talked of colonization he had in mind primarily Manchuria, China, and the Japanese colonies. When the magazine sent a questionnaire to a number of officials and writers, asking which areas of the world were most suitable for Japanese colonization and settlement, almost all the respondents stressed Manchuria and Korea, although few were willing to write off other parts of the world. One, a high official in the Ministry of Agriculture and Commerce, thought that Manchuria and Korea were the best since they were close to and under the control of Japan, climatically similar to conditions at home, and sparsely populated. Another official, working in Korea, asserted that Korea, China, Manchuria, the South Seas, and Siberia were most suitable for Japanese colonization as they were "bound to fall under Japanese control or at least Japanese direction and influence." The United States was really the most ideal place, several responded, but, given the strained relations between the countries, it did not seem possible to establish Japanese settlements there. South America, on the other hand, presented no diplomatic complications. However, all agreed that politically it was much easier to send colonists to the areas in East Asia that were under Japan's political control.[4] Universalistic expansionism never disappeared from the scene, but the vogue of continentalism was unmistakable.

Articles in *Shokumin sekai* reveal that around this time Japanese officials and writers were becoming seriously concerned with the problem of how to establish permanent colonies abroad that would redound to the benefit of the nation. Thousands of Japanese had gone to the continent of Asia after the Russo-Japanese War, dreaming of quick riches, but that stage of hasty, unplanned migration was over, and there was need to think of the future. Writer after writer stressed that the time was gone when a Japanese could go to Manchuria and taking advantage of military victories and postwar conditions of instability, make money. Now that the dust had settled, Japanese settlers had to reckon with the presence and competition of the Chinese. They would never succeed unless they were well prepared and equipped. They needed a substantial sum of initial capital, they had to have some knowledge of China and its people, and they must be prepared to stay in the new land forever.[5] These exhortations had been heard frequently when writers talked of migration to the United States. Because Manchuria and Korea were closer to home and under Japan's control, the temptation was all the greater to dream of easy and quick successes. This would not do, Takahashi Sanmin, editor of *Shokumin sekai,* said. There were still too few Japanese abroad who were truly engaged in productive activities. "People often talk of Japan's great expansion and extension; but where is our expansion?" Emigration to North America had stopped, and trade in China had not been doing well. As for Manchuria and Korea, "I have not heard of any activities by individual Japanese that we can be proud of." He thought that those who went to Manchuria and Korea were afflicted with the same ills that had characterized emigrants to America: provincialism and lack of sense of permanence. They were too prone to feel homesick, and too easily discouraged by small failures. Unless the situation was speedily remedied, it was idle to talk of the expansion of Japan.[6] Other writers called on Japanese going to China to learn first something about the Chinese, their habits and language. They must show understanding of Chinese sentiment, especially nationalism, and endeavor to work with, not against, them.[7]

It was ironical that at the precise moment the Japanese began stressing continental expansion, the United States was turning *its* at-

tention to the Asian continent, especially Manchuria. In 1908, just
when Japanese-Chinese relations were faced with a crisis over the
Tatsu Maru incident, plans were made to solidify American ties with
China by promoting further investment in Manchuria. Willard
Straight, who had done much to criticize and obstruct Japanese penetration of Manchuria while he was consul general at Mukden, was ordered home to provide necessary information on financial conditions
in that part of the world. E. H. Harriman, the banker, who was in part
responsible for Straight's recall to Washington, was desirous of obtaining such information in order to realize his plans for railway construction in Manchuria and Siberia.[8] Simultaneously, T'ang Shao-yi,
governor of Fengtien province, left for the United States, hoping to
obtain a loan for a central Manchurian bank which he and Straight
visualized as the financer of their projects.[9] Before anything was done
in that direction, however, the Chinese Emperor and the Empress
Dowager died, in November, and caused a political eclipse of Yüan
Shih-k'ai, the powerful figure who had supported T'ang's schemes.
Still, American opinion continued to entertain the hope that China
would survive the domestic turmoil and persist in its reform programs
with the encouragement of the United States. "Now of all times," according to the *New York Tribune,* "is the time when China needs
honest and disinterested moral support such as she may confidently
expect from the United States." [10]

Such support came when William Howard Taft entered the White
House and appointed Philander C. Knox as his secretary of state in
March 1909. As recent studies by Sondra Herman and Warren Kuehl
have pointed out anew, Taft was an ardent advocate of active participation in international affairs, not so much in world politics and armament competition, but in carrying out America's role as a provider of
order and source of economic benefits.[11] The United States, he said,
must do its part "in keeping the house of the world in order." There
was self-consciousness about exercising American influence not simply
in self-interest or in a military balance of power but in maintaining
stability and bringing about prosperity throughout the world. It was
assumed that there were strong and rich countries as well as those that
were weak and poor and lacking in experience or wisdom as they tried
to transform themselves. The United States could not only provide a
model of self-government and economic development but also actively help them so as to reduce to a minimum chances for disruption

of peace and order in the world. "The national prosperity and power impose upon us duties which we cannot shirk if we are true to our ideals," Taft said, and his constant reiteration of the nation's ideals, duties, and responsibilities made him a precursor of Wilsonian diplomacy.[12]

This type of liberal expansionism, which saw no contradiction between America's commercial and ideological expansion and the interests of mankind as a whole, was put into practice by a State Department that was headed by Knox and staffed by men like Huntington Wilson and Willard Straight. Knox was in full accord with Taft's emphasis on arbitration among the powerful nations and on their duty to help the weak. The basic rationale for this was the convergence, as Knox saw it, of nations' interests as a result of their economic development. In a Spencerian language in which so many of his contemporaries spoke, Knox expressed the faith that capitalism and economic expansion had linked countries and peoples closer together and made war that much more obsolete. "The development of commerce and industry," he said, "and the necessary exchange of commodities have caused nations to see that their interests are similar and interdependent, and that a like policy is often necessary as well for the expansion as for the protection of their interests." [13] Likewise, Huntington Wilson was fond of distinguishing between the "old-fashioned selfish exploitation" that characterized the foreign policies of the powers and the "new and sincere and practical effort to help" that was the emerging consciousness among Americans and other advanced peoples.[14]

China was obviously a good place to begin. It fit the image of a land suffering from the encroachment of greedy foreigners and yet trying resolutely to modernize itself. If ever a country needed America's assistance, here it was. The United States should step in and help, utilizing its superior economic resources. "If the American dollar can aid suffering humanity," Knox said in 1911, characterizing his "dollar diplomacy," and "lift the burden of financial difficulty from states with which we live on terms of intimate intercourse and earnest friendship, and replace insecurity and devastation by stability and peaceful self-development, all I can say is that it would be hard to find better employment." [15] This perfectly expressed his approach to China, and in particular to Manchuria, which attracted his attention as soon as he entered the State Department. Throughout 1909 Knox sought to free China from what appeared to be Japan's monopolistic hold on economic opportunities in Manchuria. The tactics employed included a railway neutralization scheme, enabling the Chinese to buy back all the existing railways in Manchuria with money to be supplied by an international syndicate, and the support of a Chinchow-Aigun railway, running across Manchuria, which E. H. Harriman, Jacob Schiff, and others were promoting so as to divert business from the exclusive control of the South Manchuria Railway.[16]

The fate of these schemes has been traced in detail by Charles Vevier and others and need not be repeated here. What stands out is the coincidence of the Taft-Knox policy and the continental expansionism of Japan that had been given renewed impetus by Katsura and Komura. Just as the language of universalistic expansionism had not helped Japanese in gaining acceptance by Americans on the West coast, the American rhetoric of liberal expansionism ran into solid resistance from the Japanese in Manchuria. From their point of view, Knox's schemes challenged their rights in one of the very regions that accepted Japanese expansion. Having been rejected by Americans, they were beginning to concentrate on continentalism, only to be confronted by a Taft-Knox policy. There is no doubt that this psychological factor embittered Japan's response to it. From Foreign Minister Komura's point of view, Japan was in Manchuria to stay, and the Japanese position there was "a foundation of national expansion." American policy under Taft and Knox seemed to attack this cardinal principle. Japan had to reject it; moreover, it must seek to have its rights in Manchuria recognized by other powers. Thus the Tokyo government at once turned down the Knox proposals and approached Russia for mutual confirmation of their respective spheres of influence in Manchuria.[17]

Just as the Americans rejected the notion of altering the existing racial make-up on the West coast, so the Japanese insisted on preserving "the status quo" in Manchuria, which they saw being challenged by the United States. Takahashi Sakue, writing for *Kokusaihō gaikō zasshi* (International law and diplomacy), asserted that the danger to the status quo was likely to come from American policy, especially the possibility of Chinese-American cooperation.[18] Another article in this scholarly journal expressed a generally held feeling: "All of a sudden, before we realized it, the United States has established its predominant influence in China and asserts its say on every Chinese question. . . . This is simply an amazing demonstration of America's ability." [19]

The United States and Japan in the World Arena

There is little doubt that the Japanese were beginning to consider their strained relations with the United States in terms not only of the immigration dispute but also of the Chinese question. In a book entitled *Nichi-Bei gaikō-ron* (On Japanese-American relations), Ōtsuka Zenjirō, who had spent eight years in San Francisco, noted that the Asian crisis was an inevitable product of the westward expansion of the United States. The American people, he said, had steadily incorporated territory westward, and, having annexed Hawaii and the Philippines, had now reached East Asia. Having emerged as a power in the western Pacific, they sought to play a powerful role in Asia. But their vanity and ambition were being obstructed by the Japanese. If the United States practiced more economic expansionism and stood aloof from Asian politics, Ōtsuka said, there would be no conflict with Japan. Increasingly, however, American policy sought a larger role, opposing Japan at every turn through superior resources, and driven by national pride. Since the Japanese were busily engaged in Korea and Manchuria and had no thought of attacking the Philippines or California, such an offensive in Asia on the part of the United States could cause serious conflict between the two countries. The author hoped, however, that crisis would be avoided if Japan remained closely bound to Russia, Britain, and France.[20] Another book, *Taiheiyō no yūetsusha* (The predominant power in the Pacific), noted that America's naval expansion in the Pacific was designed to aid the promotion of its trade in Asia, an aim likely to come into conflict with Japan's vital interests in China.[21]

One of the most thoughtful observers of Japanese-American relations, the historian Asakawa Kan'ichi, developed the theme of conflict between the two countries in Asia. He virtually ruled out the possibility of war on account of the California situation or the naval expansion undertaken by the two, but he was convinced they were pursuing different policies in China and that the drastic reversal in American attitude toward Japan after the Russo-Japanese War was attributable to Japan's continentalism. So long as the nation persisted in fair play and demanded only just and legitimate rights in China and Manchuria, it had nothing to fear. But if the United States were pictured on the side of justice and Japan as opposing it, a calamitous war would be unavoidable. Such a war would be waged not only against the United States and China, but also against mankind and civilization. The Japanese should not let the Americans speak for the principles of justice and fair play. Asakawa did not believe the Japanese deserved the American charge that they had seriously violated the open door doctrine in Manchuria; at the same time, he pointed out that after the war the United States rather than Japan had been standing as the friend of China. Japan could not afford to lose the sympathy of both countries; its policy should be guided by the absolute necessity of avoiding conflict with them. President Taft, Asakawa correctly noted, embodied "the new diplomacy" even more forcefully than his predecessor; as he was more sensitive to public opinion than Roosevelt, the alienation of the United States from Japan was bound to grow more intense unless the latter took steps to clarify its stand in China.[22]

In tracing the source of the tension between Japan and the United States to their deteriorating relations in China, Asakawa was following the argument that was widespread in the United States and was affecting the thinking of ever-wider circles in Japan. But his assertion, again reflecting American sentiment and held by many writers even today, that only Japan's concessions and good behavior in Asia would reduce tension, was not likely to be shared by his countrymen. Although Americans usually argued that immigration control was wholly within their country's legal rights, whereas a free hand in Asia was quite another matter, Japanese insisted that the principle of equal opportunity applied not only in China but everywhere and included the opportunity to migrate to the United States. As they saw it, the basic question was whether the Japanese should be allowed to expand universally or only in selected areas of the world. If Asakawa were to make his ideas more plausible and attractive, he had to recognize that in their view what he called the "new diplomacy" should apply not only to Japanese policy in Manchuria but also to the immigration policy of the United States. Otherwise he would have no convincing rebuttal to offer to the particularism of his countrymen who said that Japan had as much right to pursue its policy in Asia as the United States had in its territories.

Official Japanese policy resembled this approach. In 1910 the Tokyo government formally established colonial rule over Korea and secretly joined Russia in partitioning Manchuria into two spheres of influence. On the other hand, it deferred to the United States on the immigration question. The Japanese government was ready to reaffirm its policy of not permitting laborers to go to the United States, and did so officially during the negotiations for a new commercial treaty

(1910–11). The treaty of 1911 contained Japan's declaration expressing its intention to abide by the Gentlemen's agreement. Although
Foreign Minister Komura wanted the principle of most-favored-nation treatment applied to those Japanese already in the United States,
he accepted that government's contention that such matters came
under the jurisdiction of national law, implying that the United States
retained the right unilaterally to regulate the coming and activities of
Japanese immigrants. This was the price Komura decided to pay for
the new treaty which finally restored complete tariff autonomy to
Japan.[23]

Nonofficial Japanese publications during these years indicate that
such a negative approach to the emigration question was not shared
by many outside the government. In the above-quoted book, *Nichi-
Bei gaikō-ron,* Ōtsuka argued that, while voluntary restrictions on the
emigration of Japanese to the United States might be an unfortunate
necessity, one should not forget that there were already over 100,000
Japanese in the United States, including Hawaii, and that in 1909
they sent home as much as 7 million dollars. The government, he said,
"must protect these brave immigrants who are working for our nation
in the distant land of America, help their businesses succeed, and
maintain national honor." Japanese communities in America were an
extension of the homeland; the government was obligated to do what
it could to help them maintain their rights.[24] Japanese in the United
States were naturally unhappy over the home government's inclina-
tion to concentrate on continental expansion. As early as March 1908,
an editorial for *Shinsekai* (San Francisco) declared, "While we recognize the importance of Manchuria, Korea, and China as suitable areas
for our country's expansion, we doubt if the sending of impoverished
emigrants to these areas, at a time when the mother country does not
have abundant capital, will result in sufficient development and expansion." [25] Japanese settlers in America, by contrast, enjoyed greater
opportunities for speedy success. West coast prejudice was a serious
obstacle, but it would be foolish to give up expansion on the American continent just because of it. It was hoped that somehow restrictions on Japanese immigration would be reduced or removed. Japanese on the Pacific coast looked to the year 1911, when a new
commercial treaty between the two countries would be concluded, as
a good chance for ameliorating the unsatisfactory conditions of their
life. A *Shinsekai* editorial in December 1908 said: "we sincerely hope

that with the conclusion of treaty revision in 1911 our government's policy toward emigration will be given a new lease of life and produce fresh opportunities for positive activities." They were bound to be disappointed. As Foreign Minister Komura's approach to Japanese-American relations was more and more clearly revealed, this newspaper became more and more critical. It accused the Foreign Minister of stressing trade at the expense of the rights of overseas Japanese. It was foolish, it asserted, to ignore the fact that the Asian continent was rich in labor but short in capital. The Pacific Ocean and the American continent, in contrast, had everything except manpower. Japan must adopt a more realistic policy of expansion in these areas.[26] Almost a year later *Shinsekai* reminded the reader of the impending negotiations for treaty revision and attacked the home government's apparent indifference to the importance of the immigration question: the government must insist on an end to immigration restrictions and the granting of the right of naturalization to those already in the United States.[27] Neither objective was accomplished, and the Japanese community in the United States greeted the new commercial treaty of 1911 with a mixture of sorrow and resignation.[28]

It was, however, not just Japanese in America who held steadfast to the idea of continued expansion in areas outside the Asian mainland. Despite the vogue of continentalism after 1908, the idea of universalistic expansion was not forgotten. In fact, the successful extension of rights in Manchuria after 1909 and the continued stalemate on the West coast gave writers an opportunity to take stock of the position of Japan and the Japanese in the wider world. This produced a series of introspective and reflective essays on Japan's expansion. It is not too much to say that they represented the Japanese world view in the last years of the Meiji period and summed up several decades of modern Japan's quest for meaning in a changing world.

By coincidence, the year 1911 saw the initiation of two similarly entitled magazines: *Kaigai no Nihon* (Japan overseas), and *Sekai no Nihon* (Japan in the world). They are of considerable interest, having been launched just after the annexation of Korea. Japan was now a full-fledged imperialist, with colonies in Korea, Taiwan, southern Sakhalin, and Kwantung Leased Territory, and special rights and privileges in Manchuria. Treaty revision, the most fundamental goal of Meiji diplomacy, was finally being brought to conclusion. Historians have sometimes argued that henceforth the task of statesmen turned inward and domestic crises characterized Japanese politics. Such a view overlooks the intensity with which the coming of a new era was being felt by scores of publicists. Expansion remained their major preoccupation, and these journals attested to it. The opening statement in the first issue of *Kaigai no Nihon* asserted that the coming era was the time for "fresh expansion of our people outward." The nation's future, the editors warned, was strewn with difficulties unless it were well prepared to undertake further expansion. The magazine was intended to aid the people in this preparation by printing articles on overseas Japanese, disseminating information on opportunities abroad, and interesting the people at home in the ideology of national expansion.[29] Ōkuma Shigenobu, the most ubiquitous writer for these journals, asserted that with the signing of the new treaties of commerce the Japanese were guaranteed freedom of residence to engage in business throughout the world. Therefore, there was no need to undertake colonial settlement; what was needed was overseas settlement without colonialism or territorial control. The people should not be misled by the government's policy of concentration on continental expansion, Ōkuma said, but should spread throughout the world.[30] Another article, by an official of the Ministry of Communications, pointed out that the number and welfare of Japanese abroad were a barometer of national strength. A Diet member wrote that the urgent need of the moment was not territorial extension but national expansion, which involved settlement of the Japanese people in all parts of the world. A diplomat insisted that the emigration of Japanese should be based on economic, not political, considerations, and that once they were abroad they should try to assimilate new ways of thought.[31]

Kayahara Kazan, who returned from a four-year tour of America and Europe in 1910, became the leading popularizer of the idea of expansion. His observations overseas had made him a convinced advocate of peaceful expansionism. "I am naturally an imperialist," he asserted in *Kaigai no Nihon*. "Through imperialism our nation and our people must further expand." However, he warned that the time for militaristic imperialism had passed; the new imperialism must take the more peaceful form of economic expansion through such means as capital investment and emigration. Japan's peaceful expansionism should be directed at the United States, Canada, Australia, New Zealand, Brazil, and the South Seas as much as Manchuria and Korea.[32] Becoming an editorial writer for *Sekai no Nihon* in July 1911, he never ceased to repeat this refrain. His exhortation to his countrymen, as one who had personally observed the life of Japanese communities overseas, was that they had not learned how to live in the wider world. If they were truly to expand, they must study the world. Instead of judging other peoples from a narrowly Japanese perspective, the Japanese should develop a sense of objectivity and see themselves as others saw them. Such cosmopolitanism alone would equip them with intellectual discipline and power to cope with difficulties abroad.[33]

Such idealistic rhetoric hid a basic flaw in argument: it assumed that other peoples would accept the Japanese people's expansion and their definition of the ideal world. Not even Kayahara was sanguine about the chance for harmony and peace between different peoples and races. If the Japanese expanded abroad, no matter how peacefully, their encounter and interaction with the host country were bound to give rise to mutual suspicion and misunderstanding, as the California dispute had all too clearly shown. What was the use of talking about the new Japan or "Japan in the world" if the nation was contributing to racial strife? Conversely, how could racial antagonism be reduced so that the Japanese could freely expand?

There were no ready answers to these questions, but they could not be avoided in any discussion of the future of Japan's expansion, in particular in the Pacific region. In 1908 the influential magazine *Taiyō* (Sun) issued a special supplement under the title "The collision between the yellow and white races." The lead article asserted that "the history of the future will be a record of a primitive struggle between the yellow and white races." It was evident, the author pointed out, that all outstanding international questions could be reduced to racial competition. It was most urgent that the Japanese, as they undertook global activities, should understand that their presence overseas posed a threat to the West's white civilization, just as the coming of the West had threatened Asian civilization. The coming closer together of the two was inevitable, and the Japanese should be conscious of the historic meaning of their emergence as an expanding world power. In the Pacific Ocean the racial struggle took the form of Japanese-American competition, as the two peoples represented the newest and strongest powers in the Pacific. The rivalry was not likely to abate because each stood for a race and a civilization. So long as Americans feared Japanese strength in the Pacific and Japanese regarded with alarm American activities in Asia, mutual suspicion and hostility would continue.[34]

The policy of avoiding trouble with the United States by concentrating on continental expansion had only a limited appeal to those who were concerned with the racial and cultural aspects of Japanese expansionism. To stop emigration to non-Asian countries was a sign of defeat, while to stress continental expansion exclusively was tantamount to admitting inferiority. One writer suggested that the best solution was to improve the Japanese race so that the nation would win the struggle for supremacy among races; another urged extensive naval armament to prepare for emergencies.[35] None suggested the curtailment of expansion. The Japanese in the last years of Meiji were desperately trying to come to grips with the problems that had been produced by their expansive activities. Their estrangement from the United States symbolized the problem. Japanese-American relations now transcended narrow binational issues and were viewed as symptoms of modern Japan's difficulties. The nation must either overcome them or condemn itself to stationary, parochial existence. Lacking alternative frameworks of thought, the Japanese were gradually accustoming themselves to the notion of fundamental incompatibility among races and cultures.

Across the Pacific, Americans were also becoming accustomed to the idea of rivalry with Japan. Not only the California dispute but economic competition in Asia had marred the image of friendly relations between the two countries. The growing sympathy with Chinese nationalism and the Taft-Knox rhetoric of liberal expansionism insured that the rivalry would not abate. Although immigration of Japanese laborers to the mainland United States dropped drastically after 1908, agitation against them did not cease. The image of Japan as an expansionist and therefore a threat to American possessions in the Pacific was already there. Coupled with the disputes in Manchuria, there was emerging, just as in Japan, a notion of global confrontation between the two countries. The feeling was growing that they were in conflict not only in specific areas but in fundamental national orientations.

As earlier, the United States army was most sensitive to the imagined threat posed by an expanding Japan. The years after 1908 saw a continued flow of memorandums, all indicative of the utmost seriousness with which the question of Japan was viewed. The available documents of the Army War College, which functioned as a central depository of memorandums and originator of strategic concepts, reveal the depth of concern with the problem of "Orange" (Japan). A serious study of Japanese war potential was made in 1908–9, and it was concluded that the Japanese could transport to the United States, "in one expedition a force of about six divisions of infantry with all animals, two cavalry brigades with two batteries of horse artillery, and two regiments of heavy artillery." In other words, Japan was shown to be capable of waging an offensive war against the United States.[36] Information regarding Japanese army strength was obtained through the military attachés in Tokyo and other agents, both legitimate and secret. One example of the latter was a Lieutenant Commander J. C. Thompson of the United States navy who was verbally instructed by Chief of Staff Leonard Wood and Secretary of War Taft to undertake a secret intelligence mission in East Asia and report directly to them. A sum of money from the War Department's emergency fund was provided Thompson so that he might "secure the latest and reliable military information as to an Eastern Power's preparedness for war." [37] When the first batch of reports arrived from him, Leonard Wood wrote to W. W. Wotherspoon, head of the War College: "I believe a method has been established and with time and patience we will have a great deal." [38] Judging from the reports by Thompson that are extant, he was able to supply little more than obvious topographical data and generalized views on Japanese psychology and preparedness, but these were incorporated in the War College's periodical reviews of Japanese-American relations.[39] For example, in a memorandum dated December 17, 1910, on "What steps now being taken by Japan indicate an intention to engage in war with the United States?" the writers called attention to the fact that, since the Russo-Japanese War, "Japan has steadily continued the policy of expanding her army and creating a battleship fleet of the first class." It was considered axiomatic that Japan's military strengthening was aimed primarily at preparedness against the United States. This was because there seemed to be no indication that war between Japan and Russia was impending, and because of a list of grievances the Japanese felt toward the Americans.

In mentioning the possibility of war between the two countries, this memorandum recognized that its conclusions were based on vague generalizations and flimsy evidence. It noted the Japanese people's "great love of country, and national and racial pride," but could not see why that was sufficient reason for thinking that they were "preparing for war against the United States." However, the Japanese were also characterized by "secrecy and the power of concealing their motives and objects." The presence of Japan's secret agents in the United States, it was noted, indicated the existence of a plan to attack America unawares. The memorandum concluded: "It is believed that their efforts are principally directed towards obtaining information, or confirming reports already made as to the practicability of landing on our western coast and sustaining an army in Washington, Oregon, or California." [40] What such a paper reveals is the acceptance by the army's highest authorities of the possibility of war with Japan. The notion had dawned upon them during the immigration dispute, and the years after 1908 did nothing to dissipate it. While the emigration of Japanese to America dwindled, this did not diminish the anxiety that those already in the country were secret agents and collaborators. A memorandum by Hunter Liggett, chief of the War College division, dated March 27, 1911, noted that "certain Japanese have been occupying themselves with obtaining information regarding the bridges, tunnels, rolling stock, etc., of the railway lines leading to the Pacific Coast." Preparations seemed under way to blow up tunnels and bridges linking the Pacific coast with the rest of the country in the event of hostilities. There were also reports, Liggett said, "that Japanese agents are making maps and plans of every railroad and fortification in this country and our islands." The memorandum concluded by suggesting that the War Department request the various railroads to ascertain the number of Japanese employed. [41] The recommendation was made within the General Staff to dismiss as "security risks" all Japanese cooks at the hospital of the Presidio of San Francisco. [42] These steps, however, were considered too impractical, and the War Department's office of chief of engineers had admitted, in a memorandum of August 30, 1910, that "no means are known for restricting the activities of [Japanese] agents" in seeking "full information regarding our Pacific Coast." [43]

As before, communications from the public to the War Department abounded in reports of rumored Japanese activities of suspicious character. In September 1908 Fort Banks (Massachusetts) received information from a man in Nahant that a "Japanese was seen near Bay

Point sketching views in that neighborhood including the secondary stations on Mailey's Hill." Two Japanese were spotted taking photographs of another fort.[44] A New Haven real estate broker volunteered the information that a stenographer was typing a paper by a Japanese student at Yale, "about a war between the two nations which is supposed [to] take place about the year 1941." [45] Not a few correspondents wrote the secretary of war, warning of an alliance between Japanese and Negroes, which some feared would embrace other colored races of the Pacific area.[46]

Concern with Japanese activities outside the continental United States did not abate. From Mexico the United States military attaché wrote that he was examining "cartographically the territory of this Republic as a stepping-stone for a Japanese invasion of the United States." He believed that Japan had already decided on war against the United States and entered into a secret alliance with Mexico.[47] Cuba was regarded as another likely base of preparation for Japanese invasion. When the State Department relayed to the War Department the reported arrival of five Japanese, thought to be military officers, at Matanzas, Leonard Wood, chief of staff, suggested that the Cuban government be requested to keep them under surveillance.[48] Most serious, however, was the defense of Hawaii and the Philippines. Periodic surveys were made in Hawaii ascertaining such things as the number of fishing boats and firearms in Japanese possession. It was found, for instance, that on the island of Oahu 305 Japanese were believed to possess rifles and shotguns at the end of 1908, in contrast to 955 Chinese and 972 whites. In July 1909 there were 116 fishing boats belonging to Japanese, 77 of them near Pearl Harbor.[49] An officer of Fort Shafter, Oahu, wrote a four-page memorandum on "Land Defence of Oahu," and posed a hypothetical question: how to cope with a war with Japan, given the fact that there "are 20,000 (men, women and children) partisan residents." The writer suggested putting these aliens in camps as a basic solution.[50] Such memorandums were given careful attention in Washington, and President Taft as well as Secretary of War J. M. Dickinson were alive to the need to improve the defense capabilities of Hawaii.[51]

The defense of the Philippines presented special problems because of the islands' proximity to Japan and other circumstances such as the race and anti-American sentiment of the people. The suspicion was widespread that the Japanese already had a plan to conquer the Philippines and were engaged in intelligence and other types of subversive activities there. In the fall of 1909 much excitement was created among top American officials over reports that a high intelligence officer of the Japanese General Staff was in Luzon. The United States army headquarters in Manila cabled Washington that the visitor was there, "not only to spy out the land himself but also and chiefly to coordinate reports already made, and to communicate personally with scores, if not hundreds of other Japanese living and plotting here. [His visit] partakes not only of effrontery and duplicity, but is positively insulting." [52] Corroborating such reports, General Tasker H. Bliss, then commanding the army's Philippine department, asserted that the Japanese officer had approached Filipinos to ascertain their position in the event of war between the United States and Japan. Activities by certain Japanese in the Philippines, said Bliss, "present the appearance of a systematic effort to injure American prestige, stir up race feeling, create dissatisfaction with the existing government, and to acquire information concerning the topographical features of the country and surrounding waters and the state of preparedness of the government for the defense of the islands." [53] A major source of information on alleged Japanese-Filipino collusion was the army's Philippine constabulary, which employed Filipinos as agents. From time to time they reported having attended meetings at which native leaders were said to have discussed their stand in case of a Japanese-American war. In a secret memorandum addressed to the secretary of war, the headquarters of the constabulary warned, "There is no question whatever that there are, in addition to the members of the Japanese Information Division who are secretly obtaining maps and information and studying the dialects all over the Islands, also many other Japanese agents, natives either of Japan or of the Philippines, who are endeavoring to produce a pro-Japanese feeling on the part of the Filipinos. . . . [They] are not averse to stirring up an insurrection." [54]

Concern with Japan's military threat to the United States was nothing new. Top civilian and military leaders in Washington read these memorandums and consistently sought to strengthen the defenses of the Pacific territories as well as of the United States. But few thought that Japanese attack was imminent.[55] What was important, however, was that by 1910 Japan had come to be seen not only as a potential military antagonist in the Pacific but also as a rival in China. Army memorandums written at this time began to develop a comprehensive

picture of Japanese-American relations. The two were pictured as con-
flicting not only over immigration and strategic matters but also in
commercial and ideological ways. A long paper written for the Army
War College by Lieutenant C. A. Seoane, who had spent fifteen
months in China and Japan, was typical. Dated October 1911, it asserted that the "true position" of the United States was "that of a commercial power searching for open markets." Seoane echoed the sentiment of his countrymen that "[new] markets are necessary or else we
must recast our business." The crucial importance of China in this regard was not questioned, and the paper continued: "China alone remains open. And it seems essential that we should appreciate without
delay the great fact that our future will be much concerned with the
regions of this Empire of fabled wealth. We need no colonial Empire
but commercial satellites are necessary to our expanding commerce if
we are to continue to progress on the lines that our present manufacturing industries are laid." Japan was viewed as a competitor, even an
obstacle, in the way of American economic expansion, rather than as a
country with which the United States might maintain a relationship
of commercial interdependence.

China, however, was not viewed solely in economic terms. It was an
object of American expansion that was conceived in cultural and even
moral, as well as economic, terms. As Lieutenant Seoane stated, "in
addition to economic and political questions we must remember that
at last Western man in his great migration around the world has met
the East and if the said East is to take on the benefits of Western Civilization, the greater task is one that the United States and the United
States only can assume. The other White Powers are impotent."
Americans had the mission to befriend the downtrodden and help
them realize their aspirations. To do otherwise would bring to question America's quality as a nation and its status as an Asian and
Pacific power.[56] This was precisely the language used by administration officials and publicists who recognized the implications of the
growing enmity between Japan and the United States.

A seventy-eight-page report by Captain William Mitchell, then
with the army signal corps, not only sums up army thinking but also
provides a fitting resumé of developments in Japanese-American relations up to that time. Based on his observations during his tour of
Manchuria, Korea, and Japan in the fall of 1911, it stated categori-
cally, "That increasing friction between Japan and the United States

will take place in the future there can be little doubt and that this will eventually lead to war sooner or later, seems quite certain." The reasons Mitchell gave for these assertions need extensive quoting, as they were to be repeated time and again until the 1940's:

The Japanese resent the virtual exclusion of their citizens from our territory; the proposal to neutralize the Manchurian Railway and the fact that we have not officially recognized their annexation of Korea, are sore points. That we stand clearly for the territorial integrity of China is another. The fact of the whole matter is that our trade lines are crossing and they readily see that as our country becomes more developed internally . . . our over sea commerce will vastly increase, and should we push it and again create a large merchant marine, we would be in a good position to handle the trade of China with its 400,000,000 people. Japan's success in the China war and the Russian campaign has left her mistress of the East. Her men of war control the waters, while her merchant ships running to all parts of the world are successfully competing with all others, and growing very rapidly. Her army is excellent and prepared, and her merchants are gaining greatly in the continental trade of Asia.

Mitchell argued that Japanese children were inculcated in ideas of discipline, subordination, and patriotism at school, and when they came of age they entered the army, thus making it a formidable organization of well trained men. He estimated that as many as two million men could be immediately mobilized and that part of them could be shipped across the Pacific by Japan's merchant marine numbering 390 ships, aggregating over one million tons. Given such strength, should war occur between the two countries, "it is difficult to see how we could prevent an occupation of our Pacific coast states by Japan's armed forces." To cope with the alarming situation, Mitchell pointed out the absolute necessity of making plans for mobilization of at least 500,000 men to defend the West coast, and for organizing special corps of troops to be stationed at garrisons in overseas possessions.

There was one ray of hope in the otherwise gloomy picture: the growing friendship between Chinese and Americans. His observations in China had convinced him, Mitchell wrote, that the Chinese were united in their hatred of Japan; by contrast, they "regard the United States today in a better light than any foreign country. . . . They are convinced that we do not want any of their territory, and that we are the greatest guarantee of their territorial integrity." It might even be possible for Americans to provide China with military advisers, which would not only help the Chinese but bolster American prestige in Asia.[57]

Mitchell recognized the roots of Japanese-American estrangement for what they were: the growth of the two countries as expansionists both in Asia and the Pacific. In the years after 1908 official Japanese policy sought to reduce friction with the United States by stressing continentalism, but such a step was not supported by the public at home. Furthermore, it could not succeed because American policy at this very moment was asserting itself on the Asian continent. At every turn the two peoples were forced to become aware of each other's presence. They did not know how to conceptualize the resulting feeling of tension and anxiety except by referring to the language of mutual antagonism. A group of worried American Protestant missionaries in Japan met together in October 1909 and correctly diagnosed the difficulties. "In this day of extensive and increasing commingling of races and civilizations," their unanimous resolution read, "one of the prime problems is the maintenance of amicable international relations. Essential to this are not only just and honest dealings between governments, but also, as far as practicable, the prevention as well as the removal of race jealousy and misunderstanding between peoples themselves." [58] But the "commingling" of Americans and Japanese had resulted from their respective expansion in Asia and the Pacific, and no way could be found to reduce jealousy and misunderstanding in the process.

No such way could be found so long as Americans believed in opportunities and needs for expansion. It was no accident that those who disputed the existence of fundamental conflict between Japan and the United States also discounted the importance of Asian markets. "The trade of Manchuria," a typical *Nation* article stated, "may become in the future a matter of great importance to the people of the United States. . . . But do not let us act, with regard to the vague possibilities of a future that nobody can forecast, as though we were dealing with a vital or critical concern of the present." Such being the case, it was deplorable that the Americans seemed to have formed "the Japan habit, very much as the English have formed the Germany habit." Instead of magnifying the importance of America's trade with China and therefore of competition with Japan, they should "keep [their] heads level" and refrain from the sensationalism of predicting war between the two countries.[59] In a similar vein Ambassador

O'Brien lamented: "It seems unfortunately to be true that there is a considerable percentage of people in both countries who are not quite satisfied as to the sincerity and honesty of the purpose of the other. It is to be regretted that this sentiment prevails to a greater extent in the United States than [in Japan]." He alluded to "the opinion expressed without hesitation in high places at home that war with Japan is inevitable and that the plain duty of the United States is to augment her navy in the Pacific to a point not dreamed of even five years ago." O'Brien did not believe war was inevitable just because people thought so, but he feared that conflict could not be avoided unless both sides limited their expansionism. In view of the desirability of restricting Japanese immigration to the United States, he felt that country should not try to obstruct Japanese expansion in the western Pacific and East Asia. Americans should recognize that "we have no occasion to expand nor should America harbor envy or jealousy in the expansion of others." [60]

To disclaim an interest in westward expansion, however, was out of character with American thinking and practice at that time. To be sure there was no plan or desire on the part of the United States to dominate the Pacific militarily, as O'Brien feared, and the defensive strategy of War Plan Orange remained. As was made explicit in a detailed war plan adopted in May 1913, it was essential to maintain such a strategy until the Panama Canal was completed. "The character of such a war [with Japan] will at first be defensive on the part of the United States in the Philippines, Oahu, Panama, Alaska and on the Pacific coast of the United States." [61] There was no idea of extending the limits of American naval power in the Pacific. The United States navy had increased its total strength phenomenally during the two Roosevelt administrations, annual naval expenditures having been almost doubled between 1901 and 1909, from 60 to 115 million dollars. By the time Taft entered the White House, the tonnage of warships had increased to 496,000, more than four times that of 1901, which brought the United States navy second only to that of Great Britain. Naval expansion continued under Taft, though at a slower tempo; technical improvements in the fields of fire power, speed, and communication kept pace with quantitative increases, and bigger and better submarines as well as workable seaplanes were being developed. All of this, however, did not presuppose any offensive strategy but indicated an interest in preparedness. As Japan, too, continued to augment its armament, and since no other power maintained a large navy in the Pacific Ocean, Japanese-American rivalry was an accomplished fact.

To translate this rivalry in naval tonnage into actual hostility, however, would require another factor—a sense of competition and conflict—which was basically psychological and cultural. Archibald Cary Coolidge, for instance, in *The United States as a World Power,* criticized the notion of Japanese-American struggle for mastery of the Pacific as "mere claptrap," unless the struggle be derived from factors other than military. "The United States and Japan may, indeed, be rivals in the waters of the Pacific today . . . but the supposition is monstrous that they must therefore enter into a desperate struggle with each other in order that one of them may obtain an undisputed primacy, which depends on other things than force of arms." Coolidge correctly understood the basic character of the developing estrangement across the Pacific when he said, "if a large number of persons in the United States and in Japan are convinced that this 'dominion' [of the Pacific] properly belongs to their own country and not to the other, and that there must some day be a war between the two to settle the point . . . a situation and a state of mind are created which are perilous to the peace." [62]

It was precisely this state of mind that provided some Americans with a framework for viewing all aspects of Japanese-American relations and defined those relations as critical. This was especially true of America's economic expansion in Asia. Statistically speaking, American trade and investment in China were still minimal. United States exports to China in 1909 and 1911 remained roughly the same (about 19 million) in dollar figures, although in terms of the silver tael it increased from 32 to 40 million, reflecting a slight decline in the price of silver in terms of gold. In both years the American share in the Chinese market was about 8 percent; as earlier, its trade with Japan was far greater in volume than that with China. The total American exports to Japan during the three years between 1909 and 1911 amounted to about 85 million dollars, 30 million more than those to China. American imports accounted for between 12 and 16 percent of Japanese purchases in these years. In the field of loans and investment, it is true, there were signs of increasing activity after 1909, resulting in part from the vigorous leadership of the State Department. American loans to the Chinese government in Peking began that year, with a little over 7 million dollars lent to the Manchu regime before its overthrow. This was mostly America's share of the "Hukuang loan" for the nationalization of railways. The Chinchow-Aigun railway scheme, had it materialized, would have meant an additional American loan of 40 million dollars. The amount of total loans the Chinese government contracted between the end of the Russo-Japanese War and the Republican revolution is estimated to have been $125,750,000. The share of the United States, therefore, was a mere 6 percent.[63]

Although such statistics led some Americans to question the wisdom of expansion in China if it would incur the hostility of Japan, for a growing number of people the same evidence demonstrated the existence of Japanese-American rivalry. From such a point of view American commercial expansion was being hindered by Japan, whether acting alone or in conjunction with its imperialist friends. Thomas F. Millard wrote in 1910: "Our trade interests in Manchuria are considerable, have already been injured by conditions due to Russian and Japanese occupation, and may be further impaired by a continuation of it. Our trade with China is large, and certain to grow if not too badly handicapped." [64] Similarly, the *American Lumberman* (Chicago) said: "Japan . . . aspires to be to China what England so long was to the American colonies — the sole provider of manufactured commodities." [65] Such a policy was diametrically opposed to America's commercial aspirations, and unless Japan mended its ways, war with the United States could not be ruled out. Jacob Schiff, who had been instrumental in helping Japan procure American loans during the Russian war, came gradually to embrace this attitude, believing that the Japanese government was in the way of America's effort to supply capital to the Chinese. The New York speech in March 1910, in which he prophesied war between the two countries, occasioned much surprise, but it was in line with a basic view of American expansion and Japanese continentalism.[66] According to this reasoning, American expansion was becoming an article of faith, almost synonymous with anti-Japanese moves.

The basis of such reasoning was an image of China and a vision of America's task in Asia that was as much cultural and moral as economic. The United States could not discontinue its expansion in East Asia, fundamentally because it seemed to have a mission — to assist China's modern development and prevent its coming under Japanese control. As Millard eloquently put it, "The major premise of the moral obligation of western nations in the case of China is whether the institutions and ethical standards of East or West shall shape the course of civilization there." Expressed in this way, there was little doubt that the impending conflict between America and Japan had far larger implications than their economic interests. In the words of Millard, the fact "that the ultimate issue of any war between America and Japan will be whether the ideas and genius of the white or yellow races will dominate the future of civilization practically assures to America the moral support of greater European powers should such a conflict ever come." [67] That China would side with the United States and develop its institutions under American and Western inspiration seemed axiomatic. It is interesting to note that those who did not share such an image of China tended to be skeptical of the inevitability of Japanese-American conflict. Ambassador O'Brien in Tokyo wrote that China "is not able to meet her simplest obligations. She cannot or will not observe the terms of her solemn treaties, and the Government seems impotent to enforce its will even in her own provinces." He therefore failed to see why the United States should bestir itself on behalf of China and alienate Japan.[68] Similarly, George Kennan declared, "People who expect in China the rapid national transformation that took place in Japan will certainly be disappointed." The country lacked the ingredients of fiscal, military, and educational institutions essential for a modern nation. There was little point in a third power's trying to influence Chinese development, and it was incorrect to talk of Japanese designs on China.[69]

Official American policy, military thinking, and a segment of the foreign policy public were more in agreement with Millard than with Kennan. For them it was inconceivable to refrain from action in China just because it would precipitate a crisis with Japan. As Secretary of State Knox said in his famous reply to Theodore Roosevelt's letter expostulating with him against taking too inflexible a stand on Japanese rights in Manchuria: "I still believe that the wisest and best way for all concerned is for us to stand firmly on our pronounced policy and let it be known on every proper occasion that we expect fair play all round. The Japanese Government certainly is not indifferent to public opinion, and it is much better that we should continue to try to bring Japan's policy in China up to the level of ours, where we may differ, than to lower our policy to the level of hers." [70] China was serving as a symbol of confrontation between two expanding peoples of different races, traditions, and orientations. For many Americans it embodied the ultimate in the unrealized goals of universalistic expansion—unrealized chiefly because of Japanese obstruction, but never unrealizable. For Japanese, expansion into China meant not simply their determination to spread their power and influence on the Asian continent, but also a forced alternative to expansion eastward across the Pacific. Ironically, while Japanese and Americans were thus conceptualizing their encounter, forces were at work in China that were soon to bring about the end of the old order and usher in a revolutionary period of the Chinese people's foreign relations. It remained to be seen how the sense of estrangement across the Pacific might be affected by these changes, and how their respective expansion might become intertwined with the course of Chinese politics.

IX

Epilogue

The year 1911 is a convenient terminus to this analysis of the origins of Pacific estrangement. The new Japanese-American commercial treaty, providing complete tariff autonomy for Japan and the right of the United States to regulate immigration, was to remain the framework for their economic relations for the subsequent decades, until it was unilaterally abrogated by the United States in 1940. The Chinese Republican revolution, launched in October 1911, was to last even longer, establishing a setting in which Japanese and American expansion was to take place. The following year the Ch'ing dynasty ended its three-hundred-year history, the Meiji emperor died after reigning for over forty years, and elected President of the United States was Woodrow Wilson who, though no one knew it then, was to conceive of his and his country's role as the leader of a new world order.

That same year saw the signing of an arbitration treaty between the United States and Great Britain. Coming just after the renewal of the Anglo-Japanese alliance, it was designed to preclude the possibility of a Japanese-British combination against the United States, as the new alliance specified that neither signatory would fight a third power with whom it had an arbitration treaty. For the American people, however, there was added significance to the treaty with Britain. It was seen as evidence that the two countries had reached a stage at which no controversies so serious that they could be settled only on the battlefield would arise. The movement for arbitration rather than armament and war to settle international disputes had gained widespread support in the United States, not only among pacifist groups but also governmental and business leaders. It was assumed that wars were becoming obsolete, especially among civilized nations, which would seek to protect and extend their interests only through peaceful methods. As the *Outlook* asserted, "we are coming into that stage of society in which the nations are increasingly recognizing their international relations and looking forward to some form of true international unity." [1]

Had Japanese-American relations reached that stage? The editors of the *Outlook* were not certain. As they so clearly expressed it, "International arbitration assumes that certain nations have reached such a stage of civilization that any questions which are likely to arise between them may be safely submitted to the judgment of an independent court in which other nations of an equal degree of civilization are represented." An arbitration treaty with Japan was possible only on the basis that "both parties pledge themselves to respect each other's national honor, vital interests, internal administration, and territorial integrity." [2] To enumerate these conditions was to recognize the distance that still had to be traversed before potential amity rather than conflict could be taken for granted in Japanese-American relations. In view of the discord that had developed, the journal took the stand, perhaps reflecting the thinking of its contributing editor Theodore Roosevelt, that the most desirable basis for understanding was the countries' agreement to consider their racial and cultural identities as distinct and not to talk of their relations as if they were similar to American-British relations. It was better that East and West should not meet. "The East for the Oriental, the West for the Occidental, with no attempt to keep house together, but free intermingling in international trade, is the true solution of the Oriental problem." [3] This was hardly a realistic solution and it ran counter to the liberal international premises upon which the movement for arbitration treaties was based. How could one talk of the world becoming more and more civilized and unified so that there was less and less chance of war, and at the same time insist on maintaining the wall of separation between different peoples? The result of the interaction between Americans and Japanese might indicate, as speakers noted at a Clark University symposium in 1911, that "the Japanese are a strong, alert, aggressive and ambitious people, who have precisely those ambitions for supremacy which characterize white men," or that "no fundamental difference exists [between East and West] that should prevent mutual respect, appreciation, social intercourse and in time naturalization and full recognition of humanity." [4] Unfortunately, experiences of the preceding decades had encouraged the notion of their incompatibility, even as they expanded throughout the Pacific and Asia and came into closer contact with one another.

By 1911 the United States had had a long history of expansion, and its foreign affairs could be defined as an aspect of that story. The debate had been not whether to expand, but how and where. And, regardless of the divergence of opinions at home, the expansion had had a profound impact on the rest of the world. This book has dealt with the impact on Japan and its own expansionism. American territorial imperialism in the Pacific had emerged simultaneously with Japanese imperialism, and the two countries' relations had often resembled those of two empires, with complicated problems of defense and political compromises. No less important had been the development of the peaceful expansionism, sustained by economic energy and a sense of mission, that had defined the way Americans looked at their action in East Asia. It had its counterpart in Japan's own peaceful expansionism, inspired by an image of the United States as an expanding nation. The years of the administration of William Howard Taft saw the culmination of different types of American expansion, and its economic-moralistic aspect was most pronounced in Asia. This was also the time when Japan's expansionists were becoming self-consciously more particularistic. They never gave up the idea of peaceful expansion in all directions, but the unfortunate experiences in North America had turned them to greater willingness to espouse the idea of Asian empire.

In rhetoric at least, Woodrow Wilson accepted and strengthened the American liberal-expansionist tradition. "A nation is not made of anything physical," he said in 1912, but "of its strengths and its purposes. Nothing can give it dignity except its thoughts." [5] These thoughts consisted of principles such as liberty, fair play, and constitutional government, which were universal precepts governing the conduct of men. Since the United States embodied these principles, it undertook to spread them to other peoples who were no less entitled to them by being less developed. America's own interests would be served when other peoples were free and improved their well-being through free exchanges of commodities and ideas. As Wilson said of his Mexican policy, "We will serve the Mexican people without first thinking how we shall serve ourselves. . . . We must show ourselves friends [of Latin America] by comprehending their interest whether it squares with our own interest or not." [6] Under his initiative and inspiration, the self-perception of the American people as the moral leaders of the world was fostered to a greater degree than ever before. Wilsonianism was indeed a culmination of one strand of American expansionism.

Wilsonian ideals have been criticized as illusions unrelated to realities of American needs and considerations of power politics. They have also been characterized as a cover for capitalistic exploitation of the world.[7] These opinions pale in significance beside the far more fundamental dilemma of Wilsonianism: how to reconcile the universalism of certain ideals with the use of force to carry them out. The national power of the United States was at the service of ideals, in Mexico, Siberia, and, most important, Europe. Once military force was resorted to, particularistic considerations were bound to be given precedence over more abstract principles, although many, including Wilson himself, persisted in the belief that ideals could be promoted through state power. For them power itself was amoral, neutral. But American power was good because America was good. In the preface to *Drift and Mastery*, Walter Lippmann wrote, "we have not learned to use our power, and direct it to fruitful ends." [8] He was talking of the powers of industry and government, but the same concept could be and was applied to foreign affairs. The United States learned to use its power, and it could even be said that during the war it was "directed to fruitful ends." As Wilson saw it, America's military force was utilized to combat the evil power of evil nations. While attacking the old balancing-of-powers game, he supported a massive expansion in the navy and even added a new territory — the Danish West Indies — to the United States. A new world order which was to be an embodiment of Wilsonianism was being erected through military victories and on the destruction of existing societies. For all the self-consciousness about national power, however, few Americans came to grips with the fundamental tension between force and ideal, between political and ideological expansionism, that had been heightened as a result of the World War.

The war also had far-reaching implications for Japanese expansionism. Japan took advantage of the confusion in China and conflagration in Europe to extend its formal empire. Like the United States, its armies and ships were scattered throughout Asia and Europe, and its export trade increased phenomenally. To its leaders the vastly ex-

panded power and influence of the United States was a serious challenge. Even more so was Wilson's reaffirmation of the principles of
liberal expansionism, now known as the New Diplomacy. Japanese
leaders and opinion elites became aware that the postwar era was to
be a period of peaceful, rather than forceful, expansion. The transi-
tion from wartime imperialism to postwar economic expansionism
was not really as drastic or painful as historians have pictured it. There
had already been a tradition of nonimperialistic expansion in Japan.
All that was needed after 1918 was for Japan's leaders to recognize
that the international environment now favored that mode of expansion rather than tolerating the continuation of imperialism. This new
environment was to a great extent a product of American power and
ideology. Thus once again the Japanese found themselves accepting a
pattern of international behavior prescribed by Americans. "Today it
is a worldwide trend to honor pacifism and reject oppression," said
Makino Shinken, a Japanese plenipotentiary at the Paris Peace Conference. "Everywhere in the world the so-called Americanism is advanced, and conditions have definitely altered from the days of the
old diplomacy." [9]

The story of Japanese-American relations during the brief period of
peace (1918–1931) was a story of an experiment on the part of the two
to reconcile their respective economic expansionism. After they
agreed, at the Washington Conference (1921–1922), to reduce naval
armament and renounce aggressive military policy, their energies were
directed toward expanding their economic interests without the burden of territorial empire and through as peaceful a method as possible. Men like Secretaries of State Charles Evans Hughes and Frank B.
Kellogg or Secretary of Commerce Herbert C. Hoover were in this
sense all Wilsonians — perhaps even more inclined to economic expansionism without Wilson's readiness to employ force. Their counterparts in Japan, men such as Hara Kei and Shidehara Kijūrō, fully
shared the vision of a new world of economic interdependence and
political understanding among the advanced countries of the world.
Both the United States and Japan, to be sure, retained their empires,
and were not above using force to carry out policy objectives — as the
American occupation of Nicaragua and the Japanese expeditions to
Shantung revealed.[10] But these episodes were carryovers from the previous age, a legacy of imperialistic expansionism. Resistance to imperialism was strong in both countries, and the emphasis on the extension

of economic interests through peaceful methods was presenting a formidable challenge to the existing Caribbean policy of the United States. In Japan, too, a good-neighbor ideal of viewing China in the framework of economic policy was developing, and some, at least, of the governmental leaders and intellectuals were talking of the eventual necessity to give up political and territorial control over China.[11]

Unfortunately, postwar economic expansionism collapsed economically. The new world order depended on the continued supply of American capital and relative free trade among trading countries. More fundamentally, it had been related to the health of the capitalist economies and their smooth relationship in exchanging goods and capital. This in turn was dependent on the steady functioning of a gold-based exchange system. Since the United States was the predominant economic power, the availability of stable and abundant dollars was crucial in maintaining the existing system of international economic relations. All this changed after 1929, as credit shortages in Europe and the shrinkage in world trade brought about an era of managed currencies and tariff barriers. Economic expansionism seemed to have failed to justify itself. If a nation was to continue to expand, and few questioned the goal of expansion itself, more particularistic and militaristic alternatives had to be considered. Universalism gave way to regionalism, and internationalism to nationalism.

Japanese-American relations unfolded in such a framework. Those in Japan who had stood for the "Washington Conference system" failed to vindicate themselves as the national economy plunged into depression and the American market for Japanese exports shrank. Their critics argued that there could be no justification for peaceful expansionism when it brought no visible benefits. Moreover, in the case of Japanese-American relations there was one factor — immigration — that had never been part of the system of postwar expansionism. Despite adherence to principles of fair play, equal opportunity, and international harmony, the United States had not altered its policy of Japanese exclusion. If anything, it formalized the policy by enacting the new immigration act in 1924. From Japan's point of view, the right of free emigration was one of the cores of postwar international relations. The *Osaka Mainichi* had editorialized even before the end of the war that overseas emigration and enterprises were to be the sinew of postwar foreign policy.[12] Since it was now out of the question to acquire new colonies in which to settle a surplus population, the only solution to the nation's growing population problem was to fall back on the panacea of the 1890's: emigration and settlement abroad. This seemed totally in accord with the New Diplomacy of economic interdependence and political understanding among the powers. These ideas were not new; the mere fact that men such as Kayahara Kazan and Nitobe Inazō continued to write in the 1920's attested to the continuity of peaceful-expansionist thinking. But there was now a kind of determined self-consciousness about the new order. Men talked of the need to become "world citizens," and Japanese interests came to be viewed as simultaneous with world peace and international understanding.[13]

The 1920's left a lasting imprint on Japanese minds because of the unmistakable gap between such idealistic perceptions and the cruel reality of immigration restriction in the United States, which, combined with the economic crisis after 1929, shattered the dream world of peaceful expansionism. In the meantime Chinese nationalism, too, was destroying the basis of the Washington Conference system by unilaterally violating the existing treaties and threatening to expel from China those foreigners who did not accept the new dispensation. Japanese and American expansionists in China, instead of meeting the challenge jointly and cooperatively, each sought to make the most of the situation by strengthening bilateral ties with the Chinese. Japanese-American antagonism and mutual suspicion in China, dating back to the period of the Russo-Japanese War, never disappeared. The postwar structure of the peace in East Asia was supposed to have supplanted mutual hostility with an environment of understanding and cooperation, but such an environment existed more in the realm of imagination than in reality when Japan and the United States were confronted with China's revolutionary diplomacy.[14]

On September 17, 1931, Ambassador Debuchi Katsuji went to see Secretary of State Henry L. Stimson. The Japanese representative said he would soon be on leave and would not come back till next February. He asked "if there were any important things to come up while he was away." "I told him no," Stimson recorded, "but I said that before I went out of office I hoped that I might be able to at least take up some time the question of Japanese immigration." [15] Even as the two men went to bed that night, the curtain was rising on the opening act of the Manchurian crisis, which would obliterate any opportunity for solving the Japanese immigration issue in the United States, as the two nations would grapple with the question of how best to protect and promote their interests in China in totally changed circumstances. The decade of the 1930's saw Japan reverting to imperialism and regionalism, entrenching its power on the Asian mainland and ejecting Americans from China by force. Massive settlement of Japanese took place in Manchuria, while Japan's export to the United States began to decline, until, in 1940, the latter abruptly nullified the 1911 treaty of commerce. Nearly two years later, as the Japanese launched their ambitious project of imperialistic expansionism to create a pan-Asian order, their countrymen on the West coast of the United States lost their homes and businesses. They became enemy aliens, and the plan to segregate them — an idea proposed more than thirty years earlier during the first Pacific crisis — was put into effect. For Americans the attack on Pearl Harbor justified their suspicion of the Japanese character; it was but a confirmation of the long-held view that the Japanese wanted to expand by force of arms across the Pacific as well as on the continent of Asia, and had secretly prepared for the event. For Japanese the Pacific War was their answer to the westward movement of Americans. Using pan-Asianist language which, too, went back to the turn of the century, they asserted that the war signified Asia's counteroffensive against the expansion of Western power and civilization.[16]

The Second World War stopped Japan's imperialistic expansion; the return of millions of Japanese in torn clothes, poor health, and humiliation to the home islands dramatically ended fifty years of expansion. Yet, just as dramatically, postwar Japan staged a miraculous economic recovery and, less than twenty-five years after the war, Japanese merchants and commodities were all over the globe, contributing to a phenomenal growth of the nation's export trade. While other countries fought wars and suffered from civil strife, Japan, under a constitution that forbade the use of force to solve international disputes, and without once sending its armed forces overseas, was achieving the very goals of expansion sought by earlier generations. Undoubtedly the international environment now favored Japanese advances. With its security guaranteed by the former enemy, and with its three powerful neighbors engaged in cold wars, Japan was free to devote its resources to economic expansion. Nevertheless, postwar Japan's economic successes could not have been obtained if there had been no tradition of peaceful, economic expansionism. Men who directed Japanese foreign policy and conducted businesses were heirs to the prewar leaders who had experienced both imperialistic and nonimperialistic expansion. The triumph of one over the other since the Pacific War was the reaffirmation of a strong tradition, going back to the period before the first Sino-Japanese War.[17]

The United States, in contrast, emerged as the predominant military power in Asia. One of the first crucial decisions its leaders made after the Pearl Harbor attack was to send a large-scale expedition to Australia to demonstrate America's determination to stay in the southwestern Pacific. Throughout the war and after victory, the western Pacific and East Asia became primary areas for United States policy, much as the Western Hemisphere had been before 1941. The presence of American power shaped the course of Asian politics, and massive military interventions in Korea and in Vietnam, incurring expenses far out of proportion to immediate economic benefits, were accompanied by a rhetoric of empire that went back to the 1890's. But here again, the use of force, territorial control, and the language of duty, power, and national prestige were not the only ingredients of postwar American expansionism. The United States took a lead in liberalizing international trade, supplied capital to enable the devastated countries of the world to reconstruct, and abolished the quota system in immigration policy. Liberal expansionism often took the form of education; a far greater number of students than ever before studied Asian languages and civilization, and the new specialists did much to raise the level of general understanding of Asian affairs.

Perhaps the most fundamental area of postwar Japanese-American relations was the greatly expanded contact between the two peoples. For several decades they had met and interacted in the process of expansion. But instances of encounter and interaction grew to an unprecedented degree, beginning with the American occupation of Japan and continuing through the exchange of students and tourists and involving an ever-increasing number of joint activities — whether discussions of pollution, binational scholarly conferences, or movie production and theatrical performances.

It remains to be seen how deepened contact will affect the overall relations between the two countries. In the United States strong voices have called for retrenchment from overseas commitments. "Expansion," John K. Fairbank has said, "is now the great enemy of us all." [18] For an authoritative historian, one who has done much to relate America and East Asia to one another intellectually, to disparage expansion signifies the end of an era. But it is unlikely that unilateral contraction on the part of the United States will discourage expansion by others. In 1971, Japan's determined economic drive overseas caused America to adopt drastic measures to meet the challenge. Signs were everywhere that the asymmetrical relationship between the two countries after the war — the United States providing a military shield while Japan undertook economic expansion — was causing a serious strain, and that the two would have to grope for a new definition of their association. In the meantime, America's moves to seek China's cooperation in East Asia were causing the same kinds of response in Japan that had produced a sense of crisis after the Russo-Japanese War.

Whatever the future of expansion as a theme in United States–East Asian relations, one thing is certain. In a world of shrinking distances and diminishing spaces there are bound to be expansionists, whether their goals and methods be peaceful or militaristic, political or cultural. Japanese and Americans have played their roles as expansionists, and their Pacific estrangement has demonstrated the enormous difficulties of avoiding friction and suspicion, especially when two peoples represent diverse races and traditions. Nevertheless, awareness of these difficulties is a positive factor that can in time build a bridge of common humanity across the Pacific. If nothing else, the history of interaction between Japanese and Americans can bequeath to future generations of the world a legacy of warning as well as hope: warning against selfish, parochial approaches to foreign affairs, and hope that the level of understanding among peoples can be raised through the efforts of peacefully oriented and internationally minded individuals.

Notes, Bibliography, and Index

Abbreviations Used in the Notes

JFMA: Japanese Foreign Ministry Archives, Tokyo.
JWHA: Archives of War History Division, Self-Defense Agency, Japan. Tokyo.
NDA: Archives of Navy Department, United States. National Archives.
NGB: *Nihon gaikō bunsho*
NGB, NRS: *Nihon gaikō bunsho: Nichi-Ro sensō*
PRO: British Foreign Office Archives, Public Record Office. London.
SDA: State Department Archives, United States. National Archives.
WDA: Archives of War Department, United States. National Archives.
WWPA: Archives of Waiwupu (Chinese Foreign Ministry). Institute of Modern History, Academia Sinica, Taipei.

Notes

I. Introduction

1. Cited in Marilyn B. Young, *The Rhetoric of Empire: American China Policy, 1895–1901* (Cambridge, Mass., 1968), p. 97.

2. For a brief recent survey of some of the literature on imperialism, see Akira Iriye, "Imperialism in East Asia," in James B. Crowley, ed., *Modern East Asia: Essays in Interpretation* (New York, 1970), pp. 122–150. There is a good list of published works on the subject in the bibliography of David Healy, *U.S. Expansionism: The Imperialist Urge in the 1890's* (Madison, Wis., 1970).

3. See Norman A. Graebner, ed., *Manifest Destiny* (Indianapolis, 1968); Frederick Merk, *Manifest Destiny and Mission in American History: A New Interpretation* (New York, 1963); Frederick Merk, *The Monroe Doctrine and American Expansionism, 1843–1849* (New York, 1966); Richard W. Van Alstyne, *The Rising American Empire* (Oxford, 1960).

4. William H. Goetzmann, *Exploration and Empire* (New York, 1966), p. 58; Albert K. Weinberg, *Manifest Destiny* (Baltimore, 1935).

5. The standard work on early British diplomacy in China is John K. Fairbank, *Trade and Diplomacy on the China Coast: The Opening of the Treaty Ports, 1842–1854* (Cambridge, Mass., 1964). See also Douglas Hurd, *The Arrow War: An Anglo-Chinese Confusion, 1856–1860* (New York, 1968).

6. The best recent treatment of individual Americans overseas in the first century of national history is James A. Field, *America and the Mediterranean World, 1776–1882* (Princeton, 1969). Also valuable is Clifton Jackson Phillips, *Protestant America and the Pagan World: The First Half Century of the American Board of Commissioners for Foreign Missions, 1810–1860* (Cambridge, Mass., 1969).

7. Robert Kelley, *The Transatlantic Persuasion: The Liberal Democratic Mind in the Age of Gladstone* (New York, 1969). The interaction between American and European history, in particular the interaction of ideas, has

been traced by such books as Durand Echeverria, *Mirage in the West: A History of the French Image of American Society to 1815* (Princeton, 1957), and R. R. Palmer, *The Age of the Democratic Revolution: A Political History of Europe and America, 1760–1800,* 2 vols. (Princeton, 1959, 1964).

8. *American Whig Review,* 3: 612–624 (June 1846). Nineteenth-century American thinking on civilization and history has been given authoritative treatment by Louis Harz, *The Liberal Tradition in America* (New York, 1955), and Richard Hofstadter, *The Progressive Historians: Turner, Beard, Parrington* (New York, 1968).

9. William H. Seward, *Works,* ed. George E. Baker, vol. 4 (New York, 1889), pp. 165–166, 169–170.

10. See Philip S. Klein, *President James Buchanan: A Biography* (University Park, Pa., 1962), for Buchanan's foreign policy.

11. Phillips, *Protestant America,* pp. 122–132.

12. Henry Blumenthal, *A Reappraisal of Franco-American Relations, 1830–1871* (Chapel Hill, 1959), chap. 4.

13. Seward, *Works,* 4: 319, 320.

14. *American Whig Review,* 15: 508 (June 1852).

15. *Democratic Review,* 28: 325 (April 1852).

16. *North American Review,* 87: 235–236 (July 1856).

17. *Harper's Monthly,* 21: 324 (August 1860).

18. *Atlantic Monthly,* 5: 722 (June 1860).

19. Stuart Creighton Miller, *The Unwelcome Immigrant: The American Image of the Chinese, 1875–1882* (Berkeley, 1969), p. 126.

20. There are no comprehensive accounts of American foreign relations for these years, but Field, *America and the Mediterranean World,* is relevant to this period. See also David M. Pletcher, *The Awkward Years: American Foreign Relations under Garfield and Arthur* (Columbia, Mo., 1962); Milton Plesur, *America's Outward Thrust: Approaches to Foreign Affairs, 1865–1890* (DeKalb, Ill., 1971). Both of these are conventional, uni-archival studies.

21. Cited in Pletcher, *Awkward Years,* p. 70.

22. Cited in Edward L. Younger, *John A. Kasson: Politics and Diplomacy from Lincoln to McKinley* (Iowa City, 1955), p. 340.

23. See Peter Duus, "Science and Salvation in China: The Life and Work of W. A. P. Martin (1827–1916)," in Kwang-ching Liu, ed., *American Missionaries in China: Papers from Harvard Seminars* (Cambridge, Mass., 1966), pp. 11–41.

24. *Shinbun shūsei Meiji hennen-shi* (Chronicle of the Meiji period as seen in newspapers), 6: 80 (Tokyo, 1935).

25. Matsumoto Kunpei, *Kaigai seicha bōeki iken* (A view of the tea trade; Tokyo, 1896), pp. 17ff.

26. Henry M. Field, *From Egypt to Japan* (New York, 1877), pp. 59, 60, 243, 246, 248, 416, 424.

27. Cited in Pletcher, *Awkward Years,* p. 225.

28. *Andover Review,* 4: 327–328 (October 1885).

29. Josiah Strong, *Our Country: Its Possible Future and Its Present Crisis,* rev. ed. (New York, 1891), p. 225.

30. *Ibid.,* p. 222.

31. E. A. Allen, *History of Civilization,* 4 vols. (Cincinnati, 1888), 4: 726.

32. For Chinese emigration in the nineteenth century, see especially Gunther Barth, *Bitter Strength: A History of the Chinese in the United States, 1850–1870* (Cambridge, Mass., 1964); Edgar Wickberg, *The Chinese in Philippine Life, 1850–1898* (New Haven, 1965).

33. Phillips, *Protestant America,* p. 86.

34. Miller, *Unwelcome Immigrant, passim.*

35. Cited in Pletcher, *Awkward Years,* p. 178.

36. Kuroda Ken'ichi, *Nihon shokumin shisō-shi* (History of colonialism in Japan; Tokyo, 1942).

37. Yoshida Hideo, *Nihon jinkō-ron no shiteki kenkyū* (Historical study of population theories in Japan; Tokyo, 1944).

38. Marius B. Jansen, *The Japanese and Sun Yat-sen* (Cambridge, Mass., 1954); Uete Michiari, "Taigaikan no tenkai" (Changing images of the world), in Hashikawa Bunzō and Matsumoto Sannosuke, eds., *Kindai Nihon seiji shisō-shi* (Modern Japanese political thought), vol. 1 (Tokyo, 1971); Motoyama Yukihiko, "Ajiya to Nihon" (Asia and Japan), in *ibid.* For specific examples of Meiji Japanese adventurers on the Asian continent, the best source is *Tōa senkakusha shishi kiden* (Chronicle of pioneers in East Asia) ed. Kokuryūkai (Black Dragon Society), 3 vols. (Tokyo, 1933–1936).

39. Taiwan Governor-General's Office, *Meiji shoki Hong Kong Nihonjin* (Japanese in Hong Kong in the early Meiji period; Taipei, 1937), pp. 112, 270.

40. *Hennen-shi,* 6: 211.

41. *Ibid.,* 6: 25.

42. Hashimoto Jūbei, *Sanshi bōeki kairyō shigi* (A proposal for improving the silk trade; n.p. [1883]), pp. 4–5, 10–11, 15, 93.

43. Ōgoshi Seitoku, *Gaikoku bōeki kakuchō-ron* (How to expand our foreign trade; Tokyo, 1889), pp. 64–65, 70, 140–146. See also *Hennen-shi,* 6: 141–142.

44. Ōgoshi, *Gaikoku bōeki,* p. 151; Mutō Sanji, *Beikoku ijūron* (On emigration to the United States; Tokyo, 1887), preface and p. 107.

45. *Ibid.,* p. 143.

46. Nakae Chōmin, *San suijin keirin mondō* (Argument among three drunkards; Tokyo, 1887), pp. 5–6, 43–44, 48–50, 64, 82, 87, 136.

II. The Emergence of Imperialism

1. *Yorozu chōhō,* Aug. 16, 1898.

2. Julius W. Pratt, *Expansionists of 1898: The Acquisition of Hawaii and the Spanish Islands* (Baltimore, 1936); Richard Hofstadter, *Social Darwinism in American Thought* (Philadelphia, 1944). Not all Social Darwinists were imperialists, of course; men like William Graham Sumner were impelled by Social Darwinism to become strong opponents of imperialism.

3. Ernest R. May, *American Imperialism: A Speculative Essay* (New York, 1968).

4. Allan Nevins, *Henry White: Thirty Years of American Diplomacy* (New York, 1930), pp. 110–111, 119.

5. *Science,* 20: 359 (December 1892).

6. Josiah Strong, *The New Era, or the Coming Kingdom* (New York, 1893), p. 2.

7. Charles Morris, *Civilization: An Historical Review of Its Elements* (Chicago, 1890), pp. 1, 37, 477.

8. Allen, *History of Civilization,* 4: 3, 726, 752.

9. For an excellent study of America's self-confidence in the late nineteenth century and the early twentieth century, see Henry F. May, *The End of American Innocence: A Study of the First Years of Our Own Time, 1912–1917* (New York, 1959). It is my view that the kind of innocence May describes was being subtly eroded by the self-consciousness about American civilization, with problems it shared with Western civilization in general.

10. Strong, *New Era,* p. 222 (italics are Strong's).

11. *Forum,* 20: 644 (February 1896).

12. *Arena,* 2: 83, 97 (June 1890).

13. Charles H. Pearson, *National Life and Character: A Forecast* (London, 1893), pp. 13, 14, 84, 96, 130, 344. For another good example, see Henry Norman, *People and Politics of the Far East* (London, 1895).

14. *Outlook,* 60: 425 (June 1899).

15. *Harper's,* 95: 523–533 (September 1897).

16. *Atlantic,* 79: 722–732 (June 1897). See also another article Wheeler wrote for *Atlantic* (82: 146–153; August 1898). In it he said, "The United States of America find themselves forced . . . to transmute their policy of resisting intrusion into one of assuming the positive responsibilities of a moral hegemony in the West."

17. Thomas J. McCormick, *China Market: America's Quest for Informal Empire, 1893–1901* (Chicago, 1967). Another excellent discussion of Cleveland's anti-imperialism is in E. Berkeley Tompkins, *Anti-Imperialism in the United States: The Great Debate, 1890–1920* (Philadelphia, 1970).

18. *Letters of Grover Cleveland,* ed. Allan Nevins (Boston, 1933), pp. 130, 134–135, 335–336, 365–366.

19. *Ibid.,* p. 419.

20. May, *American Imperialism,* p. 181.

21. Inagaki Manjirō, *Tōhōsaku* (Eastern policy; Tokyo, 1891), pp. 18, 90, 113, 160–162. See also the original English edition: *Japan in the Pacific: A Japanese View of the Eastern Question* (London, 1890).

22. Ōishi Masami, *Fukyōsaku* (On enriching and strengthening the nation; Tokyo, 1891), pp. 50, 59, 64–70.

23. Tsuneya Seifuku, *Kaigai shokumin-ron* (On overseas colonization; Tokyo, 1891), pp. 1–2, 68, 78–87.

24. See Tokutomi Sohō's preface to Hattori Tōru, *Nanyō-saku* (Policy toward the south; Tokyo, 1890); Kayahara Kazan, *Tōhoku taiseiron* (On conditions in northeastern Japan; Yamagata, 1895), p. 66.

25. Hattori, *Nanyō-saku,* pp. 4, 39, 80–82, 135.

26. Watanabe Shūjirō, *Sekai ni okeru Nihonjin* (Japanese in the world; Tokyo, 1893), preface and p. 386. See also Mishima Kazuo, *Gōshū oyobi Indo* (Australia and India; Tokyo, 1891); Shiga Shigetaka, *Nanyō jiji* (Affairs in the South Seas; Tokyo, 1887). These authors were particularly attracted by Australia, which seemed both highly civilized and in need of development, thus offering marvelous opportunities for Japanese enterprise.

27. Takeuchi Seishi, *Shin rikkoku* (The founding of the new nation; Tokyo, 1892), pp. 13–14, 30–34, 40, 309, 535–536, 540–546.

28. *Shokumin Kyōkai hōkoku* (Report of the Colonization Society), no. 1 (1893).

29. *Ibid.*

30. *Nihon kyōkasho taikei* (Anthology of Japanese textbooks), ed. Kaigo Tokiomi, 15: 254–262, 487 (Tokyo, 1965).

31. *Ibid.*, 16: 152–154, 252–253.

32. Nagasawa Setsu, *Yankii* (Yankees; Tokyo, 1893), pp. 5–6, 8–9, 11–22, 34–35, 117, 131–132.

33. Tokutomi Sohō, *Dai-Nihon bōchōron* (On the expansion of Japan; Tokyo, 1894), pp. 5–6, 17.

34. Yanabe Kentarō, *Nik-Kan gappei shōshi* (A short history of the Japanese annexation of Korea; Tokyo, 1966), pp. 101–105.

35. Tokutomi, *Dai-Nihon bōchōron*, pp. 22–23. See also Kimitada Miwa, "Crossroads of Patriotism in Imperial Japan" (unpublished Ph.D. dissertation, Princeton University, 1967), pp. 180–183.

36. Kayahara, *Tōhoku taiseiron*, pp. 26, 29–38.

37. For Japanese diplomacy and continentalism during 1894–95, see Tabohashi Kiyoshi, *Nis-Shin sen-eki gaikōshi no kenkyū* (A study of the diplomacy of the Sino-Japanese War; Tokyo, 1951); Hilary Conroy, *The Japanese Seizure of Korea, 1868–1910* (Philadelphia, 1960).

38. Tokutomi, *Dai-Nihon bōchōron*, pp. 66–71, 137, 147–148, 155–157.

39. Minyūsha, ed., *Ensei* (Expeditions to distant lands; Tokyo, 1895), pp. 1–6, 9.

40. Matsumoto, *Kaigai seicha*, pp. 7–8.

41. *Ibid.*, pp. 62ff.

42. Cited in Sumiya Mikio, *Dai-Nihon teikoku no shiren* (Tribulations of the Japanese empire; Tokyo, 1966), pp. 136–139.

43. The best account in English is Ian Nish, *The Anglo-Japanese Alliance: The Diplomacy of Two Island Empires, 1894–1907* (London, 1967).

44. See, for instance, Sumiya, *Dai-Nihon teikoku*; Inoue Kiyoshi, *Nihon teikokushugi no keisei* (The formation of Japanese imperialism; Tokyo, 1968).

45. *Hennen-shi*, 9: 14 (Tokyo, 1936).

46. *Ibid.*, 9: 16.

47. *Ibid.*, 9: 127, 241, 244.

48. *Ibid.*, 9: 281.

49. *Ensei*, pp. 31–34, 128.

50. Minyūsha, ed., *Firipin guntō* (The Philippine Islands; Tokyo, 1896), pp. 10–11, 139–142.

51. See William A. Russ, *The Hawaiian Revolution, 1893–94* (Selinsgrove, Pa., 1959), for an excellent discussion of the subject.

52. Basic documentation on the incident is in *Nihon gaikō bunsho* (Japanese diplomatic documents; hereafter cited as *NGB*), 30: 659ff. (Tokyo, 1954). See also Hilary Conroy, *The Japanese Frontier in Hawaii, 1868–1898* (Berkeley, 1953), p. 125.

53. In 1894 the Japanese government abolished the system of "official contract emigration" under which the two governments undertook the supervision of Japanese emigration to and work in Hawaii. After June 1894 emigration to the islands was put in the hands of private companies. See *Hawai Nihonjin imin-shi* (A history of Japanese immigrants in Hawaii; Honolulu, 1964), pp. 145–148.

54. Conroy, *Japanese Frontier,* p. 120.

55. Shimamura to Ōkuma, Mar. 18 and Apr. 7, 1897, *NGB,* 30: 674–676, 703.

56. Ōkuma to Shimamura, Apr. 12, 1897, *ibid.,* 30: 704–705.

57. Ōkuma to Shimamura, Apr. 19, 1897, *ibid.,* 30: 717–724.

58. Cited in Murota to Ōkuma, May 13, 1897, *ibid.,* 30: 747–748.

59. Pratt, *Expansionists of 1898,* p. 218.

60. *Ibid.,* p. 220.

61. Robert Beisner, *Twelve Against Empire: The Anti-Imperialists, 1898–1900* (New York, 1968), pp. 148–150.

62. George F. Hoar, *Autobiography of Seventy Years,* 2 vols. (New York, 1903), 2: 307–308.

63. Pratt, *Expansionists of 1898,* pp. 225, 320.

64. *Ibid.,* p. 320.

65. Hoshi to Ōkuma, Feb. 26, 1897, *NGB,* 30: 945–947.

66. Ōkuma to Hoshi, Mar. 30, 1897, *ibid.,* 30: 947–948; Ōkuma to Katō, Mar. 30, 1897, *ibid.,* 30: 948; Ōkuma to Hoshi, June 18, 1897, *ibid.,* 30: 978–979.

67. Katō to Ōkuma, May 21, 1897, *ibid.,* 30: 968–970.

68. Ōkuma to Hoshi, June 18, 1897, *ibid.,* 30: 978–979.

69. Hoshi to Ōkuma, June 17, 1897, *ibid.,* 30: 978.

70. Ōkuma to Hoshi, June 19, 1897, *ibid.,* 30: 985–986.

71. *Akiyama Masanosuke den* (Biography of Akiyama Masanosuke; Tokyo, 1941), pp. 58ff.

72. Murota to Ōkuma, May 13, 1897, *NGB,* 30: 747–748.

73. *Hennen-shi,* 10: 93–94 (Tokyo, 1936).

74. Conroy, *Japanese Frontier,* p. 136.

75. Walter LaFeber, *The New Empire: An Interpretation of American Expansion, 1860–1898* (Ithaca, 1963); McCormick, *China Market;* William Appleman Williams, *The Roots of the Modern American Empire: A Study of the Growth and Shaping of Social Consciousness in a Marketplace Society* (New York, 1969).

76. Young, *Rhetoric of Empire;* Healy, *U.S. Expansionism.*

77. Ernest R. May, *Imperial Democracy: The Emergence of America as a Great Power* (New York, 1961).

78. John A. S. Grenville and George B. Young, *Politics, Strategy, and American Diplomacy* (New Haven, 1966), pp. 271–276.

79. McNair to Dewey, Dec. 31, 1897, Department of Navy Archives (hereafter cited as NDA), Record Group (hereafter cited as RG), 45, National Archives; Long to Dewey, Feb. 1, 1898, NDA, RG 45.

80. Dewey to Long, Mar. 31, 1898, *ibid.*

81. Memo by Sicard, May 20, 1898, *ibid.*

82. McKinley to Long, May 19, 1898; memo by McKinley, May 21, 1898, *ibid.*

83. Sewall to Day, June 8, 1898, *ibid.*

84. Memo by Sicard, Aug. 19, 1898, *ibid.*

85. *Cleveland Leader,* May 29, 1898, enclosed in Irvine to Long, June 10, 1898, NDA, RG 45; *Atlantic,* 82: 432 (September 1898).

86. Ōkuma to Katō, Kurino, and Nakagawa, Sept. 8, 1898, *NGB*, 31.2: 357–358 (Tokyo, 1954).

87. *Jiji shinpō,* May 31, 1898.

88. *Yorozu chōhō,* May 5, 1898.

89. *Ibid.,* Aug. 16, 1898.

90. *Ibid.,* May 24, 1898.

91. *Gaikō jihō (Revue diplomatique),* 1.7: 21–31 (Aug. 20, 1898).

92. *The Anti-Imperialist* (Brookline, Mass.), no. 1, p. 37 (May 27, 1899).

93. See Yamaguchi Kazuyuki, "Kenseitō naikaku no seiritsu to Kyokutō jōsei" (The formation of the Kenseitō cabinet and its policy toward the Far East), *Kokusai seiji* (International politics), no. 19, p. 98 (April 1962).

94. *Ibid.,* pp. 97–99.

95. Takayama Rinjirō, *Jidai kanken* (Thoughts on contemporary affairs; Tokyo, 1898), pp. 20, 208.

96. *Ibid.,* pp. 23–24, 220, 223–225.

III. Beyond Imperialism

1. The best account of United States naval thinking on East Asian matters is William R. Braisted, *The United States Navy in the Pacific, 1897–1909* (Austin, Tex., 1958); see especially chap. 3.

2. Hackett to Kempf, June 18, 1900, Archives of War Department (hereafter cited as WDA), RG 165.

3. Lyman to McKinley, July 20, 1900, *ibid.*

4. Remey to Long, June 6, 1900, *ibid.*

5. Chaffee to adjutant general's office, rec. Dec. 4, 1900, *ibid.*

6. Bash to Adee, Aug. 14, 1900, *ibid.*

7. Braisted, *United States Navy,* pp. 126–128; Takahira to Katō, Dec. 7, 1900, *NGB*, 33: 273–274 (Tokyo, 1956).

8. Tyler Dennett, *John Hay: From Poetry to Politics* (New York, 1933); Young, *Rhetoric of Empire*; LaFeber, *New Empire*; McCormick, *China Market*; Thomas J. McCormick, "American Expansion in China," *American His-*

torical Review, 75: 1393–1397 (June 1970); Williams, *Roots of Modern American Empire*; Jerry Israel, *Progressivism and the Open Door: America and China, 1905–1921* (Pittsburgh, 1971); L. I. Zubok, *Ekspansionistskaia politika SShA v nachale XX veka* (Moscow, 1969).

9. Woodrow Wilson, *A History of the American People*, vol. 5: *Reunion and Nationalization* (New York, 1902), pp. 294–296, 299–300.

10. Charles A. Conant, *The United States in the Orient: The Nature of the Economic Problem* (Boston, 1901), pp. 2–3, 32–33, 222–224.

11. Paul S. Reinsch, *World Politics at the End of the Nineteenth Century, as Influenced by the Oriental Situation* (New York, 1900), pp. 20, 42, 66, 79, 236–237, 326.

12. *Ibid.*, p. 214, 240; Josiah Strong, *Expansion* (New York, 1900), pp. 189, 191, 193, 202–205. The quote from Giddings is in *ibid.*, p. 186.

13. Alfred Thayer Mahan, *The Problem of Asia, and Its Effect on International Politics* (New York, 1900), pp. 31–33, 90–91.

14. Brooks Adams, *The New Empire* (New York, 1902), p. 194.

15. *Literary Digest*, 21: 3 (July 7, 1900); *ibid.*, 21: 62 (July 21, 1900); Farnham to Goodnow, July 7, 1900, WDA, RG 165.

16. For United States policy in China during the Boxer crisis, see Young, *Rhetoric of Empire*; Paul A. Varg, *The Making of a Myth: The United States and China, 1897–1912* (East Lansing, 1968).

17. Allen to Rockhill, Feb. 28, 1901, and Jan. 4, 1904, Papers of W. W. Rockhill (Harvard University).

18. Memo by Muir, Oct. 24, 1900, WDA, RG 165.

19. Braisted, *United States Navy*, p. 142; Mahan, *Problem of Asia*, pp. 11–12. (Mahan asserts that Japan does not covet the Philippines.)

20. Tsunoda Jun, *Manshū mondai to kokubō hōshin* (The Manchurian problem and strategic principles; Tokyo, 1967); Nish, *Anglo-Japanese Alliance*; John A. White, *The Diplomacy of the Russo-Japanese War* (Princeton, 1964); George Lensen, *Korea and Manchuria between Russia and Japan, 1895–1904* (Tallahassee, 1966).

21. See Tani Toshio, *Kimitsu Nichi-Ro senshi* (Secret history of the Russo-Japanese War; Tokyo, 1966), which is based on a series of confidential lectures Colonel Tani gave in 1925 at the Army War College. These lecture notes, containing many unpublished documents, are in Archives of War History Division, Self-Defense Agency (henceforth cited as JWHA). Also invaluable for background data on the war is *Kimitsu Nichi-Ro senshi* (Secret history of the Russo-Japanese War; Tokyo, 1931), compiled by the General Staff. Kurino Shin'ichirō, minister to Russia, who tried desperately to prevent rupture between the two countries, was convinced that by making some compromise on the issue of Korean fortification, Japan could expand economically, with Russia's blessings, not only in Korea but also in Manchuria and Siberia. See Hiratsuka Atsushi, *Shishaku Kurino Shin'ichirō den* (Biography of Count Kurino Shin'ichirō; Tokyo, 1942).

22. See *NGB*, 36.1: 1–49 (Tokyo, 1957), for examples of intergovernmental exchanges between the United States and Japan on the Manchurian question.

23. Memo by Ikata, February 1901, in *Kimitsu Nichi-Ro senshi,* chap. 1.

24. See Asai Masahide, ed., *Kaigun gunbi enkaku* (History of naval armament; Tokyo, 1922).

25. Kōtoku Shūsui, *Nijusseiki no kaibutsu teikokushugi* (Imperialism, the monster of the twentieth century; Tokyo, 1901), pp. 1, 4, 15–17, 31–33, 45, 91–95, 97, 103–105, 122, 126–127.

26. These book reviews are printed in the second edition of Kōtoku, *ibid.*

27. Takimoto Seiichi, *Keizaiteki teikokushugi* (Economic imperialism; Tokyo, 1901), pp. 7, 19–22, 37, 63, 72, 92, 98–103, 138–139, 153.

28. Ukita Kazutami, *Teikokushugi to kyōiku* (Imperialism and education; Tokyo, 1901), pp. 19–20, 35–36, 43–44, 49–50, 68–69, 75–84. Ukita reiterated the theme of universalistic expansionism — what he came to call "ethical imperialism" — in *Kokumin kyōiku-ron* (On national education; Tokyo, 1903).

29. Itakura Naka, *Keisei kigen* (Thoughts on government; Tokyo, 1902), p. 61.

30. Satō Torajirō, *Shin seikei* (New politics and economy; Tokyo, 1903), pp. 176–177.

31. *Ibid.,* pp. 137–138, 153–156, 212–218.

32. Satō Torajirō, *Shina keihatsu-ron* (On developing China; Yokohama, 1903), pp. 5, 54–56, 59.

33. *Ibid.,* pp. 34, 58.

34. Komura to Uchida, Mar. 2, 1903, *NGB,* 36.2: 170–171 (Tokyo, 1957).

35. Sanetō Keishū, *Chūgokujin Nihon ryūgaku-shi* (History of Chinese students in Japan; Tokyo, 1960), pp. 53, 87ff.

36. See Akira Iriye, "Chūgoku ni okeru Nihon bukkyō fukyō mondai" (Japanese Buddhist missionaries in China), *Kokusai seiji,* no. 26, pp. 87–100 (April 1965).

37. *Kimitsu Nichi-Ro senshi,* pp. 21–24.

38. *Ibid.,* pp. 25ff. Yamagata Aritomo, the army's senior leader, also considered China primarily an area for Japan's economic expansion. In a memorandum written in August 1900, he joined his voice to southern expansionism, arguing that the nation should aim at entrenching its economic interests in the provinces of Fukien and Chekiang. *Yamagata Aritomo ikensho* (Memoranda of Yamagata Aritomo; Tokyo, 1966), pp. 255–264.

39. Asai, *Kaigun gunbi enkaku,* pp. 84ff.

40. *Meiji sanjūshichihachi-nen kaisen-shi* (The naval warfare of 1904–5), ed. Navy General Staff (Tokyo, n.d.), pt. 1, vol. 1, pp. 22ff.

41. See Satō Tetsutarō, *Teikoku kokubō shiron* (A historical study of Japanese strategy; Tokyo, 1908); Shimada Kinji, *Roshia ni okeru Hirose Takeo* (Hirose Takeo in Russia; Tokyo, 1961); Shimada Kinji, *Amerika ni okeru Akiyama Saneyuki* (Akiyama Saneyuki in America; Tokyo, 1969).

42. Moriyama Nobunori, *Bei-Sei sensō* (The Spanish-American War; Tokyo, 1903), pp. 210, 215–216. See also Narita to Komura, Feb. 9, 1903, *NGB,* 36.2: 410–411. Japanese-American economic relations in general are well delineated in Kaneko Kentarō, *Yū-Bei kenbunroku* (Observations in America; Tokyo, 1900).

43. *Hawai Nihonjin,* p. 167.

44. For instance, see Hamaguchi Kichiemon, *Hokubei Nihon shōkō se-isaku* (Japan's commercial and industrial policy toward North America; Tokyo, 1901), p. 143.

45. Watanabe Kanjirō, *Kaigai dekasegi annai* (A guide to working abroad; Tokyo, 1902), p. 3.

46. *Ibid.,* pp. 5–8, 19–34.

47. Preface to *Shin to-Bei* (Going to America; Tokyo, 1904), ed. Shuppan Kyōkai.

48. Katayama Sen, *To-Bei annai* (How to go to the United States; Tokyo, 1901), pp. 1–3, 4, 9. Other examples of guidebooks for prospective emigrants to the United States are: Okumiya Takeyuki, *Hoku-Bei imin-ron* (On emigrating to North America; Tokyo, 1903); and Ōfu Onshi (pseud.), *Zai-Bei seikō no Nihonjin* (Successful Japanese in America; Tokyo, 1904). The latter was a collection of articles serialized in the newspaper *Osaka Mainichi,* and the author asserted that it was "the spirit of the times" to go abroad and establish "new Japans" everywhere in the world.

49. See *Shin to-Bei;* Yoshimura Daijirō, *Seinen no to-Bei* (Young people's going to America; Tokyo, 1902).

50. Katayama, *To-Bei annai,* pp. 22–24, 66–67.

51. Yoshimura, *Seinen no to-Bei,* pp. 24–25.

52. Watanabe Shirō, *Kaigai risshin no tebiki* (How to get ahead abroad; Tokyo, 1902), p. 57.

53. Noma Gozō, *Jūō kōgiroku* (Speeches; Okayama, 1902), pp. 103–105.

54. Katayama, *To-Bei annai,* pp. 14–15.

55. *Nichi-Bei bunka kōshō-shi* (History of cultural relations between Japan and the United States), vol. 5: *Ijū-hen* (Immigration; Tokyo, 1955), pp. 96–115.

56. See *NGB,* 33: 405–464 (Tokyo, 1956).

IV. Japanese Continentalism and Chinese Nationalism

1. Taft to Lawrence, Feb. 14, 1904, Papers of William Howard Taft (Library of Congress).

2. Sugiyama to Taft, Jan. 7, 1904, Taft Papers.

3. Original in English: Komura to Uchida, Feb. 17, 1904, *NGB,* 37.2: 54–55 (Tokyo, 1958).

4. Original in English: Uchida to Komura, Jan. 8, 26, 29, and Feb. 2, 1904, *NGB,* 37.2: 31–33; Komura to Uchida, Jan. 28, 30, 1904, *NGB,* 37.2: 37–49.

5. Komura memo, July 1904, in *NGB, Nichi-Ro sensō* (The Russo-Japanese War; hereafter cited as *NRS*), 5: 59–63 (Tokyo, 1960).

6. Tsunoda, *Manshū mondai,* p. 281.

7. Tani, *Kimitsu Nichi-Ro senshi,* chap. 10.

8. *Manshū kaihatsu yonjūnen-shi* (Forty years of Manchurian development; Tokyo, 1964), ed. Manshikai, 1: 178.

9. Irie Toraji, *Hōjin kaigai hattenshi* (History of Japanese overseas; Tokyo, 1938), 2: 451–452.

10. *Dairenshi-shi* (History of Dairen; Dairen, 1936), pp. 241ff.

11. Chinda to Ishimoto, Sept. 30, 1905, Japanese Foreign Ministry Archives (hereafter cited as JFMA), 1.7.3.45.

12. Tsunoda, *Manshū mondai*, p. 272.

13. Kayahara Kazan, *Kōjō no ichiro* (Ceaseless progress; Tokyo, 1904), pp. 228–230; Kayahara Kazan, *Dōchū seikan* (Quiet in movement; Tokyo, 1904), p. 73.

14. Kayahara Kazan, *Sayū shūchiku* (Bamboos everywhere; Tokyo, 1905), pp. 154–155.

15. Kayahara, *Kōjō no ichiro*, pp. 266–276.

16. In *Sengo keiei* (Postwar management; Tokyo, 1905), ed. Yamamoto Rikio, pp. 9–10.

17. *Ibid.*, p. 55.

18. Yano Ryūkei, *Sekai ni okeru Nihon no shōrai* (Japan's future in the world; Tokyo, 1905), pp. 49–55.

19. Yamamoto, *Sengo keiei*, pp. 82–85.

20. *Katsudō no Nihon* (Active Japan), 1.1: 7 (May 1904).

21. For the Portsmouth peace treaty, see *NGB, NRS*, vol. 5; White, *Diplomacy of the Russo-Japanese War;* Raymond A. Esthus, *Theodore Roosevelt and Japan* (Seattle, 1966); L. N. Kutakov, *Portsmutskii mirnyi dogovor* (Moscow, 1961). The antitreaty movement in Japan is described in Okamoto Shumpei, *The Japanese Oligarchy and the Russo-Japanese War* (New York, 1970), chap. 7.

22. *Katsudō no Nihon*, 2.9: 7 (March 1905).

23. Kayahara, *Dōchū seikan*, p. 90.

24. *Katsudō no Nihon*, 2.10: 2–5 (April 1905). For similar expressions of postwar expansionism, see Mizuno Ryū, *Nan-Bei tokō annai* (Guide to going to South America; Tokyo, 1906); Takegoshi Yosaburō, *Hikaku shokumin seido* (Comparative colonial systems; Tokyo, 1906); Yamane Goichi, ed., *Saikin to-Bei annai* (New guide to going to America; Tokyo, 1906).

25. *Hawai Nihonjin*, p. 167.

26. Yamato Ichihashi, *Japanese in the United States* (Stanford, 1932), p. 12; Tōgō Minoru and Satō Shirō, *Taiwan shokumin hattatsu-shi* (History of colonialism in Taiwan; Taipei, 1916), pp. 168–169; *Chōsen sōtokufu shissei nenpō: 1923* (Annual report of the Korean governor-general's office: 1923; Keijō, 1924), pp. 22–24.

27. Kayahara, *Sayū shūchiku*, pp. 131–134.

28. Shimanuki Hyōdayū, *Rikkōkai to wa nanzoya* (What is Rikkōkai?; Tokyo, 1911), pp. 80–85, 126–128.

29. Shimanuki Hyōdayū, *Saikin to-Bei saku* (New ways to go to America; Tokyo, 1904), preface and p. 24.

30. Amano Torasaburō, *To-Bei rashin* (Guide to going to America; Tokyo, 1904), p. 2.

31. Iwasaki Tatsusaburō, *Saishin to-Bei annai* (New guide to going to

America; Tokyo, 1905), preface and pp. 1–3. See also Umeta Matajirō, *Zai-Bei no kugakusei oyobi rōdōsha* (Japanese students and laborers in America; Tokyo, 1907).

32. Abe Isoo, *Hokubei no shin-Nihon* (The new Japan in North America; Tokyo, 1905), pp. 23–24, 31, 38, 100, 106, 121, 124–126.

33. Mori Rintarō, *Kōkaron kōgai* (An outline of the yellow peril concept; Tokyo, 1904), preface and pp. 2, 69.

34. *Ōkuma-haku jikyoku dan* (Count Ōkuma talks on contemporary affairs; Tokyo, 1905), pp. 48–49, 50–52, 53–57; Yamamoto, *Sengo keiei*, p. 10.

35. Komura to Hayashi, Feb. 23, 1904, *NGB, NRS,* 5: 668–670.

36. Taguchi Ukichi, *Ha-kōkaron* (Down with the yellow peril concept; Tokyo, 1904). See also Yamauchi Masaaki, *Shokumin-ron* (On colonization; Tokyo, 1905), pp. 383, 402–403.

37. *Ōkuma-haku jikyoku dan,* pp. 146–147.

38. Abe, *Hokubei,* pp. 93, 126–127.

39. Ogino Mannosuke, *Gaiyū sannen* (Three years abroad; Tokyo, 1907), p. 39.

40. Abe, *Hokubei,* pp. 27, 51ff.

41. Okudo Zennosuke, *To-Bei nikki* (Diary in America; Osaka, 1904), p. 141.

42. Abe, *Hokubei,* pp. 81–82.

43. Okudo, *To-Bei nikki,* p. 141. Other examples of critical comment on Japanese in the United States are: Tamura Shōgyo, *Hokubei sezoku-kan* (Life in North America; Tokyo, 1909); Togawa Shūkotsu, *Ō-Bei kiyū* (Travels in Europe and America; Tokyo, 1907); Nakamura Shun'u, *Ō-Bei inshō-ki* (Impressions of Europe and America; Tokyo, 1910); Tabata Kisaburō, *Zai-Bei seikō no tomo* (How to succeed in America; Tokyo, 1908).

44. *Kafū zenshū* (Collected works of Nagai Kafū), Iwanami edition, 13: 137–138 (Tokyo, 1963).

45. *Ibid.,* 3: 123, 129–130, 185, 314–320, 334. For a detailed analysis of Kafū's life in the United States, see Mitsuko Iriye, "Quest for Literary Resonance: Young Nagai Kafū and French Literature" (unpublished Ph.D. thesis, Harvard University, 1969).

46. Straight diary, Aug. 12, 1904, Willard Straight Papers, Cornell University; Straight to Mott, Sept. 18, 1904, *ibid.*; Straight to Sanborn, May 18, 1905, *ibid.*

47. Straight to Fletcher, Sept. 17, 1905, *ibid.*; Straight diary, June 22, 1905, *ibid.*

48. Meyer to Roosevelt, Jan. 20, 1905, George von Lengerke Meyer Papers, Massachusetts Historical Society.

49. Griscom to Rockhill, June 23, 1905, Rockhill Papers.

50. Ueno to Komura, Mar. 7, 1905, *NGB,* 38.2: 297–299 (Tokyo, 1959).

51. For the Japanese exclusion movement, see studies by Roger Daniels (*The Politics of Prejudice: The Anti-Japanese Movement in California and the Struggle for Japanese Exclusion,* Berkeley, 1962), Thomas A. Bailey (*Theodore Roosevelt and Japanese-American Crises,* Stanford, 1934), and

Charles E. Neu (*An Uncertain Friendship: Theodore Roosevelt and Japan, 1906–1909,* Cambridge, Mass., 1967).

52. Roosevelt to Meyer, Dec. 26, 1904, *Letters of Theodore Roosevelt,* ed. Elting E. Morison, 4: 1079 (Cambridge, Mass., 1951); Roosevelt to Lodge, June 5 and 16, 1905, *ibid.,* 4: 1205, 1221–1223; Roosevelt to Hay, Aug. 29, 1904, *ibid.,* 4: 916–917.

53. Roosevelt to Spring Rice, Mar. 19 and Dec. 27, 1904, *ibid.,* 4: 760–761, 1085–1086; Roosevelt to Trevelyan, May 13, 1905, *ibid.,* 4: 1173.

54. Tani, *Kimitsu Nichi-Ro senshi,* pp. 74–81, 618–625.

55. See documentation in *NGB,* 37.2: 124–199.

56. Hayashi to Komura, Mar. 5, 1904, *ibid.,* 37.2: 141–142; Komura to Hayashi, May 5, 1904, *ibid.,* 37.2: 142–144; Komura to Takahira, May 8, 1904, *ibid.,* 37.2: 144–145.

57. Regarding trade statistics, see *Nichi-Bei bunka kōshō-shi,* vol. 2: *Tsūshō sangyō-hen* (Commerce and industry), ed. Ohara Keishi, chap. 1 (Tokyo, 1954).

58. See Esthus, *Theodore Roosevelt,* p. 117; Paul Varg, *Open Door Diplomat: The Life of W. W. Rockhill* (Urbana, Ill., 1952), *passim.*

59. Memorial by Hsü, Dec. 2, 1904, *Ch'ing Kuang-hsü Chung-Jih chaio-she shih-liao* (Documents on Chinese-Japanese relations during the Kwang-hsü reign), 2: 1315–1316 (Taipei, 1963).

60. See Howard K. Beale, *Theodore Roosevelt and the Rise of America to World Power* (Baltimore, 1956); Chang Tsun-wu, *Kuang-hsü san-shih-i-nien Chung-Mei kung-yüeh feng-ch'ao* (The Chinese labor dispute of 1905; Taipei, 1965).

61. *North China Herald,* Aug. 11, 1905.

62. Cited in Jessie A. Miller, "China in American Policy and Opinion, 1906–1909" (unpublished Ph.D. dissertation, Clark University, 1938), p. 15.

63. These ideas were developed in Liang Ch'i-ch'ao's "Hsin-min shuo" (On the new people), which appeared as a series of articles in *Hsin-min ts'ung-pao* (New people's miscellany; Yokohama, 1901–1903).

64. For late-Ch'ing nationalism, the best survey is Mary Wright, ed., *China in Revolution: The First Phase, 1900–1913* (New Haven, 1968), pp. 1–63. See also Akira Iriye, "Public Opinion and Foreign Policy: The Case of Late Ch'ing China," in *Approaches to Modern Chinese History,* eds. Albert Feuerwerker, Rhoads Murphey, Mary C. Wright (Berkeley, 1967), pp. 216–238; John E. Schrecker, *Imperialism and Chinese Nationalism: Germany in Shantung* (Cambridge, Mass., 1971).

65. *Tung-fan tsa-chih* (The Eastern miscellany), 1.1: 1–3 (Mar. 11, 1904).

66. *Ibid.,* 1.1: 4–6.

67. *Ibid.,* 1.1: 5–7.

68. Cited in *ibid.,* 1.1: 13–15. See also Yamaguchi Ichirō, *Kindai Chūgoku tai-Nichi-kan no kenkyū* (Chinese images of Japan; Tokyo, 1969), pp. 19–22.

69. Ts'en's memorial, Feb. 10, 1904, *Ch'ing-chi wai-chiao shih-liao* (Diplomatic documents of the Ch'ing period), eds. Wang Yen-wei and Wang Liang, 181: 16–17 (Peking, 1935).

70. *Hsin-hai ko-ming ch'ien shih-nien-chien shih-lun hsüan-chi* (Collection of essays on public affairs published during the decade preceding the 1911 revolution), ed. Wang Jen-chih, 1.1: 53–58 (Peking, 1960).

71. The editorial is reprinted in *Hsin-min ts'ung pao,* combined vols. 38–39 (October 1903).

72. Kikuchi Takaharu, *Chūgoku minzoku undō no kihon kōzō: taigai boycott no kenkyū* (The structure of Chinese nationalism: A study of anti-foreign boycotts; Tokyo, 1966), pp. 13–17; *North China Herald,* July 28, 1905.

73. Cited in Beale, *Theodore Roosevelt,* p. 222.

74. These ideas are contained in numerous letters sent by various groups to the Waiwupu (Foreign Ministry). They are found in the Waiwupu Archives (henceforth cited as WWPA), at the Institute of Modern History, Academia Sinica, under the heading "Kung-yüeh an" (The labor dispute). See also Sakurai Toshiaki, "Nichi-Ro sensō to Chūgoku no minzoku undō" (The Russo-Japanese War and Chinese nationalism) in Shinobu Seizaburō and Nakayama Jiichi, eds., *Nichi-Ro sensō-shi no kenkyū* (Historiography of the Russo-Japanese War; Tokyo, 1959), pp. 447–478.

75. *Hsin-hai ko-ming,* 2.1: 61–69 (Peking, 1963).

76. Cited in *ibid.,* 2.1: 3–5. Letters from Shanghai merchants to Waiwupu, June 18 and Sept. 13, 1905, WWPA.

77. Yüan to Waiwupu, July 4, 1905, WWPA.

78. Chou to Waiwupu, Aug. 31, 1905, WWPA.

79. Ts'en to Waiwupu, Aug. 21, 1905, WWPA.

80. See Iriye, "Public Opinion."

81. Magoon to Taft, July 15, 1904, Taft Papers.

82. Hay to Taft, Dec. 17, 1904, *ibid.*

83. Resolution by Alameda County Exclusion League, June 25, 1905, *ibid.*

84. Henderson to Taft, June 25, 1905, *ibid.*

85. Hanford to Taft, June 21, 1905, *ibid.*

86. Healy to Taft, rec. June 30, 1905, *ibid.*

87. Hamilton to Taft, July 6, 1905, *ibid.*

88. Healy to Taft, July 5, 1905, *ibid.*

89. *Literary Digest,* 32: 17 (Jan. 6, 1906).

90. Te-li-fei-sen [Duliferson?] to Waiwupu, Aug. 29, 1905, WWPA.

91. Arthur H. Smith, *China and America Today: A Study of Conditions and Relations* (New York, 1907), pp. 173–174.

92. Beale, *Theodore Roosevelt,* pp. 218–219.

93. *New York Times,* Oct. 17, 1905.

94. Leavenworth to Roosevelt, May 28, 1904, Taft Papers.

95. Jenks to Taft, July 1, 1905, *ibid.*

96. Bash to Taft, Dec. 19, 1905, *ibid.*

97. Wilson to Roosevelt, September 1905, Francis M. Huntington Wilson Papers (Ursinus College).

V. Confrontation: The Japanese View

1. *Shinjidai* (The new era), vol. 1, no. 5 (November 1906). See also Hasebe Sumitaka, *Ō-Bei rekiyū nisshi* (Diary of travels to Europe and America; Tokyo, 1907), pp. 74–75, 145.

2. *Shinjidai*, 1.1: 1–2, 14–16 (July 1906).

3. *Ibid.*, 1.1: 1.

4. *Ibid.*, 2.3: 9–11 (March 1907).

5. *Katsudō no Nihon*, 4.1: 1–3 (July 1906), and 4.2: 1–4 (August 1906). See also Itō Gingetsu, *Kaikoku Nihon* (Maritime Japan; Tokyo, 1905).

6. *Jitsugyō sekai Taiheiyō* (The Pacific Ocean, the world of business), 5.1: 1–5 (Jan. 1, 1906).

7. *Ibid.*, 5.2: 1–5, 7–8 (Jan. 15, 1906).

8. *Katsudō no Nihon*, 4.4: 1–3 (October 1906).

9. *Ibid.*, 4.4: 16–19.

10. *Ibid.*, 4.5: 3–6 (November 1906). A well documented argument for emigration to Brazil as a solution to the postwar unemployment problem can be found in Mizuno, *Nan-Bei tokō annai*.

11. See *Shokumin sekai* (The world of colonialism), 1.1: 4–5 (May 1908). Yamauchi, *Shokumin-ron*, published even before the end of the war, was one of the first books on colonization. In the preface the author lamented, "In our country there are few books on the subject, although we must study theories of colonization to prepare for postwar management and lay the foundation for national economic independence." The book, over four hundred pages long, was essentially a compendium of Western authorities such as Paul Reinsch, F. Fabri, and A. Zimmermann.

12. Nitobe's introduction to Ōkawahira Takamitsu, *Nihon imin-ron* (Japanese emigration; Tokyo, 1905); also its preface and pp. 1–4, 32–33, 127, 211, 285. See also Nitobe Inazō, *Kigan no ashi* (The return of a wild goose; Tokyo, 1907), reminiscences of his experiences abroad. He argues that the greatness of the Anglo-Saxons derives from their willingness to go overseas and mingle with other peoples.

13. Tōgō Minoru, *Nihon shokumin-ron* (On Japanese colonization; Tokyo, 1906), pp. 237, 283, 343, 354, 361. The relation between peaceful and forceful expansionism is explored by Yamauchi, *Shokumin-ron*; Sasakawa Kiyoshi, *Nihon no shōrai* (The future of Japan; Tokyo, 1907).

14. *Hawai Nihonjin*, pp. 167–171, 316. The postwar era also saw renewed interest in migration to Mexico as well as the beginning of emigration to Brazil, a country that began to seem more and more appropriate as a place for Japanese settlement in the absence of strong local opposition. See Kamata Sannosuke, *Hokubei Mekishiko shokumin annai* (Guide to settlement in Mexico; Tokyo, 1908); Kikuchi Gorō, *Yamato minzoku shin hattenchi jijō* (Conditions of Japan's expanding communities abroad; Tokyo, 1912); *Burajiru ni okeru Nihonjin hatten-shi* (History of Japanese in Brazil; Tokyo, 1941), 1: 52, 253–259.

15. Bailey, *Theodore Roosevelt and Japanese-American Crises;* Neu, *An Uncertain Friendship.*

16. *Shinjidai,* 3.1: 3–8 (July 1907). See also Kawamura Tetsutarō, *Hokubei jigyō annai* (Guide to business in North America; Tokyo, 1906).

17. Memo by Hayashi, Nov. 1907, *NGB,* 40.3: 791–800 (Tokyo, 1961). That Hayashi was interested in promoting emigration can be seen in his May 1908 proposal for establishing a section within the commerce bureau of the Foreign Ministry to deal with the matter. Such a section was created soon afterward.

18. For documentation on the Gentlemen's agreement, see *Nihon gaikō nenpyō narabi shuyō bunsho* (Chronology and main documents of Japanese diplomacy), 1: 284–305 (Tokyo, 1955).

19. Itō to Hayashi, Nov. 6, 1907, *NGB,* 40.3: 789–791.

20. Aoki to Hayashi, Nov. 7, 1907, *ibid.,* 40.3: 593–596.

21. The best discussion of the Root-Takahira agreement is Esthus, *Theodore Roosevelt,* chap. 16. See also Zubok, *Ekspansionistskaia politika SShA,* pp. 356–363.

22. *Yorozu chōhō,* Oct. 8, 1906.

23. *Shinjidai,* 3.1: 81–84 (July 1907).

24. Tōgō, *Nihon shokumin-ron,* p. 323; Sasakawa, *Nihon no shōrai,* p. 136.

25. *Tokyo Nichinichi,* Feb. 1, 11, 20, 1907.

26. *Shinjidai,* 3.2: 16–21 (August 1907).

27. *Yorozu chōhō,* Jan. 18, 19, 1907.

28. *Ibid.,* Feb. 25, 28, Mar. 1, 1907.

29. *Shinsekai* (The new world), Nov. 2, 1906.

30. Kayahara Kazan, *Kaigai bunshō: Tōzai seikatsu no hihan* (Essays written abroad: a critique of Eastern and Western life; Tokyo, 1912), preface.

31. *Shinsekai,* Nov. 16, 28, 1906.

32. *Ibid.,* Dec. 23, 26, 1906.

33. *Ibid.,* Nov. 1, Dec. 22, 1906.

34. *Ibid.,* Dec. 5, 1906.

35. *Ibid.,* Nov. 15, Dec. 5, 1906; Mar. 16, 1907.

36. *Ibid.,* Nov. 5, 6, 21, 1906; Jan. 7 and 19, Mar. 4, 1907.

37. Kayahara, *Kaigai bunshō,* pp. 3–7.

38. *Shinsekai,* Feb. 10, Mar. 15, 1907.

39. *Shinjidai,* 2.5: 2–6 (May 1907).

40. *Tōyō keizai shinpō* (Oriental economist), no. 415, pp. 6–7 (June 5, 1907).

41. *Heimin shinbun* (People's daily), Apr. 13, 1907.

42. Tsunoda, *Manshū mondai,* pp. 674–704, 708–709.

43. *Ibid.,* pp. 705–706, 709, 711–713; Hata Ikuhiko, "Meiji ikō ni okeru Nichi-Bei Taiheiyō senryaku no hensen" (The Pacific strategy of Japan and the United States), *Kokusai seiji,* no. 37, pp. 96–115 (October 1968). See also Satō Seizaburō, "Kyōchō to jiritsu no aida" (Between cooperation and autonomy), *Nenpō seijigaku 1969* (Annals of the Japanese Political Science Association 1969; Tokyo, 1970), pp. 99–144.

44. Satō, *Teikoku kokubō shiron,* 1: 27, 144.

45. Cited in *Saitō Makoto den* (Biography of Saitō Makoto; Tokyo, 1933), pp. 92ff.

46. Satō Tetsutarō, *Teikoku kokubō shiron shō* (Outline history of Japanese strategy; Tokyo, 1912), 1: 26–28, 470.

47. See *NGB,* 40.1: 27–46 (Tokyo, 1960) for documentation.

48. Cited in *Chūōkōron,* 22.11: 85–86 (November 1907).

49. See a brief but perceptive essay on this subject in Saeki Shōichi, "Nichi-Bei no shinkankei" ("The new relationship between Japan and the United States"), *Kikan geijutsu* (Art quarterly), no. 10, pp. 60–71 (July 1969).

50. *Tōyō keizai shinpō,* no. 417, p. 5 (June 25, 1907).

51. *Tokyo Nichinichi,* Feb. 11, 1907.

52. *Tōyō keizai shinpō,* no. 417, p. 11.

53. *Tokyo Nichinichi,* July 7, Sept. 28, Oct. 5, 1907.

VI. Confrontation: The American View

1. Roosevelt to Strachey, Dec. 21, 1906, *Letters of Theodore Roosevelt,* 5: 532–533; William H. Harbaugh, ed., *The Writings of Theodore Roosevelt* (Indianapolis, 1967), pp. 225, 239–241.

2. Cited in *Literary Digest,* 33: 663 (Nov. 10, 1906).

3. *San Francisco Call,* Mar. 5 and 14, 1907.

4. Archibald Cary Coolidge, *The United States as a World Power* (New York, 1909), pp. 64, 65, 74–77, 352–353.

5. John H. Latané, *America as a World Power, 1897–1907* (New York, 1907), p. 320.

6. Memo by Wilson, Oct. 22, 1906, Department of State Archives (hereafter cited as SDA), National Archives, 1797/2.

7. Roosevelt to Root, Mar. 28, 1908, SDA 2542/481.

8. Memo by Wilson, July 6, 1907, SDA 1797/385–386.

9. Root to Holmes, Mar. 6, 1907, SDA 2542/55A.

10. Irish to Root, Oct. 26, 1906, SDA 1797/19.

11. Wood to Root, Feb. 24, 1907, SDA 1797/443.

12. Deming to Roosevelt, Oct. 27, 1906, SDA 1797/24–25.

13. San Francisco Merchants Exchange to Root, July 12, 1907, SDA 1797/291.

14. Tacoma Chamber of Commerce to Roosevelt and Root, Apr. 30, 1907, SDA 2542/81.

15. Memo by Root for Metcalf, Oct. 27, 1906, SDA 1797/13.

16. Pruit to War Department, Dec. 31, 1906, WDA, RG 94.

17. Lane to War Department, Feb. 15, 1907, WDA, RG 165.

18. Wilson to Roosevelt, n.d., WDA, RG 165.

19. McKay to Taft, July 15, 1907, WDA, RG 94.

20. Simon to War Department, July 29, 1907, WDA, RG 94.

21. Thorne to Roosevelt, Dec. 28, 1907, SDA 1797/431.

22. Kaeding to Taft, rec. Dec. 19, 1906, WDA, RG 165.

23. Blaker to Roosevelt, Dec. 12, 1907, WDA, RG 94.

24. Robotham to Roosevelt, Oct. 22, 1907, SDA 1797/384.

25. Denby to Root, July 2, 1907, SDA 1797/347.

26. Tower to Root, July 10, 1907, SDA 1797/348.

27. Hans to Roosevelt, Jan. 1, 1908, SDA 1797/275; Mrs. van Heekeren to War Department, Jan. 28, 1908, WDA, RG 94.

28. Harris to Taft, June 12, 1907, WDA, RG 94.

29. Hot Air Club of Dexter to Taft, June 18, 1907, WDA, RG 94.

30. Military Intelligence Division compilations, Feb. 6, 1906, and Oct. 2, 1907, WDA, RG 165.

31. General Staff memo for Secretary of War, Feb. 14, 1907; Reber's report, 1907; M.I.D. to Reber, Feb. 3, 1907, WDA, RG 165.

32. Reber's report, May 31, 1907, WDA, RG 165.

33. M.I.D. to Chamberlain, Feb. 21, 1907; Chamberlain's reports, Apr. 5, July 9 and 29, Sept. 5, Nov. 1, 1907, WDA, RG 165.

34. Attaché's report, May 28, 1907, WDA, RG 165.

35. M.I.D. memo, May 7, 1907; M.I.D. to Swift, May 17, 1907; Swift's reports, June 27, Nov. 27, Dec. 7 and 10, 1907, WDA, RG 165.

36. Van Deman's memo, Apr. 3, 1907, WDA, RG 165.

37. M.I.D. to twenty-two forts, Apr. 9, 1907; Fort McIntire's report, May 10, 1907, WDA, RG 165.

38. Spalding to Adjutant General, Sept. 18, 1907, WDA, RG 165.

39. Fort Clark's report, Aug. 27, 1907, WDA, RG 165.

40. Fort Liscum's report, Aug. 31, 1907, WDA, RG 165.

41. Fort Columbia's report, Aug. 16, 1907, WDA, RG 165.

42. Gatchell to Adjutant General, July 13 and 18, 1907; Adjutant General to Gatchell, July 15, 1907, WDA, RG 94.

43. Haan to Wotherspoon, Jan. 3, 1908, WDA, RG 165.

44. Braisted, *United States Navy*, chap. 5.

45. Memo by Sperry for Strauss, Feb. 4, 1907, WDA, RG 165.

46. Memo by Wotherspoon, June 29, 1907; M.I.D. memo on strategic planning, filed Jan. 6, 1908, WDA, RG 165.

47. Bigelow to Lodge, June 10, 1907; Lodge to Bigelow, June 12, 1907, Henry Cabot Lodge Papers, Massachusetts Historical Society.

48. See Nish, *Anglo-Japanese Alliance*, pp. 363–377, for a discussion of the Anglo-Japanese alliance in relation to the United States.

49. Memo by Wilson, Oct. 12, 1907, SDA 2542/161; Neu, *Uncertain Friendship*, p. 205.

50. Taft to Roosevelt, Oct. 5, 1907, SDA 1797/380–383.

51. White to Lodge, Oct. 30, 1907, Lodge Papers.

52. Grey to Bryce, Mar. 30, 1908, Archives of the Public Record Office (hereafter cited as PRO), F.O. 800/81; Grey to McDonald, Nov. 14, 1908, PRO, F.O. 800/68.

53. Homer Lea, *The Valor of Ignorance* (New York, 1909), pp. 157–162, 171, 176, 205.

54. *Ibid.*, p. 180. On Lea's type of crisis literature, see a perceptive discussion in Fred Jaher, *Doubters and Dissenters: Cataclysmic Thought in America, 1885–1918* (New York, 1964).

55. Ernest Hugh Fitzpatrick, *The Coming Conflict of Nations, or the Japanese-American War* (Springfield, Ill., 1909), pp. 22, 32, 129, 143–144, 164, 197, 287, 298–300.

56. Stevens to Brownson, Dec. 24, 1907, SDA 12611/4.

VII. The Role of China

1. Roosevelt to Wood, Jan. 22, 1906, *Letters of Theodore Roosevelt*, 5: 135.

2. Memo by Wilson for Root, July 6, 1907, SDA 1797/385–386.

3. O'Brien to Root, Nov. 29, 1907, SDA 2542/262.

4. *Komura gaikōshi* (Japanese diplomacy under Komura; Tokyo, 1968), ed. Foreign Ministry, pp. 743–755.

5. O'Brien to Root, Nov. 13, 1908, SDA 2542/779.

6. Tōgō, *Nihon shokumin-ron*, pp. 361–362, 385. See also Sasakawa, *Nihon no shōrai*, pp. 133–136.

7. See also *Tōyō keizai shinpō*, no. 415, p. 2; no. 417, p. 4.

8. See Wilson's memo for Adee, Aug. 1, 1907, SDA 1797/328.

9. Tsunoda, *Manshū mondai*, pp. 301–305.

10. See Kurihara Ken, *Tai-Man-Mō seisaku-shi no ichimen* (Aspects of Japanese policy toward Manchuria and Mongolia; Tokyo, 1966), chaps. 2–3.

11. Tsurumi Yūsuke, *Gotō Shinpei*, 2: 814–820, 826–833 (Tokyo, 1938). Gotō's ideas on expansion and colonialism are well summarized in his *Nihon shokumin seisaku ippan: Nihon bōchō-ron* (Japanese colonial policy: On Japanese expansion; Tokyo, 1944). See also Hara Kei's diary entries of Aug. 12 and Oct. 28, 1906, for circumstances of Gotō's appointment as president of the South Manchuria Railway. *Hara Kei nikki* (Hara Kei Diary; Tokyo, 1950), 2: 192, 204.

12. Tsurumi, *Gotō Shinpei*, 2: 762–797; Gotō's memo of Aug. 30, 1908, Gotō Shinpei Papers, Tokyo Institute for Municipal Research.

13. Eshiya to Hagihara, Jan. 30, 1907, JFMA 1.7.3.56; Dairen office of South Manchuria Railway to Nakamura, Jan. 27, 1908, *ibid.*; Abe to Hayashi, Aug. 13 and 15, Sept. 11, 1907, *NGB*, 40.2: 393–395 (Tokyo, 1961); Hayashi to Abe, Sept. 16, 1907, *ibid.*, 40.2: 396.

14. Hayashi to Gotō, Jan. 25, 1908, *ibid.*, 41.1: 633–635 (Tokyo, 1960); Amano to Hayashi, Apr. 21, 1908, JFMA 1.7.3.56; Katō to Hayashi, May 12, 1908, *ibid.*

15. Hayashi to Amano, Apr. 16, 1908, *ibid.*; Hayashi to Katō, Apr. 16, 1908, *ibid.*; Katō to Hayashi, Apr. 21, 1908, *ibid.*

16. See Charles Vevier, *The United States and China 1906–1913: A Study of Finance and Diplomacy* (New Brunswick, N.J., 1955), chap. 3.

17. *Tokyo Nichinichi*, July 9 and 30, Aug. 19, Oct. 1, 1907.

18. *Tōyō keizai shinpō*, no. 403, pp. 3–7 (Feb. 5, 1907); no. 404, pp. 3–5 (Feb. 15, 1907). Consul General Hagihara Shuichi at Mukden lamented in May 1906 that poverty had prevented Japan from taking advantage of the fruits of war. For instance, roads and bridges in Port Arthur were in poorer condition than under Russian rule. See *Hagihara Shuichi shi tsuikai-roku* (In memory of Hagihara Shuichi) ed. Kubota Masakane (Tokyo, 1913), p. 377.

19. *Jitsugyō sekai Taiheiyō*, 5.1: 1–5 (Jan. 1, 1906).

20. *Ibid.*, 5.2: 1–5 (Jan. 15, 1906).

21. *Ibid.*, 5.3: 14–15 (Feb. 1, 1906).

22. Hatano Yoshihiro, "Nichi-Ro senso go ni okeru kokusai kankei no dōin" (International relations after the Russo-Japanese War), *Kokusai seiji*, no. 1, pp. 153–182 (October 1957).

23. *Katsudō no Nihon*, 4.3: 8–9 (September 1906).

24. *Ibid.*, 4.4: 16–19 (October 1906).

25. Tsunoda, *Manshū mondai*, pp. 347–348.

26. Report by South Manchuria Railway, 1907, in JFMA 1.6.1.7.2.

27. *Jitsugyō sekai Taiheiyō*, 5.3: 14–15 (Feb. 1, 1907).

28. *Tōyō keizai shinpō*, no. 415, pp. 2–4.

29. *Katsudō no Nihon*, 4.1: 3–7 (July 1906).

30. *Shina kindai no seiji keizai* (Modern China's politics and economy; Tokyo, 1931), ed. Nikka Jitsugyō Kyōkai (Sino-Japanese Business Association), pp. 198–215.

31. See Wright, *China in Revolution*, pp. 1–63.

32. Segawa to Komura, Dec. 12, 1908, JFMA 3.10.1.23.

33. Hayashi to Hayashi, Aug. 15, 1906, *NGB*, 39.1: 826–838 (Tokyo, 1959).

34. See Iriye, "Chūgoku ni okeru Nihon Bukkyō fukyō mondai."

35. For documentation on the *Tatsu Maru* incident, see *NGB*, 41.2: 1–124 (Tokyo, 1961).

36. See Iriye, "Public Opinion."

37. *Hennen-shi*, 13: 369–370 (Tokyo, 1936).

38. Memo by Hayashi, 1907, *NGB*, 40.3: 800–803; A. M. Pooley, ed., *The Secret Memoirs of Count Tadasu Hayashi* (New York, 1915), p. 307.

39. Hayashi to Hayashi, Apr. 30, 1907, JFMA 1.6.1.4.2.5.

40. For documentation on Japanese attitudes toward Chinese domestic politics, see JFMA 1.6.1.4.2.1, and 1.6.1.4.2.5.

41. Thomas F. Millard, *America and the Far Eastern Question* (New York, 1909), pp. 11–12, 21, 27, 29, 31, 37, 38, 60, 218, 354.

42. A. Dobrov, *Dalnevostochnaia politika SShA v period russko-iaponskoi voin'* (Moscow, 1952); G. Sevostianov, *Ekspansionistskaia politika SShA na Dal'nem Vostoke* (Moscow, 1958); Zubok, *Ekspansionistskaia politika SShA.*

43. The statistical information in these paragraphs is taken from *Nichi-Bei bunka kōshō-shi*, 2: 22–24, 339–347. A recent discussion of American images of economic opportunities in China and Japan is Robert McClellan, *The Heathen Chinee: A Study of American Attitudes toward China, 1890–1905* (Columbus, Ohio, 1971).

44. Rockhill to Root, Oct. 11, 1906. *Papers Relating to the Foreign Rela-*

otions of the United States, 1906, part 1, pp. 225–226 (Washington, D.C., 1909).

45. Memo by Straight, n.d., Straight Papers.

46. Straight to Phillips, Dec. 18, 1907, *ibid.*

47. Straight to Denby, Dec. 3, 1907, *ibid.* In 1908 the division of Far Eastern affairs and the bureau of trade relations of the State Department concluded, "Very little energy, enterprise, or systematic effort is given by the American manufacturer or merchant interested in Far Eastern trade relatively to the painstaking and organized efforts of private commercial enterprises of other countries." Quoted in Michael H. Hunt, "Frontier Defense and the Open Door: Manchuria in Chinese-American Relations, 1895–1911" (Ph.D. dissertation, Yale University, 1971), p. 185.

48. *Manshū kaihatsu yonjū-nen-shi,* 1: 201.

49. For American investment in China, see Charles F. Remer, *Foreign Investments in China* (New York, 1933). American financial schemes in China are given an excellent treatment in Hunt, "Frontier Defense." For the South Manchuria Railway episode of 1905, when the Japanese government refused E. H. Harriman's proposal for joint management of the railway, see Tsunoda, *Manshū mondai,* pp. 269–272. Gotō Shinpei, president of the South Manchurian Railway, welcomed foreign investment in Manchuria. What he and others opposed was direct foreign investment involving control over Japanese railways and enterprises. See Gotō's memo, Aug. 30, 1908, Gotō Papers.

50. Hayashi to Itō, November 1907, *NGB,* 40.3: 792–800.

51. Straight to Wilson, Dec. 30, 1907, Straight Papers.

52. Straight to Phillips, Sept. 8, 1907, *ibid.*

53. Cited in Miller, "China in American Policy and Opinion," p. 17.

54. Smith, *China and America Today,* pp. 48, 61, 65, 67.

55. *Ibid.,* pp. 101–102; Arthur H. Smith, *The Uplift of China* (New York, 1907), p. 201; Miller, "China in American Policy and Opinion," p. 71.

56. James' memo cited in Smith, *China and America Today,* pp. 213–218.

57. *Ibid.,* pp. 215–216; Coolidge, *The United States as a World Power,* pp. 340, 367.

58. *Ibid.,* pp. 339, 368; Millard, *America and the Far Eastern Question,* pp. 13, 30. See also Joseph K. Goodrich, *The Coming China* (Chicago, 1911).

59. Millard, *America and the Far Eastern Question,* p. 357; Taft to Roosevelt, Oct. 5, 1907, SDA 1797/380–383.

60. Taft's speech is reprinted in *Journal of the American Association of China,* 2.5: 20–26 (November 1907).

61. *Ibid.,* 2.5: 17–22, 27–31.

62. Straight to Harriman, Oct. 7, 1907, Straight Papers.

63. Millard, *America and the Far Eastern Question,* p. 319. See also J. O. P. Bland, *Recent Events and Present Politics in China* (Philadelphia, 1912), p. 208.

64. Straight to Wilson, Jan. 31, 1908, Straight Papers.

65. Coolidge, *The United States as a World Power,* p. 365.

VIII. The United States and Japan in the World Arena

1. Tsunoda, *Manshū mondai*, pp. 428–440.
2. *Manshū kaihatsu yonjū-nen-shi*, pp. 84–87.
3. *Ibid.*, pp. 78–79, 92; *Antung kyoryūmin jūnen-shi* (Ten years of Japanese settlement in Antung; Antung, 1919), *passim*; Itō Takeichirō, *Manshū jūnen-shi* (History of Manchuria in the past ten years; Dairen, 1916), pp. 226–228.
4. *Shokumin sekai*, 1.1: 22–24 (May 1908); *ibid.*, 1.3: 11–18 (July 1908).
5. *Ibid.*, 1.3: 5–10, 50–54.
6. *Ibid.*, 1.2: 23–24 (June 1908).
7. *Ibid.*, 1.2: 24–26; 1.3: 1–3.
8. Phillips to Straight, Sept. 9, 1908, Straight Papers.
9. See JFMA 5.3.2.65 for documentation, and Hunt, "Frontier Defense," chaps. 9, 10.
10. Cited in Takahira to Komura, Nov. 30, 1908, *NGB*, 41.1: 108.
11. Warren F. Kuehl, *Seeking World Order: The United States and International Organization to 1920* (Nashville, 1969); Sondra R. Herman, *Eleven against War: Studies in American Internationalist Thought, 1898–1921* (Stanford, 1969).
12. Herman, *Eleven against War*, chap. 2; Charles A. Beard, *The Idea of National Interest: An Analytical Study in American Foreign Policy* (New York, 1934), pp. 103–107, 376.
13. *Ibid.*, p. 376.
14. *Ibid.*, pp. 107–110.
15. Dana Munro, *Intervention and Dollar Diplomacy in the Caribbean, 1900–1921* (Princeton, 1964), p. 235.
16. Vevier, *The United States and China*, chap. 7; Walter V. Scholes and Marie V. Scholes, *The Foreign Policies of the Taft Administration* (Columbia, Mo., 1970), chaps. 9–11.
17. *Komura gaikō-shi*, pp. 820–823; Zubok, *Ekspansionistskaia politika SShA*, pp. 326–331, 363–367.
18. *Kokusaihō gaikō zasshi* (International law and diplomacy), 9.3: 172–179 (November 1910). See also Takahashi Sakue, *Nichi-Bei no shinkankei* (The new relationship between Japan and the United States; Tokyo, 1910); Takeshima Keishirō, *Rekkyōkan no Nihon* (Japan among the powers; Tokyo, 1912).
19. *Kokusaihō gaikō zasshi*, 9.9: 689–690 (May 1911).
20. Ōtsuka Zenjirō, *Nichi-Bei gaikō-ron* (On Japanese-American relations; Tokyo, 1910), pp. 55–59.
21. Sanbe Yūsuke, *Taiheiyō no yūetsusha* (The predominant power in the Pacific; Tokyo, 1911), pp. 199–201.
22. Asakawa Kan'ichi, *Nihon no kaki* (Japan's woes; Tokyo, 1909), pp. 6–7, 11, 37, 54–55, 141–142, 181, 220–225, 227–229. See also *Shinsekai*, Mar. 13, 1908.

23. *Komura gaikō-shi*, pp. 896–911.
24. Ōtsuka, *Nichi-Bei gaikō-ron*, pp. 88–92.
25. *Shinsekai*, Mar. 14, 1908.
26. *Ibid.,*Mar. 2, 19, 1909.
27. *Ibid.*, Oct. 7, 1909. See also *ibid.*, Mar. 16, June 15, 1910.
28. *Ibid.*, Feb. 26, 28, Mar. 4, 1911.
29. *Kaigai no Nihon* (Japan overseas), 1.1: 3 (January 1911).
30. *Ibid.*, 1.1: 4–5.
31. *Ibid.*, 1.2: 8, 44, 47–48 (February 1911).
32. *Ibid.*, 1.4: 139–143 (April 1911). This type of presumably nonaggressive imperialism was given the epithet "ethical imperialism" by Ukita Kazutami, who collected his essays on the subject and published them in 1908 as *Rinri-teki teikokushugi* (Ethical imperialism; Tokyo, 1908).
33. *Sekai no Nihon* (Japan in the world), 2.7: 1–5 (July 1911).
34. *Taiyō* (The sun), 14.3: 2–9, 64, 115–117, 128–129 (Feb. 15, 1908).
35. Unno Sachinori, *Nihon jinshu kaizō-ron* (On improving the Japanese race; Tokyo, 1910); Kawashima Seijirō, *Kokubō kaigun-ron* (On naval defense; Tokyo, 1911).
36. Major H. G. Learnard, "Preparedness of Japan to wage an aggressive war against a Trans-Pacific Power" (Army War College, 1913–1914), WDA, RG 165.
37. Various memoranda on Thompson's secret mission (1909–1911) are filed in WDA, RG 165.
38. Wood to Wotherspoon, Dec. 28, 1908, WDA, RG 165.
39. Reports by agent "S," June 27, 1910, and Feb. 9, 1911, WDA, RG 165.
40. Army War College memo for Taft, Dec. 17, 1910, WDA, RG 165.
41. Memo by Liggett, Mar. 27, 1911, WDA, RG 165.
42. Wood to Meyer, Mar. 16, 1911, WDA, RG 165.
43. Office of chief engineer memo, Aug. 30, 1910, WDA, RG 77.
44. Hodgin to adjutant general's office, Sept. 12, 1908, WDA, RG 94.
45. Judge to Dickinson, June 22, 1910, WDA, RG 94.
46. Anonymous letter to Dickinson, rec. Dec. 4, 1909, WDA, RG 94; Mangann to Dickinson, Mar. 1909, WDA, RG 94.
47. Memo by Frederick, Nov. 13, 1910, WDA, RG 165. The Magdalena Bay episode of 1911, involving rumored attempts by private Japanese to purchase land in the area and producing the so-called Lodge corollary to the Monroe Doctrine, was part of the developing suspicion of Japanese-Mexican intrigues against the United States. In view of the tension between the United States and Mexico and the image of Japanese on the American continent as potential subversives, it was not surprising that Senator Henry Cabot Lodge as well as military personnel were extremely sensitive to any sign of Japanese-Mexican collusion. See William Reynolds Braisted, *The United States Navy in the Pacific, 1909–1922* (Austin, Tex., 1971), pp. 51–57. The Soviet historian Zubok cites Tsarist official dispatches reporting on America's uneasiness with Japanese activities in Mexico. See his *Ekspansionistskaia politika SShA*, p. 435.

48. Wood to Dickinson, Nov. 5, 1910, WDA, RG 94.
49. Jones to Frear, July 12, 1909, WDA, RG 94.
50. Fort Shafter's memo, Mar. 15, 1910, WDA, RG 94.
51. Taft to Dickinson, May 26, 1910, WDA, RG 94.
52. Duvall to Adjutant General, Sept. 3, 1909; Duvall to War Department, Jan. 24, 1910, WDA, RG 94.
53. Memo by Bliss for Dickinson, Feb. 14, 1910, WDA, RG 94.
54. Reports by Filipino agents, WDA, RG 94.
55. Oliver to Dickinson, Sept. 5, 1909; Taft to Dickinson, Oct. 11, 1909, WDA, RG 94.
56. Lieutenant C. A. Seoane, "A Military and Political Report upon the Far East" (War College Division, filed Oct. 28, 1911), WDA, pp. 1–5.
57. Captain William Mitchell, "Report of Observations in Manchuria, Korea, and Japan" (Jan. 2, 1912), WDA, RG 165.
58. *Outlook*, 96: 259 (Oct. 1, 1910).
59. *Nation*, 90: 254–255 (Mar. 17, 1910).
60. O'Brien to Knox, Feb. 5, 1910, SDA 711.94/138.
61. Office of Chief of Staff, "Plan in case of war in the Pacific before the Panama Canal is completed" (May 19, 1913), WDA.
62. Coolidge, *The United States as a World Power*, pp. 369–370.
63. Jerome Ch'en, *Yüan Shih-k'ai, 1859–1916: Brutus Assumes the Purple* (Stanford, 1961), pp. 109–110; *Nichi-Bei bunka kōshō-shi*, 2: 404–406.
64. *Forum*, 44: 67–89 (July 1910).
65. *American Lumberman*, August 1908, in SDA 12611/12–13.
66. O'Brien to Knox, Mar. 16, 1910, SDA 711.94/145.
67. Millard, *America and the Far Eastern Question*, pp. 59, 353.
68. O'Brien to Knox, Feb. 5, 1910, SDA 711.94/138.
69. *Outlook*, 98: 583–586 (July 15, 1911).
70. Cited in Tyler Dennett, *Roosevelt and the Russo-Japanese War* (New York, 1925), pp. 321–323.

IX. Epilogue

1. *Outlook*, 98: 242 (June 3, 1911).
2. *Ibid.*, 98: 244.
3. *Ibid.*, 97: 64 (Jan. 14, 1911).
4. George H. Blakeslee, ed., *Japan and Japanese-American Relations* (New York, 1912), pp. 166, 208.
5. Cited in Harley Notter, *The Origins of the Foreign Policy of Woodrow Wilson* (Baltimore, 1937), p. 75.
6. *Ibid.*, pp. 257, 269.
7. Robert E. Osgood, *Ideals and Self-Interest in American Foreign Relations* (New York, 1953); Arno Mayer, *Political Origins of the New Diplomacy, 1917–1918* (New Haven, 1959); Arno Mayer, *Politics and Diplomacy of Peacemaking: Containment and Counterrevolution at Versailles, 1918–1919*

(New York, 1967); N. Gordon Levin, *Woodrow Wilson and World Politics: America's Response to War and Revolution* (New York, 1968).

8. Walter Lippmann, *Drift and Mastery: An Attempt to Diagnose the Current Unrest* (New York, 1914), p. xviii.

9. Itō Miyoji, *Suiusō nikki* (Suiusō diary; Tokyo, 1966), pp. 326, 334–335.

10. For the 1920's, see Akira Iriye, *After Imperialism: The Search for a New Order in the Far East, 1921–1931* (Cambridge, Mass., 1965).

11. See Akira Iriye, "Kayahara Kazan and Japanese Cosmopolitanism," in Albert M. Craig and Donald H. Shively, eds., *Personality in Japanese History* (Berkeley, 1970), pp. 373–398.

12. *Osaka Mainichi*, Aug. 2, 1918.

13. See Akira Iriye, "The Failure of Economic Expansionism, 1918–1931" (paper presented at the conference on Taisho Japan, Durham, N.C., 1969).

14. Iriye, *After Imperialism*.

15. Stimson's memo of conversation with Debuchi, Sept. 17, 1931, Henry L. Stimson Papers, Yale University.

16. Fascinating material on this subject may be found in *Shōwa sensō bungaku zenshū* (Anthology of wartime literature), vol. 4 (Tokyo, 1964).

17. I have elaborated on this theme in "Heiwateki hattenshugi to Nihon" (Peaceful expansionism in Japan), *Chūōkōron*, 84.10: 74–94 (October 1969).

18. John K. Fairbank, "Sino-American Images" (paper presented at American Historical Association annual meeting, Washington, D.C., 1969).

Bibliography

This list includes only items mentioned in the text and footnotes of this book. They represent most, but by no means all, of the relevant material consulted. Primary and secondary sources are listed together, with archival documents grouped separately.

MANUSCRIPT SOURCES

Gotō Shinpei Papers. Tokyo Institute for Municipal Research.
Japanese Foreign Ministry Archives. Tokyo.
Archives of War History Division, Self-Defense Agency, Japan. Tokyo.
Henry Cabot Lodge Papers. Massachusetts Historical Society. Boston.
George von Lengerke Meyer Papers. Massachusetts Historical Society. Boston.
Archives of Navy Department, United States. National Archives.
British Foreign Office Archives, Public Record Office. London.
W. W. Rockhill Papers. Harvard University.
State Department Archives, United States. National Archives.
Henry L. Stimson Papers. Yale University.
Willard Straight Papers. Cornell University.
William Howard Taft Papers. Library of Congress.
Archives of Waiwupu (Chinese Foreign Ministry). Institute of Modern History, Academia Sinica, Taipei.
Archives of War Department, United States. National Archives.
Francis M. Huntington Wilson Papers. Ursinus College, Philadelphia.

PRIMARY AND SECONDARY WORKS

Abe Isoo 安部磯雄. *Hokubei no shin-Nihon* 北米の新日本 (The new Japan in North America). Tokyo: Hakubunkan, 1905.

Bibliography

Adams, Brooks. *The New Empire*. New York: Macmillan, 1902.
Akiyama Masanosuke den 秋山雅之介傳 (Biography of Akiyama Masa-nosuke). Tokyo, 1941.
Allen, E. A. *History of Civilization*. 4 vols. Cincinnati, 1888.
Amano Torasaburō 天野寅三郎. *To-Bei rashin* 渡米羅新 (Guide to going to America). Tokyo: Kōseisha, 1904.
American Whig Review, New York, 1846–1852.
Andover Review, Boston, 1885.
Anti-Imperialist, Brookline, Mass., 1899.
Antung kyoryūmin jūnen-shi 安東居留民十年史 (Ten years of Japanese set-tlement in Antung). Antung, 1919.
Arena, New York, 1890.
Asahi Shinbun 朝日新聞, ed. *Nihon to Amerika* 日本とアメリカ (Japan and America). Tokyo: Asahi Shinbunsha, 1971.
Asai Masahide 淺井將秀, ed. *Kaigun gunbi enkaku* 海軍軍備沿革 (History of naval armament). Tokyo, 1922.
Asakawa Kan'ichi 朝河貫一. *Nihon no kaki* 日本の禍機 (Japan's woes). Tokyo: Jitsugyō no Nihon-sha, 1909.
Atantic Monthly, Boston, 1860, 1897–1898.
Bailey, Thomas A. *Theodore Roosevelt and Japanese-American Crises*. Stanford: Stanford University Press, 1934.
Barth, Gunther. *Bitter Strength: A History of the Chinese in the United States, 1850–1870*. Cambridge, Mass.: Harvard University Press, 1964.
Beale, Howard K. *Theodore Roosevelt and the Rise of America to World Power*. Baltimore: Johns Hopkins Press, 1956.
Beard, Charles A. *The Idea of National Interest: An Analytical Study in American Foreign Policy*. New York: Macmillan, 1934.
Beisner, Robert. *Twelve Against Empire: The Anti-Imperialists, 1898–1900*. New York: McGraw-Hill, 1968.
Blakeslee, George H., ed. *Japan and Japanese-American Relations*. New York: G. F. Stechert, 1912.
Bland, J. O. P. *Recent Events and Present Politics in China*. Philadelphia: Lippincott, 1912.
Blumenthal, Henry. *A Reappraisal of Franco-American Relations, 1830–1871*. Chapel Hill: North Carolina University Press, 1959.
Braisted, William R. *The United States Navy in the Pacific, 1897–1909*. Austin: University of Texas Press, 1958.
——— *The United States Navy in the Pacific, 1909–1922*. Austin: Univer-sity of Texas Press, 1971.
Burajiru ni okeru Nihonjin hattenshi ブラジルに於ける日本人發展史 (His-tory of Japanese in Brazil). 2 vols. Tokyo, 1941.
Chang Tsun-wu 張存武. *Kuang-hsü san-shih-i-nien Chung-Mei kung-yüeh feng-ch'ao* 光緒三十一年中美工約風潮 (The Chinese labor dispute of 1905). Taipei, 1965.
Ch'en, Jerome. *Yüan Shih-k'ai, 1859–1916: Brutus Assumes the Purple*.

Stanford: Stanford University Press, 1961.

Ch'ing-chi wai-chiao shih-liao 清季外交史科 (Diplomatic documents of the Ch'ing period). Wang Yen-wei 王彥威 and Wang Liang 王亮, eds. 125 vols. Peking, 1932–1935.

Ch'ing Kuang-hsü Chung-Jij chiao-she shih-liao 清光緒中日交涉史科 (Documents on Chinese-Japanese relations during the Kwang-hsü reign). 2 vols. Taipei, 1963.

Chōsen sōtokufu shisei nenpō: 1923 朝鮮總督府施政年報 (Annual report of the Korean governor-general's office: 1923). Keijō, 1924.

Chūōkōron, Tokyo, 1907, 1969.

Cohen, Warren I. *America's Response to China*. New York: John Wiley, 1971.

Conant, Charles A. *The United States in the Orient: The Nature of the Economic Problem*. Boston: Houghton Mifflin, 1901.

Conroy, Hilary. *The Japanese Frontier in Hawaii, 1868–1898*. Berkeley: University of California Press, 1953.

———*The Japanese Seizure of Korea, 1868–1910*. Philadelphia: University of Pennsylvania Press, 1960.

Coolidge, Archibald Cary. *The United States as a World Power*. New York: Macmillan, 1909.

Craig, Albert M., and Donald H. Shively, eds. *Personality in Japanese History*. Berkeley: University of California Press, 1970.

Crowley, James B., ed. *Modern East Asia: Essays in Interpretation*. New York: Harcourt, Brace, Jovanovich, 1970.

Dairenshi-shi 大連市史 (History of Dairen). City of Dairen, ed. Dairen, 1936.

Daniels, Roger. *The Politics of Prejudice: The Anti-Japanese Movement in California and the Struggle for Japanese Exclusion*. Berkeley: University of California Press, 1962.

Democratic Review, New York, 1852.

Dennett, Tyler. *Roosevelt and the Russo-Japanese War*. New York: Doubleday, 1925.

———*John Hay: From Poetry to Politics*. New York: Dodd, Mead, 1933.

Dobrov, A. *Dalnevostochnaia politika SShA v period russko-iaponskoi voin'*. Moscow, 1952.

Duus, Peter. "Science and Salvation in China: The Life and Work of W. A. P. Martin (1827–1916)," in Liu, *American Missionaries in China*.

Echeverria, Durand. *Mirage in the West: A History of the French Image of American Society to 1815*. Princeton: Princeton University Press, 1957.

Esthus, Raymond A. *Theodore Roosevelt and Japan*. Seattle: University of Washington Press, 1966.

Fairbank, John King. *Trade and Diplomacy on the China Coast: The Opening of the Treaty Ports, 1842–1854*. Cambridge: Harvard University Press, 1964.

———*"Sino-American Images"* (paper presented at American Historical

Association annual meeting, Washington, D.C., 1969).

Feuerwerker, Albert, Rhoads Murphey, and Mary C. Wright, eds. *Approaches to Modern Chinese History*. Berkeley: University of California Press, 1967.

Field, Henry M. *From Egypt to Japan*. New York, 1877.

Field, James A. *America and the Mediterranean World, 1776–1882*. Princeton: Princeton University Press, 1969.

Fitzpatrick, Ernest Hugh. *The Coming Conflict of Nations, or the Japanese-American War*. Springfield: H. W. Bokker, 1909.

Forum, Philadelphia, 1896, 1910.

Gaikō jihō 外交時報 (*Revue diplomatique*), Tokyo, 1898.

Goetzmann, William H. *Exploration and Empire*. New York: Knopf, 1966.

Goodrich, Joseph King. *The Coming China*. Chicago: A. C. McClurg, 1911.

Gotō Shinpei 後藤新平. *Nihon shokumin seisaku ippan: Nihon bōchō-ron* 日本植民政策一斑・日本膨脹論 (Japanese colonial policy: On Japanese expansion). Tokyo: Nihon Hyōron-sha, 1944.

Graebner, Norman A., ed. *Manifest Destiny*. Indianapolis: Bobbs-Merrill, 1968.

Grenville, John A. S., and George B. Young. *Politics, Strategy, and American Diplomacy*. New Haven: Yale University Press, 1966.

Hagihara Shuichi shi tsuikai-roku 萩原守一氏追懷錄 (In memory of Hagihara Shuichi). Kubota Masakane 久保田政周, ed. Tokyo, 1913.

Hamaguchi Kichiemon 濱口吉右衞門. *Hokubei Nihon shōkō seisaku* 北米日本商工政策 (Japan's commercial and industrial policy toward North America). Tokyo: Hakubunkan, 1901.

Hara Kei nikki 原敬日記 (Hara Kei diary). 9 vols. Tokyo: Kangensha, 1950.

Harbaugh, William H., ed. *The Writings of Theodore Roosevelt*. Indianapolis: Bobbs-Merrill, 1967.

Harper's Monthly, New York, 1860, 1897.

Harz, Louis. *The Liberal Tradition in America*. New York: Harcourt, Brace, 1955.

Hasebe Sumitaka 長谷部純孝. *Ō-Bei rekiyū nisshi* 歐米歷遊日誌 (Diary of travels to Europe and America). Tokyo, 1907.

Hashikawa Bunzō 橋川文三 and Matsumoto Sannosuke 松本三之介, eds. *Kindai Nihon seiji shisō-shi* 近代日本政治思想史 (Modern Japanese political thought), vol. 1. Tokyo: Yūhikaku, 1971.

Hashimoto Jūbei 橋本重兵衞. *Sanshi bōeki kairyō shigi* 蠶糸貿易改良私議 (A proposal for improving the silk trade). n.p. [1883].

Hata Ikuhiko 秦郁彦. "Meiji ikō ni okeru Nichi-Bei Taiheiyō senryaku no hensen" 明治以降における日米太平洋戰略の變遷 (The Pacific strategy of Japan and the United States), *Kokusai seiji* 國際政治 (International politics), no. 37 (October 1968).

Hatano Yoshihiro 波多野善大. "Nichi-Ro sensō go ni okeru kokusai kankei no dōin" 日露戰爭後における國際關係の動因 (International relations after the Russo-Japanese War), *Kokusai seiji*, no. 1 (October 1957).

Hattori Tōru 服部徹. *Nanyō-saku* 南洋策 (Policy toward the south). Tokyo, 1890.

Hawai Nihonjin imin-shi ハワイ日本人移民史 (A history of Japanese immigrants in Hawaii). Honolulu, 1964.

Healy, David. *U.S. Expansionism: The Imperialist Urge in the 1890's.* Madison, Wis.: University of Wisconsin Press, 1970.

Heimin shinbun 平民新聞 (People's daily), Tokyo, 1907.

Herman, Sondra R. *Eleven against War: Studies in American Internationalist Thought, 1898–1921.* Stanford: Stanford University Press, 1969.

Hiratsuka Atsushi 平塚篤. *Shishaku Kurino Shin'ichirō den* 子爵栗野愼一郎傳 (Biography of Count Kurino Shin'ichirō). Tokyo, 1942.

Hoar, George F. *Autobiography of Seventy Years.* 2 vols. New York: Scribner's, 1903.

Hofstadter, Richard. *Social Darwinism in American Thought.* Philadelphia: University of Pennsylvania Press, 1944.

———*The Progressive Historians: Turner, Beard, Parrington.* New York: Knopf, 1968.

Hsin-hai ko-ming ch'ien shih-nien shih-lun hsüan-chi 辛亥革命前十年時論選集 (Collection of essays on public affairs during the decade preceding the 1911 revolution). Wang Jen-chih 王忍之, ed. 2 vols. Peking, 1960–1963.

Hsin-min ts'ung-pao 新民叢報 (New people's miscellany), Yokohama, 1901–1903.

Hunt, Michael H. "Frontier Defense and the Open Door: Manchuria in Chinese-American Relations, 1895–1911" (Ph.D. thesis, Yale University, 1971).

Hurd, Douglas. *The Arrow War: An Anglo-Chinese Confusion, 1856–1860.* New York: Macmillan, 1968.

Ichihashi, Yamato. *Japanese in the United States.* Stanford: Stanford University Press, 1932.

Inagaki Manjirō. *Japan in the Pacific: A Japanese View of the Eastern Question.* London, 1890.

———稲垣滿次郎. *Tōhōsaku* 東方策 (Eastern policy). Tokyo, 1891.

Inoue Kiyoshi 井上清. *Nihon teikokushugi no keisei* 日本帝國主義の形成 (The foundation of Japanese imperialism). Tokyo: Iwanami Shoten, 1968.

Irie Toraji 入江寅次. *Hōjin kaigai hatten-shi* 邦人海外發展史 (History of Japanese overseas). 2 vols. Tokyo: Imin Mondai Kenkyūkai, 1938.

Iriye Akira 入江昭. "Chūgoku ni okeru Nihon bukkyō fukyō mondai" 中國における日本佛教布教問題 (Japanese Buddhist missionaries in China), *Kokusai seiji*, no. 26 (April 1965).

———*After Imperialism: The Search for a New Order in the Far East, 1921–1931.* Cambridge, Mass.: Harvard University Press, 1965.

———"Public Opinion and Foreign Policy: The Case of Late Ch'ing China," in Feuerwerker, et al., eds., *Approaches to Modern Chinese History.*

———"The Failure of Economic Expansionism, 1918–1931" (paper presented at the conference on Taisho Japan, Durham, N.C., 1969).

———"Heiwateki hattenshugi to Nihon" 平和的發展主義と日本 (Peaceful expansionism in Japan), *Chūōkōron*, vol. 84, no. 10 (October 1969).

———"Kayahara Kazan and Japanese Cosmopolitanism," in Craig and Shively, eds., *Personality in Japanese History*.

Iriye, Mitsuko. "Quest for Literary Resonance: Young Nagai Kafū and French Literature" (Ph.D. dissertation, Harvard University, 1969).

Israel, Jerry. *Progressivism and the Open Door: America and China, 1905–1921*. Pittsburgh: University of Pittsburgh Press, 1971.

Itakura Naka 板倉中. *Keisei kigen* 經世危言 (Thoughts on government). Tokyo, 1902.

Itō Gingetsu 伊藤銀月. *Kaikoku Nihon* 海國日本 (Maritime Japan). Tokyo: Ryūbunkan, 1905.

Itō Miyoji 伊東巳代治. *Suiusō nikki* 翠雨莊日記 (Suiusō diary). Tokyo: Hara Shobō, 1966.

Itō Takeichirō 伊藤武一郎. *Manshū jūnen-shi* 滿洲十年史 (Ten years of Manchuria). Dairen, 1906.

Iwasaki Katsusaburō 岩崎勝三郎. *Saishin to-Bei annai* 最新渡米案內 (New guide to going to America). Tokyo: Daigakukan, 1905.

Jaher, Fred. *Doubters and Dissenters: Cataclysmic Thought in America, 1885–1918*. New York: Macmillan, 1964.

Jansen, Marius B. *The Japanese and Sun Yat-sen*. Cambridge, Mass.: Harvard University Press, 1954.

Jiji shinpō 時事新報, Tokyo, 1898.

Jitsugyō sekai Teiheiyō 實業世界太平洋 (The Pacific Ocean, the world of business), 1906.

Journal of the American Association of China, Shanghai, 1907.

Kaigai no Nihon 海外の日本 (Japan overseas), Tokyo, 1911.

Kamata Sannosuke 鎌田三之助. *Hokubei Mekishiko Shokumin annai* 北米墨士哥殖民案內 (Guide to settlement in Mexico). Tokyo: Seikō Zasshi-sha, 1908.

Kaneko Kentarō 金子堅太郎. *Yū-Bei kenbunroku* 遊米見聞錄 (Observations in America). Tokyo: Yao Shoten, 1900.

Katayama Sen 片山潜. *To-Bei annai* 渡米案內 (How to go to the United States). Tokyo: To-Bei Kyōkai, 1901.

Katsudō no Nihon 活動の日本 (Active Japan), Tokyo, 1905–1907.

Kawamura Tetsutarō 河村鉄太郎. *Hokubei jigyō annai* 北米事業案內 (Guide to business in America). Tokyo: Hakubunkan, 1906.

Kawashima Seijirō 川島清治郎. *Kokubō kaigun-ron* 國防海軍論 (On naval defense). Tokyo, 1911.

Kayahara Kazan 茅原華山. *Tōhoku taiseiron* 東北大勢論 (On conditions in northeastern Japan). Yamagata, 1895.

———*Kōjō no ichiro* 向上の一路 (Ceaseless progress). Tokyo: Yūrindō, 1904.

———*Dōchū seikan* 動中靜觀 (Quiet in movement). Tokyo: Tōadō, 1904.

———*Sayū shūchiku* 左右修竹 (Bamboos everywhere). Tokyo: Ryūbun-kan, 1905.

———*Kaigai bunshō: Tōzai seikatsu no hihan* 海外文章・東西生活の批判 (Essays written abroad: a critique of Eastern and Western life). Tokyo: Isobe Kōyōdō, 1912.

Kelley, Robert. *The Transatlantic Persuasion: The Liberal-Democratic Mind in the Age of Gladstone*. New York: Knopf, 1969.

Kikuchi Gorō 菊池悟郎. *Yamato minzoku shin hattenchi jijō* 大和民族新發展地事情 (Conditions of Japan's expanding communities abroad). Tokyo: Shibunsha, 1912.

Kikuchi Takaharu 菊池貴晴. *Chūgoku minzoku undō no kihon kōzō: taigai boycott no kenkyū* 中國民族運動の基本構造・對外ボイコツトの研究 (The structure of Chinese nationalism: a study of antiforeign boycotts). Tokyo: Daian, 1966.

Kimitsu Nichi-Ro senshi 機密日露戰史 (Secret history of the Russo-Japanese War). General Staff, ed. Tokyo, 1931.

Klein, Philip S. *President James Buchanan: A Biography*. University Park: Pennsylvania State University Press, 1962.

Kokusaihō gaikō zasshi 國際法外交雜誌 (International law and diplomacy), 1910–1911.

Komura gaikō-shi 小村外交史 (Japanese diplomacy under Komura). Foreign Ministry, ed. Tokyo, 1968.

Kōtoku Shūsui 幸德秋水. *Nijusseiki no kaibutsu teikokushugi* 二十世紀の怪物帝國主義 (Imperialism, the monster of the twentieth century). Tokyo: Keiseisha, 1901.

Kuehl, Warren F. *Seeking World Order: The United States and International Organization to 1920*. Nashville: University of Tennessee Press, 1969.

Kurihara Ken 栗原健. *Tai Man-Mō seisaku-shi no ichimen* 對滿蒙政策史の一面 (Aspects of Japanese policy toward Manchuria and Mongolia). Tokyo: Hara Shobō, 1966.

Kuroda Ken'ichi 黑田謙一. *Nihon shokumin shisō-shi* 日本植民思想史 (History of colonialism in Japan). Tokyo: Kōbundō, 1942.

Kutakov, L. N. *Portsmutskii mirnyi dogovor*. Moscow, 1961.

LaFeber, Walter. *The New Empire: An Interpretation of American Expansionism, 1860–1898*. Ithaca: Cornell University Press, 1963.

Latané, John H. *America as a World Power, 1897–1907*. New York: Harper, 1907.

Lea, Homer. *The Valor of Ignorance*. New York: Harper, 1909.

Lensen, George. *Korea and Manchuria between Russia and Japan, 1895–1904*. Tallahassee: Diplomatic Press, 1966.

Levin, N. Gordon. *Woodrow Wilson and World Politics: America's Response to War and Revolution*. New York: Oxford University Press, 1968.

Lippmann, Walter. *Drift and Mastery: An Attempt to Diagnose the Current Unrest*. New York: Mitchell Kennerley, 1914.

Literary Digest, New York, 1900–1907.

Liu, Kwang-ching, ed. *American Missionaries in China: Papers from Har-*

vard Seminars. Cambridge, Mass.: East Asian Research Center, 1966.

Mahan, Alfred Thayer. *The Problem of Asia, and Its Effect on International Policies.* Boston: Little, Brown, 1900.

Manshū kaihatsu yonjūnen-shi 滿洲開發四十年史 (Forty years of Manchurian development). Manshikai 滿史會, ed. 2 vols. Tokyo, 1964.

Matsumoto Kunpei 松本君平. *Kaigai seicha bōeki iken* 海外製茶貿易意見 (A view of the tea trade). Tokyo, 1896.

May, Ernest R. *Imperial Democracy: The Emergence of America as a Great Power.* New York: Harcourt, Brace & World, 1961.

―――*American Imperialism: A Speculative Essay.* New York: Atheneum, 1968.

―――, and James C. Thomson, eds. *American-East Asian Relations: A Survey.* Cambridge, Mass.: Harvard University Press, 1972.

May, Henry F. *The End of American Innocence: A Study of the First Years of Our Own Time, 1912–1917.* New York: Knopf, 1959.

Mayer, Arno. *Political Origins of the New Diplomacy, 1917–1918.* New Haven: Yale University Press, 1959.

―――*Politics and Diplomacy of Peacemaking: Containment and Counterrevolution at Versailles, 1918–1919.* New York: Knopf, 1967.

McClellan, Robert. *The Heathen Chinee: A Study of American Attitudes toward China, 1890–1905.* Columbus: Ohio State University Press, 1971.

McCormick, Thomas J. *China Market: America's Quest for Informal Empire, 1893–1901.* Chicago: Quadrangle, 1967.

―――"American Expansion in China," *American Historical Review,* vol. 75 (June 1970).

Meiji sanjūshichihachi-nen kaisen-shi 明治三十七八年海戰史 (The naval warfare of 1904–5). Navy General Staff, ed. Tokyo, n.d.

Merk, Frederick. *Manifest Destiny and Mission in American History: A New Interpretation.* New York: Knopf, 1963.

―――*The Monroe Doctrine and American Expansionism, 1843–1849.* New York: Knopf, 1966.

Millard, Thomas F. *America and the Far Eastern Question.* New York: Scribner's, 1909.

Miller, Jessie A. "China in American Policy and Opinion, 1906–1909." Ph.D. thesis, Clark University, 1938.

Miller, Stuart Creighton. *The Unwelcome Immigrant: The American Image of the Chinese, 1785–1882.* Berkeley: University of California Press, 1969.

Minyūsha 民友社, ed. *Ensei* 遠征 (Expeditions to distant lands). Tokyo, 1895.

―――, ed. *Firipin guntō* 比律賓群島 (The Philippine Islands). Tokyo, 1896.

Mishima Kazuo 三島一雄. *Gōshū oyobi Indo* 濠洲及印度 (Australia and India). Tokyo, 1891.

Miwa Kimitada. "Crossroads of Patriotism in Imperial Japan" (Ph.D.

dissertation, Princeton University, 1967).

Mizuno Ryū 水野龍. *Nan-Bei tokō annai* 南米渡航案内 (Guide to going to South America). Tokyo: Kyōkadō, 1906.

Mori Rintarō 森林太郎. *Kōkaron kōgai* 黄禍論梗概 (An outline of the yellow-peril concept). Tokyo: Shunyōdō, 1904.

Morison, Elting E., ed. *The Letters of Theodore Roosevelt*, vols. 4, 5. Cambridge, Mass.: Harvard University Press, 1951–1952.

Moriyama Nobunori 森山信規. *Bei-Sei sensō* 米西戰爭 (The Spanish-American War). Tokyo: Komura Matashichi, 1903.

Morris, Charles. *Civilization: An Historical Review of Its Elements*. Chicago, 1890.

Motoyama Yukihiko 本山幸彦. "Ajiya to Nihon" アジアと日本 (Asia and Japan), in Hashikawa and Matsumoto, eds., *Kindai Nihon seiji shisō-shi*.

Munro, Dana. *Intervention and Dollar Diplomacy in the Caribbean, 1900–1921*. Princeton: Princeton University Press, 1964.

Mutō Sanji 武藤山治. *Beikoku ijūron* 米國移住論 (On emigration to the United States). Tokyo, 1887.

[Nagai] *Kafū zenshū* 荷風全集 (Collected works of Nagai Kafū). 28 vols. Tokyo: Iwanami Shoten, 1962–1965.

Nagasawa Setsu 長沢節. *Yankii* ヤンキー (Yankees). Tokyo, 1893.

Nakae Chōmin 中江兆民. *San suijin keirin mondō* 三酔人經綸問答 (Argument among three drunkards). Tokyo, 1887.

Nakamura Shun'u 中村春雨. *Ō-Bei inshō-ki* 歐米印象記 (Impressions of Europe and America). Tokyo: Shunjūsha, 1910.

Neu, Charles E. *An Uncertain Friendship: Theodore Roosevelt and Japan, 1906–1909*. Cambridge, Mass.: Harvard University Press, 1967.

Nevins, Allan. *Henry White: Thirty Years of American Diplomacy*. New York: Harper, 1930.

————, ed. *Letters of Grover Cleveland*. Boston: Houghton, Mifflin, 1933.

New York Times, 1905.

Nichi-Bei bunka kōshō-shi 日米文化交渉史 (History of cultural relations between Japan and the United States). Vol. 2: *Tsūshō sangyō-hen* 通商産業編 (Commerce and industry). Tokyo, 1954. Vol. 5: *Ijū-hen* 移住編 (Immigration). Tokyo: Yōyōsha, 1955.

Nihon gaikō bunsho 日本外交文書 (Japanese diplomatic documents). Tokyo, 1954–1961.

Nihon gaikō bunsho: Nichi-Ro sensō 日本外交文書・日露戰爭 (Japanese diplomatic documents: The Russo-Japanese War). 5 vols. Tokyo, 1958–1960.

Nihon gaikō nenpyō narabi shuyō bunsho 日本外交年表並主要文書 (Chronology and main documents of Japanese diplomacy). Foreign Ministry, ed. 2 vols. Tokyo, 1955.

Nihon kyōkasho taikei 日本教科書大系 (Anthology of Japanese textbooks). Kaigo Tokiomi 海後宗臣, ed., vols. 15, 16. Tokyo: Kōdansha, 1965.

Nish, Ian. *The Anglo-Japanese Alliance: The Diplomacy of Two Island*

Empires, 1894–1907. London: University of London Press, 1967.

Nitobe Inazō 新渡邊稻造. *Kigan no ashi* 歸雁の蘆 (The return of a wild goose). Tokyo, 1907.

Noma Gozō 野間五造. *Jūō kōgiroku* 縦横公議録 (Speeches). Okayama: Chūgoku Minpō-sha, 1902.

Norman, Henry. *People and Politics of the Far East*. London, 1895.

North American Review, Boston, 1856.

North China Herald, Shanghai, 1905.

Notter, Harley. *The Origins of the Foreign Policy of Woodrow Wilson*. Baltimore: Johns Hopkins Press, 1937.

Ōfu Onshi 櫻府隱士 (pseud.). *Zai-Bei seikō no Nihonjin* 在米成功之日本人 (Successful Japanese in America). Tokyo: Hōbunkan, 1904.

Ogino Mannosuke 荻野萬之助. *Gaiyū sannen* 外遊三年 (Three years abroad). Tokyo: Kōzanbō, 1907.

Ōgoshi Seitoku 大越成德. *Gaikoku bōeki kakuchō-ron* 外國貿易擴張論 (How to expand our foreign trade). Tokyo, 1889.

Ōishi Masami 大石正巳. *Fukyōsaku* 富强策 (On enriching and strengthening the nation). Tokyo, 1891.

Okamoto Shumpei. *The Japanese Oligarchy and the Russo-Japanese War*. New York: Columbia University Press, 1970.

Ōkawahira Takamitsu 大河平隆光. *Nihon imin-ron* 日本移民論 (Japanese emigration). Tokyo: Bunbudō, 1905.

Okudo Zennosuke 奧戸善之助. *To-Bei nikki* 渡米日記 (Diary in America). Osaka, 1904.

Ōkuma-haku jikyoku dan 大隈伯時局談 (Count Ōkuma talks on contemporary affairs). Tokyo: Hakubunkan, 1905.

Okumiya Takeyuki 奧宮健之. *Hoku-Bei imin-ron* 北米移民論 (On emigrating to North America). Tokyo: Tōkyōdō, 1903.

Ōsaka Mainichi 大阪毎日, 1918.

Osgood, Robert E. *Ideals and Self-Interest in American Foreign Relations*. Chicago: University of Chicago Press, 1953.

Ōtsuka Zenjirō 大塚善次郎. *Nichi-Bei gaikō-ron* 日米外交論 (On Japanese-American relations). Tokyo: Sagamiya, 1910.

Outlook, New York, 1899, 1911.

Palmer, R. R. *The Age of the Democratic Revolution: A Political History of Europe and America, 1760–1800*. 2 vols. Princeton: Princeton University Press, 1959, 1964.

Papers Relating to the Foreign Relations of the United States. Washington, D.C.

Pearson, Charles H. *National Life and Character: A Forecast*. London, 1893.

Phillips, Clifton Jackson. *Protestant America and the Pagan World: The First Half Century of the American Board of Commissioners for Foreign Missions, 1810–1860*. Cambridge, Mass.: East Asian Research Center, 1969.

Plesur, Milton. *America's Outward Thrust: Approaches to Foreign Affairs*,

1865–1890. DeKalb: Northern Illinois University Press, 1971.

Pletcher, David M. *The Awkward Years: American Foreign Relations under Garfield and Arthur*. Columbia, Mo.: University of Missouri Press, 1962.

Pooley, A. M., ed. *The Secret Memoirs of Count Tadasu Hayashi*. New York: Putnam's Sons, 1915.

Pratt, Julius W. *Expansionists of 1898: The Acquisition of Hawaii and the Spanish Islands*. Baltimore: Johns Hopkins Press, 1936.

Reinsch, Paul S. *World Politics at the End of the Nineteenth Century, as Influenced by the Oriental Situation*. New York: Macmillan, 1900.

Remer, Charles F. *Foreign Investments in China*. New York: Macmillan, 1933.

Russ, William A. *The Hawaiian Revolution, 1893–1894*. Selinsgrove, Pa.: Susquehanna University Press, 1959.

Saeki Shōichi 佐伯彰一. "Nichi-Bei no shinkankei"「日米の新關係」 (The new relationship between Japan and the United States), *Kikan geijutsu* 季刊藝術 (Art quarterly), no. 10 (July 1969).

Saitō Makoto den 齋藤實傳 (Biography of Saitō Makoto). Tokyo, 1933.

San Francisco Call, 1907.

Sanbe Yūsuke 三瓶勇佐. *Taiheiyō no yūetsusha* 太平洋の優越者 (The predominant power in the Pacific). Tokyo: Hōbunkan, 1911.

Sanetō Keishū さねとうけいしゆう. *Chūgokujin Nihon ryūgaku-shi* 中國人日本留學史 (History of Chinese students in Japan). Tokyo.: Kuroshio Shuppan, 1960.

Sasakawa Kiyoshi 笹川潔. *Nihon no shōrai* 日本の將來 (The future of Japan). Tokyo: Kōdōkan, 1907.

Satō Seizaburō 佐藤誠三郎. "Kyōchō to jiritsu no aida" 協調と自立の間 (Between cooperation and autonomy), in *Nenpō seijigaku 1969* 年報政治學 1969 (Annals of Japanese Political Science Association 1969). Tokyo, 1970.

Satō Tetsutarō 佐藤鉄太郎. *Teikoku kokubō shiron* 帝國國防史論 (A historical study of Japanese strategy). Tokyo: Tōkyō Insatsu, 1908.

——— *Teikoku kokubō shiron shō* 帝國國防史論抄 (Outline history of Japanese strategy). Tokyo: Tōkyō Insatsu, 1912.

Satō Torajirō 佐藤虎次郎. *Shin seikei* 新政經 (New politics and economy). Tokyo: Tōkyōdō, 1903.

——— *Shina keihatsu-ron* 支那啓發論 (On developing China). Yokohama: Yokohama Shimpō-sha, 1903.

Science, Cambridge, Mass., 1892.

Schrecker, John E. *Imperialism and Chinese Nationalism: Germany in Shantung*. Cambridge, Mass.: Harvard University Press, 1971.

Sekai no Nihon 世界の日本 (Japan in the world), Tokyo, 1911.

Sengo keiei 戰後經營 (Postwar management). Yamamoto Rikio 山本利喜雄, ed. Tokyo: Waseda Gakkai, 1905.

Sevostianov, G. *Ekspansionistskaia politika SShA na Dal'nem Vostoke*. Moscow, 1958.

Seward, William H. *Works*. George E. Baker, ed., vol. 4. New York, 1889.

Shiga Shigetaka 志賀重昂. *Nanyō jiji* 南洋時事 (Affairs in the South Seas). Tokyo, 1887.

Shimada Kinji 島田謹二. *Roshia ni okeru Hirose Takeo* ロシヤにおける廣瀬武夫 (Hirose Takeo in Russia). Tokyo: Kōbundō, 1961.

――*Amerika ni okeru Akiyama Saneyuki* アメリカにおける秋山眞之 (Akiyama Saneyuki in America). Tokyo: Asahi Shinbun-sha, 1969.

Shimanuki Hyōdayū 島貫兵太夫. *Saikin to-Bei saku* 最近渡米策 (New ways to go to America). Tokyo: Nihon Rikkōkai, 1904.

――*Rikkōkai to wa nanzoya* 力行會とは何ぞや (What is Rikkōkai?). Tokyo: Keiseisha, 1911.

Shina kindai no seiji keizai 支那近代の政治經濟 (Modern China's politics and economy). Nikka Jitsugyō Kyōkai 日華實業協會, ed. Tokyo, 1931.

Shinbun shūsei Meiji hennen-shi 新聞集成明治編年史 (Chronicle of the Meiji period as seen in newspapers). 15 vols. Tokyo, 1934–1936.

Shinjidai 新時代 (The new era), Tokyo, 1906.

Shinobu Seizaburō 信夫淸三郎 and Nakayama Jiichi 中山治一, eds. *Nichi-Ro sensō-shi no kenkyū* 日露戰爭史の硏究 (Historigraphy of the Russo-Japanese War). Tokyo: Kawade Shobō, 1959.

Shinsekai 新世界 (The new world), San Francisco, 1906–1911.

Shin to-Bei 新渡米 (Going to America). Shuppan Kyōkai 出版協會, ed. Tokyo, 1904.

Shokumin Kyōkai hōkoku 殖民協會報告 (Report of the Colonization Society). Tokyo, 1893.

Shokumin sekai 植民世界 (The world of colonialism), Tokyo, 1908.

Sholes, Walter V. and Marie V. *The Foreign Policies of the Taft Administration*. Columbia: University of Missouri Press, 1970.

Shōwa sensō bungaku zenshū 昭和戰爭文學全集 (Anthology of wartime literature), vol. 4. Tokyo, 1964.

Smith, Arthur H. *China and America Today: A Study of Conditions and Relations*. New York: F.H. Revell, 1907.

――*The Uplift of China*. New York: Young People's Missionary Movement, 1907.

Strong, Josiah. *Our Country: Its Possible Future and Its Present Crisis*. Rev. ed., New York, 1891.

――*The New Era, or the Coming Kingdom*. New York, 1893.

――*Expansion*. New York, 1900.

Sumiya Mikio 隅谷三喜男. *Dai-Nihon teikoku no shiren* 大日本帝國の試鍊 (Tribulations of the Japanese empire). Tokyo, 1966.

Tabata Kisaburō 田畑喜三郎. *Zai-Bei seikō no tomo* 在米成功の友 (How to succeed in America). Tokyo, 1908.

Tabohashi Kiyoshi 田保橋潔. *Nis-Shin sen'eki gaikōshi no kenkyū* 日清戰役外交史の硏究(A study of the diplomacy of the Sino-Japanese War). Tokyo: Tōkō Shoten, 1951.

Taguchi Ukichi 田口卯吉. *Ha-kōkaron* 破黃禍論 (Down with the yellow-peril concept). Tokyo: Keizai Zasshi-sha, 1904.

Taiwan Governor-General's Office. *Meiji shonen Hong Kong Nihonjin* 明治初年香港日本人 (Japanese in Hong Kong in the early Meiji period). Taipei, 1937.

Taiyō 太陽 (The Sun), Tokyo, 1908.

Takahashi Sakue 高橋作衞. *Nichi-Bei no shinkankei* 日米之新關係 (The new relationship between Japan and the United States). Tokyo: Shimizu Shobō, 1910.

Takayama Rinjirō 高山林次郎. *Jidai kanken* 時代管見 (Thoughts on contemporary affairs). Tokyo, 1898.

Takegoshi Yosaburō 竹越與三郎. *Hikaku shokumin seido* 比較殖民制度 (Comparative colonial systems). Tokyo, 1906.

Takeshima Keishirō 竹島慶四郎. *Rekkyōkan no Nihon* 列强間の日本 (Japan among the powers). Tokyo: Seikyōsha, 1912.

Takeuchi Seishi 竹內正志. *Shin rikkoku* 新立國 (The founding of the new nation). Tokyo, 1892.

Tamura Shōgyo 田村松魚. *Hokubei sezoku-kan* 北米世俗觀 (Life in North America). Tokyo, 1909.

Tani Toshio 谷壽夫. *Kimitsu Nichi-Ro senshi* 機密日露戰史 (Secret history of the Russo-Japanese War). Tokyo: Hara Shobō, 1966.

Tōa senkakusha shishi kiden 東亞先覺者志士紀傳 (Chronicle of pioneers in East Asia). Kokuryūkai 黑龍會, ed. 3 vols. Tokyo, 1933–1936.

Togawa Shūkotsu 戶川秋骨. *Ō-Bei kiyū* 歐米紀遊 (Travels in Europe and America). Tokyo, 1907.

Tōgō Minoru 東鄉實. *Nihon shokumin-ron* 日本植民論 (On Japanese colonization). Tokyo: Bunbudō, 1906.

Tōgō Minoru, and Satō Shiro 佐藤四郎. *Taiwan shokumin hattatsu-shi* 臺灣殖民發達史 (History of colonialism in Taiwan). Taipei, 1916.

Tokutomi Sohō 德富蘇峰. *Dai Nihon bōchō-ron* 大日本膨脹論 (On the expansion of Japan). Tokyo, 1894.

Tokyo Asahi shinbun 東京朝日新聞, 1907.

Tokyo Nichinichi shinbun 東京日日新聞 1906–1907.

Tompkins, E. Berkeley. *Anti-Imperialism in the United States: The Great Debate, 1890–1920.* Philadelphia, University of Pennsylvania Press, 1970.

Tōyō keizai shinpō 東洋經濟新報 (Oriental economist), Tokyo, 1907.

Tsuneya Seifuku 恒屋盛服. *Kaigai shokumin-ron* 海外植民論 (On overseas colonization). Tokyo, 1891.

Tsunoda Jun 角田順. *Manshū mondai to kokubō hōshin* 滿洲問題と國防方針 (The Manchurian problem and strategic principles). Tokyo: Hara Shobō, 1967.

Tsurumi Yūsuke 鶴見祐輔. *Gotō Shinpei* 後藤新平. 4 vols. Tokyo, 1937–1938.

Tung-fang tsa-chih 東方雜誌 (Eastern miscellany), Shanghai, 1904.

Uete Michiari 植手通有. "Taigaikan no tenkai" 對外觀の轉回 (Changing images of the world), in Hashikawa and Matsumoto, eds., *Kindai Nihon seiji shisō-shi.*

Ukita Kazutami 浮田和民. *Teikokushugi to kyōiku* 帝國主義と教育 (Imperialism and education). Tokyo: Minyūsha, 1901.

―――*Kokumin kyōiku-ron* 國民教育論 (On national education). Tokyo: Minyūsha, 1903.

―――*Rinriteki teikokushugi* 倫理的帝國主義 (Ethical imperialism). Tokyo: Ryūbunkan, 1908.

Umeta Matajirō 梅田又次郎. *Zai-Bei no kugakusei oyobi rōdōsha* 在米の苦學生及勞働者 (Japanese students and laborers in America). Tokyo: Jitsugyō no Nihon-sha, 1907.

Unno Sachinori 海野幸德. *Nihon jinshu kaizō-ron* 日本人種改造論 (On improving the Japanese race). Tokyo: Fuzanbō, 1910.

Van Alstyne, Richard W. *The Rising American Empire.* Oxford: Oxford University Press, 1960.

Varg, Paul A. *Open Door Diplomat: The Life of W. W. Rockhill.* Urbana: University of Illinois Press, 1952.

―――*The Making of a Myth: The United States and China, 1897–1912.* East Lansing: Michigan State University Press, 1968.

Vevier, Charles. *The United States and China, 1906–1913: A Study of Finance and Diplomacy.* New Brunswick, N.J.: Rutgers University Press, 1955.

Watanabe Kanjirō 渡邊觀次郎. *Kaigai dekasegi annai* 海外出稼ぎ案内 (A guide to working abroad). Tokyo: Naigai Shuppan Kyōkai, 1902.

Watanabe Shirō 渡邊四郎. *Kaigai risshin no tebiki* 海外立身の手引 (How to get ahead abroad). Tokyo: Unteisha, 1902.

Watanabe Shūjirō 渡邊修二郎. *Sekai ni okeru Nihonjin* 世界における日本人 (Japanese in the world). Tokyo, 1893.

Weinberg, Albert K. *Manifest Destiny.* Baltimore: Johns Hopkins Press, 1935.

White, John A. *The Diplomacy of the Russo-Japanese War.* Princeton: Princeton University Press, 1964.

Wickberg, Edgar. *The Chinese in Philippine Life, 1850–1898.* New Haven: Yale University Press, 1965.

Williams, William Applemen. *The Tragedy of American Diplomacy.* New York: World, 1959.

―――*Roots of the Modern American Empire: A Study of the Growth and Shaping of Social Consciousness in a Marketplace Society.* New York: Random House, 1969.

Wilson, Woodrow. *A History of the American People.* Vol. 5: *Reunion and Nationalization.* New York: Harper, 1902.

Wright, Mary, ed. *China in Revolution: The First Phase, 1900–1913.* New Haven: Yale University Press, 1968.

Yamabe Kentarō 山邊健太郎. *Nik-Kan heigō shōshi* 日韓併合小史 (A short history of the Japanese annexation of Korea). Tokyo: Iwanami Shoten, 1966.

Yamagata Aritomo ikensho 山縣有朋意見書 (Memoranda of Yamagata Aritomo). Tokyo: Hara Shobō, 1966.